TRIBAL BENGAL

Life in the Sub-Himalayan Terai Duars

Krishnopriyo Bhattacharya

TRIBAL BENGAL

Life in the Sub-Himalayan Terai Duars

Krishnopriyo Bhattacharya

NIYOGI BOOKS

Published by
NIYOGI BOOKS
Block D, Building No. 77,
Okhla Industrial Area, Phase-I,
New Delhi-110 020, INDIA
Tel: 91-11-26816301, 26818960
Email: niyogibooks@gmail.com
Website: www.niyogibooksindia.com

Text and Photographs©: Krishnopriyo Bhattacharya
Editorial and Design: Write Media

ISBN: 978-93-86906-79-3
Year of Publication: 2019

Printed at: Niyogi Offset Pvt. Ltd., New Delhi, India

In memory of

Krishnobijay Bhattacharya

and

Mahasveta Devi

Contents

PART 2

The Proto-Australoids and Others

Foreword

This book concerns a part of India that many tend to just pass through or think of as a transport corridor that brings people and goods along either Highway 31 or the railway tracks that connect mainland India with Assam and the other northeastern states. The visual image is that of the 'chicken neck', as the area has come to be known. Before the independence of India, the geopolitical map was different and movement was either south-north or up and down between the Bengal plains and the Himalayan region. During those earlier days, this area was known as the Duars (*dwar* in Sanskrit), doors or passages to the Himalayas. But, regardless of whether we think of present-day east-west movement or the earlier forms of north-south travels, it is still a matter of passing through, of being on a journey going somewhere else. I was reminded of this as I read *Across the Chicken Neck: Travels in Northeast India*. The author, Nandita Haksar, travels from Nepal, 'across' the Duars and into Northeast India, which is the actual destination and topic of the book. One can point to a similar lacuna in research that not only passes through these northernmost tracts of West Bengal, but makes it the centre of the investigation.

In view of this, it is a privilege and an honour for me to write the foreword to this wonderful book by someone who has stayed on and, with passion and scholarly zeal, carried out research for decades on the indigenous or tribal people living in the region. This is a labour of love. It is a double honour as I have had the great pleasure of knowing the author since early 1990 when, as a fresh doctoral student from Sweden, I landed on his doorstep in Lebubagan in Alipurduar. This happened some 25 years ago and my friend, Krishnopriyo Bhattacharya, was already an established authority and deeply committed scholar in the field of tribal North Bengal. He has since published several books and articles, along with his duties as an officer in the Scheduled Castes and Tribes Welfare Department (now bifurcated and renamed as Backward Classes Welfare and Tribal Development), Government of West Bengal. This is a most impressive achievement.

One of the main challenges in research is the terminology or categories we use. For social anthropologists, and others within the social sciences, this is especially tricky as we usually deal with people who are alive and hence 'speak back'. Categories once taken for granted are now being questioned or challenged on scientific as well as political grounds. What is a tribe? Is it meaningful to hold on to a term that suggests a historical journey of mankind from barbaric times to civilisation, where tribe or tribal is supposed to be an earlier stage that most of us passed through long ago? Hence, many scholars and activists today stay away from it, arguing, for example, that it is an inherently racist term. Others take a more pragmatic stand, stating that tribe or Scheduled Tribe (ST) is an administrative term that after five decades of affirmative action programmes has taken on new, and less stigmatising, meaning and that many people now self-identify as tribal or struggle for recognition as tribal. Through the global indigenous peoples' movement, activists have further come to use the term 'tribal' as being synonymous with indigenous, hence claiming that the rights of indigenous people, established through ILO Convention No. 169 of the United Nations Declaration on the Rights of Indigenous Peoples, should apply to the tribal people in India as well. Being tribal is, therefore, a political assertion and a claim, rather than a demeaning term imposed by powerful outsiders (scholars, government officers or others).

It is important to keep these different histories in mind and not immediately jump to conclusions regarding the usage of the term 'tribe'. In this book, listing people as tribal in no way suggests that these communities are inferior or backward to the dominant Hindu or Muslim communities, but rather that they have qualities and experiences that are different and distinct. Krishnopriyo has further divided the tribal communities into two categories: those that have a longer history in the area and those that were brought by the British to work in the tea plantations that were established towards the end of the 19th century. The first group is the Indo-Mongoloids, mainly speaking Tibeto-Burman languages and the second group, the Proto-Australoids, speak languages classified as Dravidian and Austric. Suffice it to say, racial as well as linguistic categories have their problems, yet, as Krishnopriyo's stories and photographs so clearly reveal, the divide still makes sense.

Stories define us as individuals and collectives. We are constantly told (and tell) stories about ourselves and others. Stories create divides, instigate violence at times, but also unite people and evoke a sense of common humanity. Through the fate of one single person, we can recognise the human that is in us all, the greatness as well as the pettiness that is inherent in us. An old Rabha woman once told me that human life is like a drop of dew on a leaf, so easily it slips. During my fieldwork among the members of this tribe, I spent some weeks close to the Bhutan border in one of the more remote villages that could only be reached by foot and by crossing several rivers. I came down with a really bad attack of malaria. Over several days of extremely high fever, I kept dreaming about trying to cross the main river. It was especially wild at the time during the monsoon, and I kept failing over and over again. In real life, I was more fortunate and, through the help of my friend Bholanath Rabha and some villagers, I did eventually manage to reach Alipurduar town for medical treatment. Bholanath later told me that the villagers thought I was a lost case and that they had started to discuss where and how to bury me. I sometimes tell this story to friends, as it seems unlikely now that my life would have ended there and then. The story reminds me of the precariousness of life and the harsh realities of the life of the Rabhas among whom malaria is a killer. They had all seen it happen many times.

Several of the stories Krishnopriyo narrates in this book are about single individuals and, through them, we learn something about their respective communities as well as the tribal predicament in the Duars more generally. The book is organised around wonderfully rich photographic material as well as information drawn from historical and ethnographical sources. Brought together, it really is a treasure for the scholar, the policy-maker as well as for the general public.

The chapter on the Ho community, to give an example, reveals the contemporary predicament of the Ho people. The Hos are one of the smaller tea garden communities in the Duars, brought there from the Singhbhum (Bihar) and Mayurbhanj (Odisha) areas in eastern India to work in the tea plantations during the colonial period. Krishnopriyo centres the chapter around Gouri Kolmunda, a girl who is doing her Masters in Bengali at the North Bengal University (NBU), located outside the large town of Siliguri. As Krishnopriyo notes, this is an extraordinary achievement, coming from a rural area that is lacking in educational infrastructure and being the first in the family and the community to advance to this level. The travel itself from her home in the tea garden, Zurrantee, to the university is a major challenge. Krishnopriyo takes us with him on his own journey searching for the community and eventually getting to know their situation in North Bengal. One critical aspect, he discovers, is the ongoing Mundaisation, that is, the Hos picking up cultural traits and even titles from the larger Munda community. This, as Krishnopriyo points out, might risk the long-term survival of the Hos as a distinct community in this part of the country.

Along with his own observations, Krishnopriyo draws on various secondary sources, quoting, for example, ET Dalton's famous *Descriptive Ethnology of Bengal* from 1872. In a seamless and jargon-free manner, Krishnopriyo weaves an account that is highly personal and yet captures the material and existential predicament of the tribal people of North Bengal. The critical reader might find several things to disagree with, and this is indeed a good thing. The author speaks from somewhere, he offers a perspective, his own, and hence invites others to come forth and tell their stories.

The late author Mahasweta Devi has, perhaps better than anyone else, brought attention to the discrimination and exploitation of tribal people in West Bengal and India more widely. She was an activist and a writer and will best be remembered by her stories. The one that has been with me since I read it some 20 years ago is about the tribal girl, Douloti, born into bonded labour and eventually forced into a life of prostitution to repay the debt of her ageing father. The story is part of the collection *Imagined Maps* translated into English and introduced by Gayatri Spivak Chakrabarty. In the opening conversation between the author and the translator, Mahasweta Devi explains that her political project is to make the tribal communities come together, 'to unite, unite, unite'. Only through a strong united tribal movement can they push for real changes and improve their situation. Mahasweta Devi was a friend of Krishnopriyo and, during an audience with the author in her apartment situated close to the Ballygunge railway station in Kolkata, she asked me how the land resettlement case in Samuktala was going. Krishnopriyo was instrumental—in his official capacity as government inspector—to ensure that the land that had been illegally transferred to non-tribal individuals was returned to the original landowners, most of them Santals. Mahasweta Devi spoke very fondly about Krishnopriyo, claiming him as her North Bengal companion in fighting for the tribal cause.

The tribal world of the Duars is changing rapidly in front of our eyes. Development, as it is called, comes in different shapes and forms, sometimes for the good—bringing schools, hospitals and material improvements—but often also in the less benign way of displacement, loss of land, livelihoods and ways of being in the world. During my initial stay in India as an exchange PhD student at the NBU, the first thing anyone asked when I spoke of my interest in tribal issues was whether I had visited the Totos in Totopara, said to be the most original and primitive tribe, now on the verge of extinction due to a diminishing population. This naturally made me curious, but I felt I did not want to go there without any proper reason. This was at the height of postcolonial critique and anthropology was challenged with serving imperial interests by constantly focusing on that which was most exotic and different. I never got around to visiting the Totos, something I regret today.

Krishnopriyo, however, has been a frequent visitor and has been following at close range the changes the community has been going through for decades. First of all, he disputes the thesis about the Totos' dwindling population. They, he asserts, have, in fact, shown a positive trend and had, in 2014, a population of 1,564, a number higher than ever before. The problem is hence not the decline, but rather the loss of land and the tribe being marginalised and turned into a minority in their own place. Today, the majority of people in Totopara are Nepalis and other newcomers. In this especially rich chapter, Krishnopriyo is bringing attention to the late anthropologist BK Roy Burman's unpublished doctoral thesis *Dynamics of Persistence and Change of a Small Community: The Totos* (1961, Calcutta University). This is a remarkable study that I have only had a chance to read a few chapters of in a badly copied version. It is certainly time for the thesis to be published and made available to a larger readership. As Krishnopriyo pointed out to me a few years ago, it is highly intriguing that the pioneering work of one of India's most renowned anthropologists has remained unpublished for half-a-century. Perhaps the author wanted it that way. Be this as it may, the study gives us a wonderful baseline in thinking about change and development among tribal communities during the postcolonial period. Krishnopriyo should get the credit for reminding us about this scholarly treasure.

Photo-ethnography is a relatively recent term that points to the visual representation of different cultures or societies. The usage of photographs and films has a long tradition in anthropology. Thinking back to the colonial studies of India's tribal people, such as the book by Dalton that I mentioned earlier, there was usually rich photographic material that accompanied the text. As pointed out by several scholars, the colonial visual record commonly depicts people in an exotic, stereotypical manner, often accompanied with derogatory captions pointing to the cultural or phenotypical traits of the particular community. Yet the visual record still fascinates and can offer a window into certain aspects of the historical transformations that these societies have gone through. Here I think of Joy LK Pachuau and Willem van Schendel's recent book *The Camera as Witness: A Social History of Mizoram, Northeast India* (2015), a wonderful account of the modern history of Mizoram through photographs. Krishnopriyo is a dedicated photographer and he has single-handedly produced a rich visual archive of tribal Bengal. The photographs are mostly of people whom he knows and has interacted with over the years. They capture the every day at particular moments and bring a poetic tension to the stories narrated in the book. Some of the people photographed are now dead, among them is my old host, Shree Tileswar Rabha, a person I hold in the highest regard. For many, this book will similarly be one of remembrance.

In sum, I am truly happy that *Tribal Bengal: Life in the Sub-Himalayan Terai Duars* is complete and would like to thank the publisher, Niyogi Books, for seeing the project through. This is not an ordinary book but one of those rare treasures you will keep returning to over and over again.

Bengt G Karlsson
Stockholm University

Preface

The photo-ethnography on Indian tribal people was once done by the scholar-photographer, Sunil Janah. A part of his work was presented in *The Tribals of India through the Lens of Sunil Janah,* in 1993. I took another look at this amazing book while I was capturing tribal faces with my lens. The documentation attempted here has been inspired by Janah's work. However, I rarely aspired to be clubbed among the echelons of the photo-ethnographers; on the contrary, my endeavour will be happily fulfilled if this work is treated as a piece of photo journalism.

My home and workplace are situated in North Bengal and I have been officially engaged in a job among the tribals for quite sometime now. Hence, my quest for documenting the tribal communities of the area from the vantage point of an intimate witness to their day-to-day life, amid joys and sorrows. I am grateful that these people allowed me to observe their society, beliefs, customs and the contemporary dilemmas they face. They are some of the earliest people in this subcontinent who are struggling, despondently yet desperately, to combat with the rapidly-changing socio-economic scenario of the country.

Like all projects generated by self-interest, this one, too, was predestined to be a self-sponsored one. Being bereft of any formal training in both, anthropology and photography, my enterprise is destined to fit among amateur researches on such a widely dealt-with subject. In undertaking the study, I am well aware of the fact that it might violate many of the sophisticated and academically endowed traditions of tribal historiography in India. But the one thing that I look forward to earnestly is the avid interest of the common reader who I hope will be less nitpicking but more patient in lending an empathetic eye and ear to the cheers and malaise of the fast-fading tribal people of this part of West Bengal.

North Bengal as a whole is an interesting tribal zone of not only West Bengal but of India as well. It is one of the finest tribal galaxies of our country for reasons best known to anthropologists and people concerned with human resources. Being a watchdog of the tribal affairs in North Bengal, I wrote a book, *B for Bengal, T for Tribes*, over a decade ago. The book presented photographs and small anthropological notes of 25 tribal communities of Bengal. Mahasveta Devi wrote its foreword and the slender volume fell out of print within a short spell of time. The eagerness with which this book was received motivated me to write *Tribal Bengal: Life in the Sub-Himalayan Terai Duars*. As I am an amateur photographer, the pictures presented in this book may not be the best shots technically and may not even capture the best moods. My quest was to identify the communities and get them framed together, keeping in mind the fact that they are on the verge of detribalisation. I had to face considerable hardship in looking for communities from the present-day social galaxy, a task similar to the unfeasibility of identifying medicinal plants in an uncharacteristic patch of the Indian rainforest. Tribal people in West Bengal, except a few large groups and otherwise typical ones, do not have tribal features today because of their prolonged inhabitation in mixed societies. We will be wrong if we assume 'Toto society', 'Santal society', 'Munda society' and the others as isolated, iconically different from the mainstream slice of Indian society. The tribal people do not necessarily live in their own society any more under the changing circumstances. In most cases, they live and share cultures in a mixed society in a rapidly globalising environment.

West Bengal is now home to about 5.3 million tribal people; they form five per cent of the total tribal population of India. In the state itself, they comprise 5.80 per cent of the total population. It can, therefore, be said that one in every 17 people of Bengal belongs to any of the tribal communities. In West Bengal, the tribal people are also known as Adivasi (from the Sanskrit words, *adi*, which means beginning and *vasi*, dweller), ST (Scheduled Tribe), Madhesia or Madesia (people of central provinces) and so on. There are altogether 40 such communities in West Bengal today whom the Government of India recognises as 'Scheduled Tribes'. Among these, three are notified as primitive tribes (Toto, Lodha and Birhor).

The 'tribal world' of Bengal features interesting socio-cultural and linguistic diversity. Together with the Indo-Mongoloids, there are people hailing from the Proto-Australoid and other Dravidian-speaking races. There is a significant number of people who speak the Tibeto-Burman, Dravidian and Austric languages, but the crude reality of their socio-economic location in Indian society has compelled them to opt for the Indo-Iranian language. It is due to this lingual variety that Bengal wonderfully exhibits the essential features of diversified India and its tribal people are also examples of the rich human heritage of this country. There are several pertinent language issues for the Bengal tribes, which are, however, not the focus of this book.

The official stand of the state of West Bengal contributes to yet another perspective on the tribal people living there. This relates to the demographic issue, which could easily roll on to some serious socio-economic debates. The proportion of the tribal population has been gradually decreasing, as is evident from the census reports of the last 50 years (1961–2011). The proportion of tribals was 5.88 per cent to the total population of the state in 1961; it became 5.50 per cent in 2001. The fall was not necessarily sudden or accidental. The marginalisation of tribals has been the phenomenon revealed by several decadal census surveys. In 1971, the figure was 5.72 per cent and, in 1981, it went down to 5.63 per cent. In 1991, it fell to 5.59 per cent. Even with the inclusion of two new communities, Tamang and Limbu, as the STs in 2003, the situation did not change. The 2011 census revealed that the proportion of tribal people is 5.80 per cent in Bengal. It is observed that, possibly owing to the paucity of data and documents, West Bengal is little known for its tribal facet. Tribals or Adivasis are more or less a matter that pertains to the Government. Tribals find very little space in the media as well, including the social media.

The tribal destinations of Bengal may be spatially viewed from five major focus areas. The first category is the Jungle Mahal of South Bengal, mainly consisting of West and East Medinipur and the Bankura and Purulia districts, where one would find the Santal, Birhor, Lodha, Kharia and other so-called 'Nishada' communities. The districts of Murshidabad and Bardhaman may be seen as its buffer zone. Middle Bengal, comprising the Dinajpur and Malda districts, is home to the Santal, Sauria Paharia and once again the 'Nishada' communities. This would be the second zone. The third, fourth and fifth categories pertain to Sub-Himalayan Bengal and are the focus area of this book. Of these three categories, the entire undivided district of Darjeeling should go first because of its preponderance of colourful hill tribes such as the Bhutias, the Sherpas, the Tamangs, the Lepchas and the Limbus. The Terai region of the Siliguri subdivision of the district of Darjeeling could be identified as the second category for its multi-ethnic tea tribes and other communities. The third zone is the great Jalpaiguri-Duars where we find both Indo-Mongoloid and Proto-Australoid people speaking wonderful languages and enjoying folk life. Here, the tribal people live in tea plantations, in plain villages and also in remote forest-villages. The zone also includes two small hill patches, at Buxa hill and Totopara, which are regarded as the homes of the Dukpa and Toto communities, respectively. Apart from these five spatial zones, the tribals are also found in many buffer areas in their pre-urbanised lifestyles.

Tribal Bengal: Life in the Sub-Himalayan Terai Duars is a documentation of photographs and texts on these people. The communities presented in this volume stand at 41. Of these, 40 are from Scheduled Tribes and one is affiliated to a tribal community that has not yet been recognised as a ST. I feel that the number of STs in West Bengal should have been 45, for six have been clubbed under a single head of 'Bhutia'. Against this backdrop, I have skipped five ST communities (Mru, Mahli, Chakma, Hazang and Khond) and included one non-ST (Dhimal). The reason for this exclusion is their non-availability in my journey. Dhimal has been included because of the tribe's meaningful existence as a community and its prolonged struggle for recognition as a ST.

Looking back, I am not really sure when I started studying the tribal people across the countryside of the Terai-Duars. It was perhaps going on simultaneously with my other sociological studies and my encounters with them during my work as a public servant, amid other job assignments. My field notes roughly show that the period of photographic work would have been during the public holidays in 2005–17. Many of the tribals said very little on their histories and traditional cultures, hence the text portion of this book is mingled with excerpts from available anthropological literature and my personal observations. My focus in this book is on exploring photographic documentation and presenting contemporary stories on the pleasures and plights of the tribals. Yet, I feel I have so many more stories to tell and so many incidents to share on these fascinating people.

Krishnopriyo Bhattacharya
Siliguri

PART 1

Indo-Mongoloids

DHIMAL
DRUKPA
GARO
LEPCHA
LIMBU
MAGH
MECH (BORO)
RABHA
SHERPA
TAMANG
TIBETAN
TOTO
YOLMO

The Diminishing Dhimals

Their language is one of the vanishing tongues of India and the community, in this continent, is on the verge of marginalisation. Being only a little more than a thousand in number in India, the Dhimals continue to pursue their scriptless traditional language. Getting information on India's Dhimals is not a problem because we have the great Naxalbari in North Bengal as a landmark for entry to their 'country'. If you plan to visit this very tiny Dhimal country, you have to take a break at Naxalbari, the place in the foothills of Bengal's Himalayas from where the historic Naxalbari peasant upsurge took a worldwide momentum in 1967. Naxalbari is still synonymous with a red village. However, Naxalbari and its history is not our point of focus here. We are looking at the Dhimal tribe, on whom BH Hodgson wrote an interesting article in the Journal of the Asiatic Society of Bengal (1849).

When you reach the Naxalbari bus stand, a four-kilometre walk towards the river Mechi will take you to the Ketugabur and Siubarjote villages, which are situated

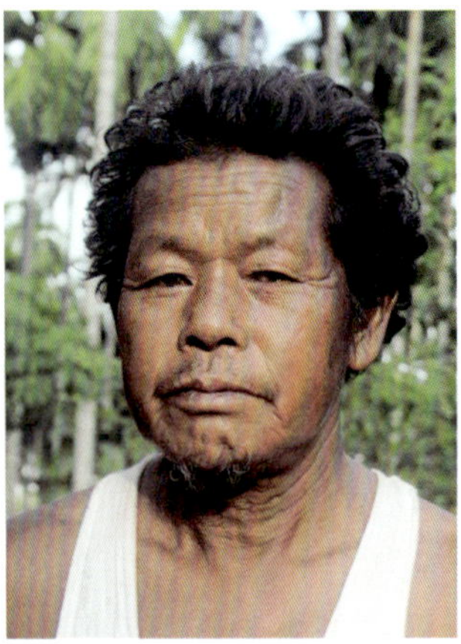

on the eastern side of the river. Surrounded by green paddy fields, you will encounter beautiful North Bengal peasantry instead of Naxalite guerrillas. Here live the Dhimals amid the Rajbanshis, Nepali-speaking races and many others. From these two hamlets, the community has spread to a few clustering villages nearby. This tribal territory is not very far from Siliguri city, just a one-and-a-half-hour road journey. The bus route is known as Siliguri-Panitanki or, more popularly, the Siliguri-Nepal route. From Naxalbari, Nepal's nearest township is Kankorvita.

Dhimal is an integral part of the tribal galaxy of North Bengal. The people here have been seeking official recognition as a Scheduled Tribe in West Bengal for the last three-and-a-half decades but they have not yet been granted the status by the Government of India despite their 200-year-old written history of being indigenous inhabitants of the Indo-Nepal borderland. The Dhimals are outspoken on this issue. My friend Garjan Mallik, a high school teacher and the founder-secretary of the Dhimal culture preservation organisation, has dedicated his life to this cause.

Dhimal drew my attention during the 1980s when I started working on the tribal people as a government servant in the Alipurduar region, which is about 200 kilometres from the actual Dhimal country. As a first catchline on these people, news came to me about their agitation for the ST status and that, too, from Naxalbari, which was one of my dream destinations. In 1998, I was posted at the Naxalbari block as a Backward Classes Welfare (BCW) Inspector. It was a thrilling experience to come across the legends of the Naxal insurrection and to meet the Dhimals, the living antecedents of the great Himalayan Mongoloids.

 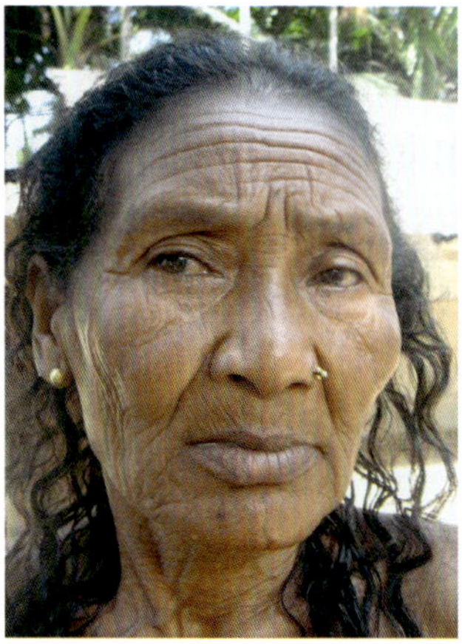 

The population of the Dhimal community in India is microscopic and their voice is such a low-tuned one that the Anthropological Survey of India could not locate them for its People of India project of 1992, though it had identified 4,635 Indian communities. Of Indo-Mongoloid origin, Dhimal could, therefore, be seen as a very small tribe of West Bengal. Like the Totos and the Birhors, the Dhimals are also a tribe of smaller count located in West Bengal. They are, however, a closed community and not much is known about them. They are not found anywhere else in Bengal or in India apart from the region close to the banks of the rivers Mechi and Manjha in the Naxalbari area on the outskirts of Siliguri in Darjeeling. The area is situated on the international border of India and Nepal. The Dhimals are found in Nepal in large numbers—16,781 (Central Bureau of Statistics, Nepal, 1993, population figure is of 1991). They believe that they settled in the North Eastern Himalayan region in 1000 BC before the Aryans invaded the Indian subcontinent.

The Indian, or rather the Bengal-Dhimals, use 'Mallik' as their surname. The tribe has a language of its own, which falls under the Tibeto-Burman linguistic family. Parts of the Dhimal vocabulary have also been found in the languages of the Totos of the Duars, the Tharus, the Rajbanshis and the Limbus of Nepal. Only a small section of the Dhimals in the Naxalbari area can converse in their own language. As a result, the language is facing an untimely death. Most of them today speak the local variety of Rajbanshi-Bengali as they live amid the Rajbanshi-speaking people in Bengal. Nepali has a major influence on their language not only in Nepal but in Bengal as well.

It seems that the Dhimals are losing their traditional values and culture with each passing day. They, however, continue to pursue some of their folklores during festivals. The Dhimals living in Nepal sing 'Jarisona', which is a part of an age-old tradition and is sung at the beginning and end of each of their important social functions. Turia and Poto songs are also sung. Among their colourful folk dances are Poyapoka (fishing dance), Utanga (jumping dance) and Vinadherko (mud dance). While the Dhimals of Nepal still perform these dances, only a limited few of the present generation of the Dhimals of Bengal do so. The tribe has a unique marriage ritual, known as the '10 payment' rite, where 10 persons from 10 different sections of society are paid a price for the bride. Without this customary payment to the 10 persons or to the office-bearers of the village council, the marriage is not approved. There are three types of marriages—by offering betel nut, by force or by elopement. In the Dhimal community, there are 14 exogamous (where marriage within the same clan is prohibited) clans or *thor*s—Donga, Ding, Talipa, Anglaiti, Latar, Rathum and so on. Each of these has its own story of emergence.

The Dhimals once had a variety of musical instruments such as *chyabrung, bomana* or *murchunga, urni tumjhai, dandara, sairenja, wasuli* and *dhol*, which were used in pairs. They were originally shifting cultivators but later settled as farmers. However, with time, many of them began looking for off-farm jobs in order to earn more. They have colourful costumes that are not in much use today. The

men wear *doura*, while the women of the tribe wear *bona*. Dhimals also wear sarees, dhotis, shirts and trousers. Their traditional festivals, Sirijat or Ashari puja (generally held in the month of Bengali Ashar) and Dhamdhani mela (held in May-June) have ample social significance. In the latter, there is a custom of selecting brides from the young girls.

No one from the present-day Indian Dhimals could explain the historical line-ups from which the community name of Dhimal has been derived. Hodgson, being a pioneer of Dhimal history in India, also could not make things better in his time. However, the British scholar mentioned the name of a place known as Dhimali between the rivers Konki and Mahananda, which, according to him, might have had a resemblance with the name of the community. Mahananda is a river passing through the terrains while Konki flows through the midland, between Nepal and Bihar. Hodgson found Dhimals at this Dhimali.

Garjan Mallik once narrated an interesting folktale to me. The story goes that there were two Dhimal brothers who were returning to the hills. It had been a long hard trek and the elder brother was exhausted so he decided to take a break and drink a local beer. The younger one found nothing wrong in that and followed his brother. The elder brother resumed his journey in a short while whereas the other brother fell asleep. The former left instructions for his brother to follow the banana trees that had been felled on his trail to get to the passage. But the drowsy youngster got absolutely lost and, finding no other alternative for his trail towards the hill, he remained on the plains and made his home there. The other brother traversed the thick forest and went to the hill. There, he found his tribe of the Limbus or Rais while the younger brother gave birth to the Dhimal community. Hence there is brotherhood between the Dhimal and the Limbu/Rai people. A similar story was told by some Dhimals of the Jhapa district of Nepal to Bed Prakash Upreti in 1966 as a folktale on their origin. This account suggests that the Dhimals are an offshoot of a large-sized tribe of the past.

I conclude with a narrative of my encounter with Khudan Mallik who happens to be the first Indian Dhimal and, perhaps, the only person from the Indian tribal fraternity who has had the privilege of meeting Chairman Mao Zedong and his wife in Beijing in 1967 during the wave of the Cultural Revolution in China. Khudan's village, Rambhola-jote, is a short distance from Naxalbari. Khudan believes that he was born for the cause of the revolution and will die for it. His village does not have a public transport system and lacks many other civic amenities. Here, people grow paddy with plough cattle and also go fishing. They worship the village deities. Their commerce centres around the one and only Naxalbari *hat* (market), held every Saturday. Though in his eighties, Khudan visits this market often. I went to his house on a motorcycle, through a very difficult road. The village

is little known to its nearest urban gentry, Siliguri and was obviously unknown to the world 50 years ago. Rambhola-jote was one of the nerve-centres of the Naxalbari insurrection.

Khudan remembers this historic meeting. He was explained Mao's words by his companion, Kanu Sanyal; Zhou-En-lai was the interpreter during the session. Mao's electrifying words left the young man of 27 years spellbound: '... Revolution is not a dinner party, nor an essay, nor a painting, nor a piece of embroidery, it cannot be so refined, so leisurely and gentle, so temperate, kind, courteous, restrained and magnanimous. A revolution is an insurrection, an act of violence by which one class overthrows another.'

Khudan's childhood was that of an average Indian tribal peasant growing up in a village. His father, a landlord in this remote village, was popularly known as a *dhami* (a person who performs religious rites). In 1967, Khudan went on an expedition to China and camped there for four months as part of a four-member delegation of Indian rebel communists. The legendary Naxalite leader, Kanu Sanyal, was his mentor in this secret mission to China. Khudan was given training on how to operate machine guns, automated rifles and pistols, use grenades, plant mines and make explosives at the military base-camps of the People's Liberation Army of communist China. His memories of visits to several Chinese cities and factories are still vivid. Before this China expedition, he was already a rebel communist revolutionary and was wanted by the Indian police. He was imprisoned in connection with the land reforms movement in 1966.

I found Khudan to be a simple old man, loved and respected by the villagers. His stories make him absolutely unforgettable.

Dukpas of the Buxa Hills

The beautiful Buxa hills in Alipurduar, North Bengal, beckon. If you can climb them, you will get a magnificent view of Bhutan. In the winter, they sometimes appear larger than the mystic Jayanti, the Switzerland of the Duars. For me, they were our private mountains and none other than the people of the Alipurduar jurisdiction could have any stake in them. The Buxa hills were like my own reading room where I did not allow outsiders.

As there was no public transport system on the Alipurduar-Buxaduar route, it was always a matter of arranging a vehicle on your own for a hill trip. I first climbed the Buxa hills in 1980, when I was at Kamakshyaguri, from where the state of Assam is not far, just an hour by road. This is the last stop of the Kamrup Express in Bengal when it goes towards Guwahati. We all were in an adventurous mood because it was India's Independence Day. The veteran Birinchi Dukpa of Buxaduar hoisted India's national flag on that day on the hilltop.

The Buxa hills were known for their numerous orange orchards; the orange-growers were the indigenous Dukpas. Mathey Dukpa was one such orange-grower and to

him goes the credit for introducing me to the Dukpa community. Mathey had a kind heart and was friendly with all the visitors to the region. Prior to visiting these hills, my notion about the Dukpas or Drukpas was that this community was only found in Bhutan, I had no knowledge of the Indian Drukpas. In the Buxa hills, I found several Dukpa villages whose names, Lepchakha, Chunabhati, Adma, Tashigaon and Topgaon, seemed almost musical to me.

At Chunabhati, a mere three kilometres from Buxaduar, I saw Dukpa women weaving their own *kira* (female costume) in traditional handloom. Once I saw a lady Christian missionary working among the people. Her name was Hellein Hukka. She had settled in this remote village and had set up a church and a small clinic here. Hellein told me that after having trained in Tibetology, at the Namgyal Institute of Tibetology, Darjeeling, she came to this region in the 1950s. She married Norbu Dukpa, a local Dukpa man and virtually became a Florence Nightingale of the area. There were at least 3,000 Dukpa people here. Hellein used to go to her homeland, Finland, occasionally, and bring cookies for the villagers.

The term *dukpa* is a corrupt form of the word *drukpa*, meaning the people of Druk-yuel or the inhabitants of the land of the Thunder-Dragon, that is, Bhotan country. Here, Bhotan or Bhutan or 'Druk-yuel' has been referred to as a 'land of Thunder Dragon'. In Tibetan, *pa* signifies man or inhabitant. 'Drukpa' was formed by suffixing *pa* with Druk (Bhutan). Later, 'Drukpa' became 'Dukpa' in common jargon. While searching for literature on the Dukpas or their ancestors, about 30 years ago, I found a story on the origin of the Tibetans. The Dukpas, I was told, had a link with the Tibetan people.

When I started researching on the written literature of the Dukpas I found that I was the only visitor writing about the Dukpas of the Buxa hills in postcolonial India. These people were virtually unknown to the tribal historians. During 1982–83, I wrote an article for a local Bengali magazine on the Dukpas and its English version was published in the Bulletin of the Cultural Research Institute of Kolkata in 1992. Later, on 31 May 2003, my first radio talk on the Dukpas was broadcast by All India Radio, Siliguri. It was probably the first radio talk on this community. There was no material for me at that time to cite a reference to strengthen my paper. I studied texts on Buddhism, Bhutan and Tibet to gain some primary knowledge of this community. I even read Montgomery Martin's Eastern India volumes for the first time to locate the Dukpas.

When most of the scholars were dwelling upon George Abraham Grierson's volumes on the Linguistic Survey of India in order to understand the language of the tribals, I had to manage with RC Nigam's study on Indian languages. Here I found little information on the dialect of the Dukpas. Yet, my interest remained focussed on the contemporary socio-economic state of affairs of the tribe. The Dukpas are Indo-Mongoloid and their language is Lohke. *Lho* means south in Tibetan. As Bhutan lies in the south of Tibet, the people of Bhutan were identified as 'Lho'. This could be the reason the Drukpas were often called Lhopa-Bhutias. The term *bhotia* means the people of Tibet while *bhutia* refers to the people of Bhutan. However, Drukpa is also the name of a sect in Himalayan Buddhism. In fact, the entire community of the Drukpas is believed to have a religious backdrop. The kingdom of Bhutan is ruled by the Dukpa family.

According to Mathey, the Dukpas are socially divided into two major ecological groups—Sharchop and Ngalop. Those who migrated from the east were called Sharchops and the people from the west were known as Ngalops. Their total population is not separately known, but a study that I conducted reveals that there are nearly 5,000 Dukpas who live in these hills. The tribe has more than 20 occupational and territorial sub-groups and is a patrilineal society with women playing an important role. Among the Dukpas, a funeral is considered more important than any other social event. Like all Tibetans, the Dukpas celebrate their week-long new year festival, Loshar, in February/March. Nimlo is observed in December and Za-eem during the monsoons. The other important festival is Thiugap (name of a star). The community has many rituals to mark the appearance of this holy star. Thiugap is believed to purify the water bodies of the earth with its supernatural power.

The Dukpas are craftsmen and their womenfolk weave garments on their looms. *Bakhu* is the traditional male garment while the women wear *kira* and *guchhum*. The Dukpa women call their necklace *zishe* while the earrings are known as *sokong* and their bracelets, *dok-chung*. The Dukpa men generally carry a sword called *patang* and a dagger known as *chengi*. *Kathla* is a knife that is used to cut betel nut and is popular with both men and women. Fine wood curving is also an art that they practice. They make good archers and play traditional games such as *sushum* (scimitar throwing) and *pangdo* (shotput). Another sport, *pangchong*, is similar to long-jump.

Though most of the Dukpas are Buddhists, there are a few who practice Christianity. The Buddhist temples are known as *chorten*. The Buddhist *lama* (priest) performs rituals during births, marriages and funerals even for the Christian converts. The community as a whole is a Scheduled Tribe and has been clubbed under the 'Bhutia' category. Most of them use the surname Dukpa or Bhutia. They converse in their own language but Nepali is used for wider communication. These tribal people divide a day into six parts—*tolle* (dawn to 6 am); *nin-too* (6 to 10 am); *ninche* (10 to 12 noon); *ninche-eno* (12 to 6 pm); *namso* (6 to 7 pm) and *phiru* (7 to dawn). *Chhang*, an intoxicating millet-beer prepared by the Dukpas, can be had any time of the day.

Garos and the Changing Times

The Garos of West Bengal are a group of a few thousand people (2,039, according to the 2011 census) and the majority of them live in the Cooch Behar and Alipurduar districts. In undivided Jalpaiguri, there were 1,117 inhabitants and 553 in Cooch Behar (2011 census). The numbers of this tribe are dwindling and a sharp fall in their population has been noticed from 1991 (3,673 ethnic Garos) to 2011 (2,039 Garos). Like the neighbouring Rabhas, the people of this region are divided into two ecological categories—the forest villagers and the village Garos. The West Bengal Garos migrated from the Garo hills of Meghalaya and Mymensingh of Bangladesh. However, they believe that their ancestors had originally migrated from Tibet and that the Garo hills became their homeland later. According to the 1981 census, there were 405,449 Garos in Meghalaya. They are recognised as a Scheduled Tribe in West Bengal, Assam, Tripura, Meghalaya, Nagaland and Mizoram.

As per the anthropological classification, the Garos belong to the Indo-Mongoloid racial stock just like the Rabhas and the Meches (Boros) and, like them, have

a script-less dialect, which belongs to the Bodo group of speeches of the Sino-Tibetan linguistic family. It is said that the word *Garo* is derived from the name of their leader Garu. They believe that the Garos migrated to the Garo hills from Tibet, under the leadership of Garu. Another view regarding the origin of the tribe is that the race originated from a Hindu fakir and a Tibetan woman. The Garos follow a matriarchal social structure, similar to the Rabhas. Yet, matriliny for both the tribes is undergoing a rapid change and patriliny tends to be the order of the day in West Bengal.

The West Bengal Garos are primarily farmers and a sizeable number live in the villages of the Duars, working as forest labourers. Some educated Garos have taken up teaching and business as their professions. The social division of this tribe is called *chatchi* and there are five *chatchi*s—Sangma, Marak, Momin, Areng and Shira. The last three are, however, not found among the present generation. These five are further sub-divided into *machong*s—Abeng, Maji, Rongma, Hadima, Tegiti, Ajibock, Chisim and Nengmaiya. Marriages normally do not take place within the same *chatchi* or even within the same *machong*. The bridegroom (*nokram*) generally goes to the bride's (*nokna*'s) parental house.

A major section of the Garos, under the influence of Christian missionaries, converted to Christianity and, therefore, the tribe has been divided into two major religious groups—Christians and non-Christians. A study reveals that they attend socio-religious festivals, namely, Wangala, Ranchagala and Duduka. In Meghalaya, the Garos celebrate the famous Wangala festival during winter with great enthusiasm. This is a crop-harvesting festival dedicated to the sun god and goddess, Misi Saljong. Wangala is also known as the festival of 100 drums.

The Amiable Lepchas

The phrase, 'The children of Kanchenjunga', has become synonymous with the history of the Lepchas. They are considered to be a native tribe of the Darjeeling and Kalimpong hills, though they claim that Sikkim is their homeland. The Sikkimese Lepchas are now concentrated in the district of Dzongu. They call themselves Rong (dwellers of rocky land), Rongkup or Mutanchi Rongkup. The Lepchas believe that their early homeland was situated in a valley called Ma-yel, near Kanchenjunga.

The members of the community are said to be extremely simple, amiable, cheerful, helpful, cooperative, careful and they do not harbour hostile thoughts. Being convinced of the bounty of their cultural heritage, Dr Archibald Campbell, a British medical superintendent in the Indian Army, who was the first to publish a list of Lepcha words, compiled a Lepcha vocabulary in English in 1840. This is one of

the few tribes of Bengal who has the glory of having their own alphabet and written history. Apparently, the Lepcha or Rong or Rong-ke languages, which belong to the Tibeto-Burman family, were the common languages across Sikkim, Tibet, Bhutan and several other regions. Those who acquired the language interacted with a wide range of people. Lepcha was the language used in business and for documenting judicial proceedings in English courts. The Lepchas, however, use Tibetan and Devnagri script for writing. Nepali is popular among them for their day-to-day communication, as it is with many other hill tribes.

LG

The traditional Lepcha house, rectangular on the ground with an oval roof, is called *dookey-moo-lee* and is rarely seen today. A model has been kept as an exhibit at the Lepcha museum in Kalimpong's Bom *busti* (settlement). *Chi* (made from a kind of millet) and *dyo* (made from various medicinal roots, herbs or other fermentable plants) are the customary homemade alcoholic drinks that the Lepchas enjoy.

The conventional term used for the male attire is *dom-pra* and the female wears a dress that is known as *dom-dyam*. These costumes are now seldom used by the members of the tribe. The Lepchas have two types of hats made of bamboo, *thaktop* and *sambu*, which they wear in the rainy season. They also make umbrellas out of bamboo mats. Their term for umbrella is *goom, tuku* or *tuk-tuku*. The traditional jewellery pieces of the tribe are *neckong* (silver earrings), *kow* (necklace), *leyap* (gold and silver ornament), *tho* (stone necklace) and *zu* (locket). Lepcha women are very fond of their jewellery and a green bead necklace (*potimala*) is the symbol of marriage in their society.

There are as many as 68 clans or *agit*s (also called *putsel ptso*); some of these are Fonning, Monlumu, Tassangmu, and Namchumu. The Lepchas also use their *agit*s as a last name. The name of each *agit* is believed to have emerged out of ancestral territory. Therefore, each group worships its respective mountain gods of the past. The Lepchas were originally nature worshippers, but only a few among them practice it today. Most members of the tribe have taken up Buddhism. Their traditional priest is known as *bongthing* while the *lama* presides over all socio-religious functions in Buddhist families. The naming ceremony is observed usually on the third day after birth. In Lepcha marriages, or during any other socio-cultural occasion, both the *lama* and the *bongthing* perform rituals. There are a few among them who are Christians. Though they practice Buddhism, they also follow the tradition of worshipping their tribal deities such as Itpomu, Narzong-nyou and Tsandong.

In 2011, the Lepcha population of West Bengal was 33,962. Of these, 32,862 were found to be the inhabitants of the Darjeeling district. According to the 1981 census, 57.12 per cent among them were Buddhists, 35.70 per cent were Christians and 7.12 per cent were Hindus, while the remaining members pursued 'other religions'.

Lapon Sonam Tshering Lepcha of Kalimpong is a well-known and widely travelled lyricist, folk singer and musician who has composed 500 songs in the Lepcha language and written 10 books on Lepcha culture. His last book is said to have been published when he turned 85. Sonam Tshering joined the British Army as a soldier in the Gorkha Rifles during the Second World War, at the age of 17. He had a short life in the army and turned into a cultural legend of the Lepchas later. The only solitary Lepcha museum in India at Kalimpong, between Sikkim and Bhutan, near Darjeeling, is his brainchild. Scholars of Lepcha history across the world know this golden treasure better than the locales.

The Lepchas refer to Sonam Tshering as *Lapon* (guru) and, even though he was presented two national awards, the Padma Shri (2006) and the Sangeet Natak Akademi award (1986) from the President of India, he continues to live a simple and tribal way of life. In 2014, he was awarded the Banga Bhushan from the Bengal Chief Minister, Mamata Banerjee. The old man can, even now, accompany you on a high altitude mountain expedition. One day in August 2012, Sonam Tshering went with me, amid rain and blizzard, to the ruins of the Damsang Fort where the last Lepcha king, Gyaboo Achyok Pano, lived. It is situated at an altitude of 6,500 feet and is now covered with dense forest. Not far from Kalimpong, the fort lies near a small hill station, Pedong, and is believed to have been built by the king sometime in the last part of the 17th century for the protection of the Lepcha kingdom from the neighbouring Bhutanese. It is said that the fort got its name from the great Tamsang Thing (an incarnation narrated in Lepcha history), who once killed Laso-mung, the powerful devil, and saved the Lepchas. Later, the Damsang Fort was invaded by the Bhutanese and King Gaeboo Achyok was assassinated. The Lepchas still celebrate the birth anniversary of this king on 20 December.

Sonam Tshering pioneered the Lepcha festival on the eve of the birthday of the legendary Gyaboo Achyok, in Kalimpong. The festival, has, over the years, become a huge international conference of the Lepcha community, where people meet and exchange views. With Sonam Tshering's initiative, Sikkim revived Tendong-Lho-Rum-Faat, the state festival, at the Mount Tendong hilltop. It is held on 8 August every year and the day has been declared a state holiday since 1995. For the Bengal Lepchas, this festival is celebrated in Kalimpong under the auspices of the Indigenous Lepcha Tribal Association. Sonam Tshering's hymn has become the national song of the Lepcha community. He believes that the Indian Lepchas are at the crossroads of cultural imperialism and hence it is time to enumerate their untold stories.

The Colourful Limbus

The Limbus, it is generally agreed, are one of the most colourful communities in the world and their existence is under severe threat, just like that of the Totos of the Bengal Duars. Like many other Indian marginal communities, they are the obvious victims of cultural imperialism. My attention was first drawn to this community when I heard the name of Renulina Subba, the 'iron lady' from Darjeeling. Renulina was a Member of the Legislative Assembly (MLA) in West Bengal during the 1980s. Her name often appeared in the media for her Tarzan-like activities. She once climbed up the Assembly house wall to protest her expulsion from a session. I was interested in this lady as I had got to know her as a Limbu.

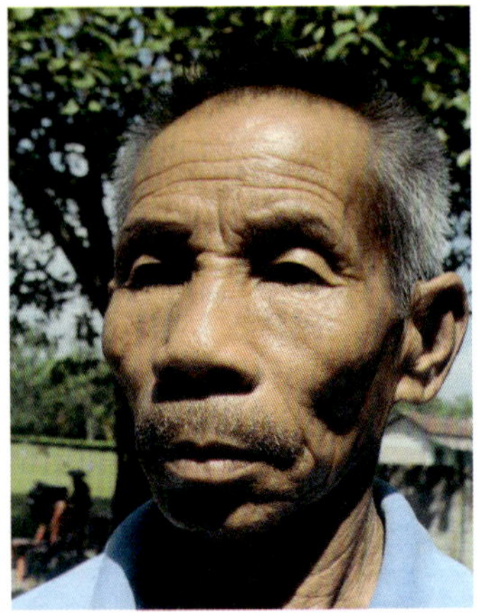

I met Chhatre Subba, a Limbu, during the Gorkhaland statehood movement in the Darjeeling hills. He subsequently became a rebel and was in the news for this reason. I was emotionally involved with this militant as he was from a Limbu family. Later, I came across Professor Tanka Bahadur Subba, another Limbu, who wrote on Anthropology. After pursuing a long scholarly journey in India and overseas, he is currently the Vice Chancellor of an Indian Central University. I had got to know him as a research scholar in the University of North Bengal. His book, *Politics of Culture: A Study of Three Kirata Communities in the Eastern Himalayas* (1999), showed me how the Limbu-Kiratas, together with the Rais and the Yakhas, had to struggle for existence against the cultural aggression of the Gorkhas and the Namgyals of Sikkim. Another book, *Kirata-jana-krti* by Suniti Kumar Chatterjee, also gave me a wider knowledge of the Kiratas. However, even before reading these books, I had bought a paperback on the tribe, *The Limbus* (1979) by Charu Chandra Sanyal, from a Jalpaiguri bookshop for Rs. 10 way back in 1981.

Over a period of time, I got to know more about the tribal affairs of North Bengal and learned that the Limbu community was originally called Kiranti and Yakthumba or Yakthumpa. They are believed to be one of the constituents of the

Kirata race, of the Vedic age. For the Limbus, *li* means bow and *lilong* means archer. Thus the term *limbu* means archer. In the term Yakthumba, a synonym of the Limbus, there are three separate phonemes, that is, *yak* (hill), *thum* (place), *ba* or *pa* (inhabitant). The Limbus use Subba as their surname (Subbas were tax collectors). Subba, according to scholars, was the title accorded to the Limbus of Nepal who accepted the Prithvi Narayan Shah Government's norms of land settlement. Similarly, a section of the Boro-speaking Mech community in the Duars also got the status of a Subba from the Bhutia chiefs of what was then Bhutan. On this basis, the descendants, Mech Subbas, use the surname Subba today. For the Limbus, however, the title of Subba was already in the traditional tribal administrative structure for years.

The migrational history of the Limbus could easily be reckoned from their days in East Nepal and Tibet. Imansing Chemjong, a Kirati scholar and the architect of the Limbu identity, argued in his works that the geographical history of the

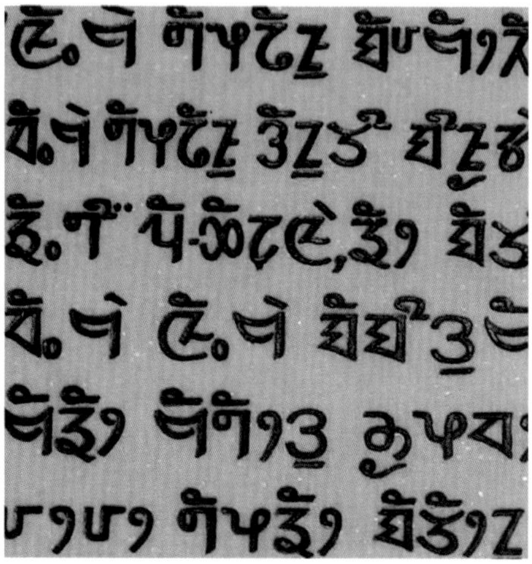

Limbu settlement is something more than that. Quoting the *Markandeya Purana,* he wrote: 'The famous seven Kirat [a] kingdoms during the *Mahabharata* time were Aswa-kut or Kabul, Kulya or Kulu Valley, Matsya or North Bihar, Paundra or Bengal, Sumer or Assam, Malak or Mlek or Lohit, Kinnaur Kirat [a] or Garhwal and Nepal' (*History and Culture of Kirata People*, Parts I and II, Fidim, CH Jabegou, 1966). Chemjong's name is held in high regard in Limbu society as he rediscovered the century-old Limbu script, Sri Junga Saksak. Books by TB Subba and Charu Chandra Sanyal also gave me further insights into the Limbu-Kirata people.

In North Bengal, I found Lukshan, a place on the western banks of the river Kuchi Daina, in the Duars's Nagrakata block of the Jalpaiguri district, which borders Bhutan, to be a beautiful Limbu country. Here, in the tea gardens, there are at least 200 Limbu families living in a big cluster. Being in the majority, they were often given the post of Lukshan Gram Panchayat Pradhan. Lukshan is the main nerve centre of Limbu identity in Bengal and has been the headquarters of the Limbu Subba Vikas Samiti (LSVS) for the last two decades. I met Jetha Subba, Bishnu Subba, Ganesh Subba, Harkabir Subba and many more Limbu people working for

the cause of the Limbus. In 2010, the LSVS built the picturesque Yuma Mangheem, the first Limbu pagoda of Bengal at Lukshan, which has now virtually become a Limbu landmark in Sub-Himalayan Bengal and a tourist destination. Inside this pagoda, there is an eight-storeyed altar, which is beautifully covered with marble and looks like a mini-pyramid. The Mangheem has been conceptualised after the ancient Pythagorean tetrarchs.

The Limbus follow the Yuma Sam religion and Yuma is considered to be the Limbu version of Goddess Parvati, the Kirateswar's (Lord Shiva's) consort. The Limbus are divided into 13 endogamous sub-tribes, each of which is again broken up into a number of exogamous septs. The names of the septs are extremely curious; two or three are totemistic (each clan has a name derived from a plant, fruit or animal and the clan members do not eat, kill or do any harm to these animals or plants), a few are local or territorial and only one is eponymous. These are Tambling, Nembek, Chongbung, Kambos, Fadopia, Fagurai, Tamarkhota, Samba, Nembang, Hanggam, Chenjong, Horha, Tameling and so on.

The West Bengal Limbus are popularly found in the tea belts of Darjeeling, Kalimpong and the Kurseong hills and in some interior parts of Siliguri. They also reside, in small numbers, in the eastern part of the Duars. They have their own language, which, according to linguists, belongs to the pronominalised eastern category of the Tibeto-Burman speech family. They had their own set of alphabets in the past. The Limbus were known for their mastery in archery. They observe three types of marriages—*magi biha* (negotiated by parents), *chheri biha* (elopement) and *jari biha* (taking away another's wife). Among these three, *magi biha* is widely practiced. Instead of garlanding her, the bridegroom presents a coin, along with a metal pot, to his bride, who keeps these with care as a holy sign of the marriage. The supreme male deity of this tribe is Niwa-Buma who, they believe, created the universe.

They have a close social relationship with the Rais, the other group of the Kirati race. Some say that the Limbu population is dwindling because of their inter-community marriages. I encountered a Limbu lady in Siliguri who married a Bengali-Hindu-Namsudra and was surprised when she came to my office for a Scheduled Caste certificate for her daughter. It was painful to give this certificate to a girl whose mother was a tribal Limbu woman.

In West Bengal, the Limbus are said to be a Scheduled Tribe community. Earlier, a section of them were regarded as belonging to the Other Backward Classes (OBCs). In 2016, the West Bengal Government formed a State Limbu Development Board for the betterment of the tribe. According to the census of 2011, the Limbu population of West Bengal was 46,847.

While researching on this tribe, I came across an old man, Purney Subba, as I drove up to Margaret's Hope Tea Estate in Darjeeling. His name had appeared in a Kolkata-based English daily and I was curious to meet him. In its metro page the newspaper had said, 'Purney tea launched'

and given a small picture of the man. The story read: 'The Purney limited edition of tea was launched by the Goodricke Group today to mark Margaret's Hope Garden's 150th year and the brew fetched a maximum of Rs. 7,000 a kg. The management has decided to name a special edition autumn tea after the garden's oldest surviving worker, Purney Subba, 98.'

This, indeed, was an example of how an indigenous centenarian has been branded as a product in the market. Since the product happened to be tea, it amounted to an international tea market. In the story itself, there was an echo of successful branding. The story continued further: 'Of the 60 kg tea launched today, 40 kg was sold. Marcus Wulf of Schroeder and Mamann from Germany and Leafull Corporation Limited from Tokyo, Japan, bought 20 kg each. The German buyer

wanted to buy 20 kg at Rs. 6,500 and later the Japanese buyer bought another 20 kg for Rs. 7,000.'

I had no idea about the price structure of our tea and, therefore, could not asses the cost index. However, the story provided the answer: 'Autumn tea is usually sold for less than Rs. 500 a kg'. Regarding the corporate branding of the product, it explained, 'The special tea is called FTGFOP1 PS Special. All Darjeeling tea is sold as FTGFOP (Fine Tippy Golden Flowery Orange Pekoe), PS stands for Purney Subba.'

Purney Subba never went to any school and cannot sign his name. During my three-hour-long sessions with him and his family, I did not discuss the Fine Tippy Golden Flowery Orange Pekoe story, as I felt it was a meaningless topic for him. The old man was ill and lying in his bed with knee pain. Most of my questions were answered by his two sons. The tea producing company had, apparently, assured 20 per cent of the sale proceeds to Purney's family and the rest of the money would be used for the welfare of the tea garden people.

Purney Subba used to get four paisa a day as wages back in the 1930s when he started working at Margaret's Hope Garden as a labourer. His two sons added that Purney retired after 40 years of work sometime in the 1970s, when his daily wages had risen to Rs. 7. The old man has eight children, five sons and three daughters. At the end of my session, he was brought in front of his house and given a chair to sit. All those present at home assembled for a family photo shoot. I took a few pictures. By the end of the session, the senior Limbu had forgotten his knee pain and was posing happily with a filter-tipped cigarette for the camera.

The Fascinating Maghs

The Burmese Maghs are well-known in Bengal for their repeated attacks and their piracy between the 15th and the 17th centuries. Their old motherland was the eastern Arakan hills, from where they migrated to Chittagong and Tripura. It is said that many of the forefathers of the present day Maghs of West Bengal migrated to India during the riots and insurgencies in Chittagong. The Bengal Maghs, often known as Barua Maghs, are believed to be the third group of the Maghs. The Bengal Maghs could be better referred to as the 'offspring of Bengali women by Burmese men or, more generally, of Arakanese mothers by Bengalee fathers'. They have intermarried for generations with the Bengalis, speak in Bengali and are, in fact, Bengali in all respects. The Maghs are known for their mastery in cooking.

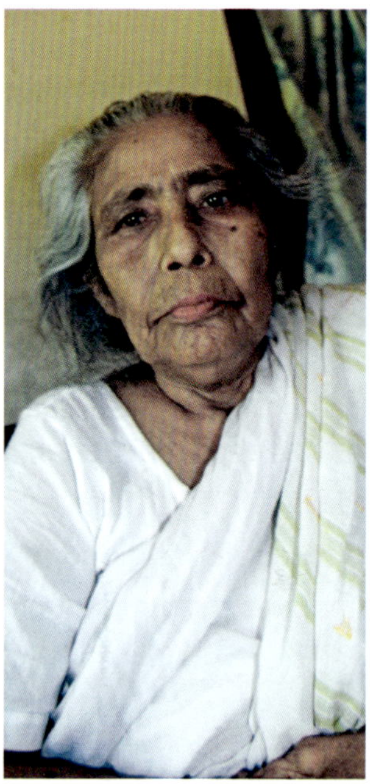

The Bengal Maghs do not have any similarity with the Jhumia Maghs or Raong Maghs of the Arakan and Chittagong hills. In West Bengal, they are recognised as a Scheduled Tribe. They are mostly Buddhists. According to the 2011 census, there are 8,032 Maghs in West Bengal. Their population is increasing; in 1991, there were 4,332 ethnic Maghs in this state and, in 2001, it rose to 8,214 and to 8,032 in 2011. The concentration of the Magh population is higher in the districts of undivided Jalpaiguri, Bardhaman and North 24 Parganas.

I visited a large Magh settlement in Hyderpara, Siliguri, where they appeared Bengali-speaking and worshippers of the Lord Buddha. Except for their Indo-Mongoloid features and dialects, they do not seem very different from the Bengalis at large.

The Autochthonous Meches

Considered the oldest Indo-Mongoloid tribe of Northeast India and the northern part of West Bengal, the Meches or the Bodos (Boros) are found in large numbers in Assam where they achieved political mileage for the Bodo statehood movement. They are also one of Assam's large-sized and developing tribal communities. There are two opinions about their route of migration to West Bengal: they either came from Assam through the Brahmaputra basin or along the river Mechi from Nepal. A concentration of the Meches of West Bengal is still found at the adjacent areas of the Duars in Assam and on the banks of the Mechi in the Indo-Nepal border near Siliguri. Though they do very little for the demographic ups and downs in the region, the Meches could successfully place themselves in North Bengal as a distinct community for their rich cultural way of life.

According to researchers, the word *mech* has been derived from the Sanskrit word *mlechha* (untouchable). The Aryans allegedly called them Mlechhas. This

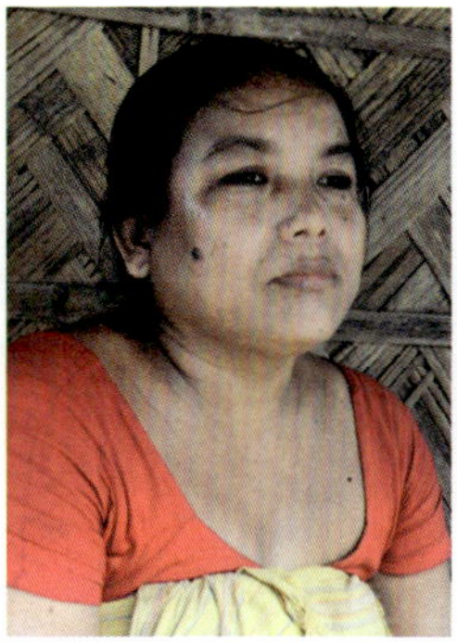

name was probably given to them because the Mech people, non-observers of the Hindu caste regulations, were considered a barbaric tribe. On the other hand, there were some who maintained that the word *mech* was an original one and not a derivation of the Sanskrit word *mlechha*. According to them, the community name Mech had been given to identify the people who lived on the banks of the river Mechi, which flows along the border of India and Nepal. The Meches of West Bengal, however, prefer to identify themselves as the Bodos or the Boros, as their counterparts in Assam. The word *bodo* or *boro* is said to be related to the word describing the inhabitants of various parts of the Bod or Tibet. The name of their language is Bodo; Bodo speech is a dialect that has linguistic links with the Sino-Tibetan language family and has been classified by linguists as a dialect of the Assam-Burmese group of speeches, belonging to the Sino-Tibetan language family. Not having any script of its own, literary works on Bodo are transcribed in Roman and Devnagri scripts. In West Bengal, Mech literature is written in Bengali script. The Meches of West Bengal can speak Bengali but they seldom communicate in the local tongue among themselves.

Some anthropologists claim that the Bodos or the Meches are the descendants of the Kachhari tribe of Northeast India and that they have been living in the undivided Jalpaiguri district of West Bengal since the seventh century, together

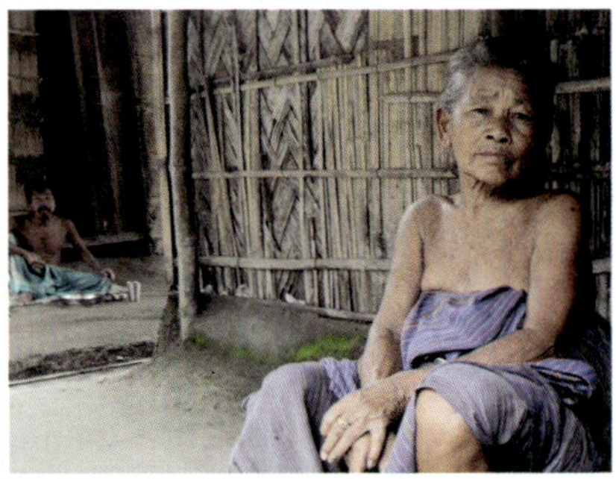

with their counterparts. Census surveys reveal that 90 per cent of the Meches of West Bengal are the Jalpaiguri-Duars-Meches. According to the 2011 census, the total population of the Meches in West Bengal is 41,242, of which 37,726 are the inhabitants of the district of undivided Jalpaiguri alone. A few members of the tribe are, however, found in the Siliguri subdivision of the district of Darjeeling and elsewhere. In Siliguri-Terai, they are found at Matigara block's Mansara-jote and the Naxalbari's Kotia-jote. The Meches also live in the villages in Baikunthapur forest's buffer zone, in Malbazar's Kathambari area.

I recently found a Mech village at Champasari's (near Siliguri) North Palash at the western bank of the river Mahananda where 50 Mech families lived. The Meches settled here after a long life of struggle in the villages of Gulma and Baikunthapur forests and became peasants. I met some aged people who still have grapeshot injuries in their bodies caused by the forest guards during various encounters. The forefathers of these people were basically the collectors of forest produce and frequent encounters took place when all the natural forests came into the orbit of the Indian Forest Act.

Up until the end of the 20th century, the Meches were reportedly found to be *jhum* (shifting) cultivators. They were once famous as cotton cultivators and also earned their livelihood through weaving and fishing. Though the community has now transformed itself to one of settled agriculture, the practice of agriculture, fishing, weaving and rearing of silkworm still exists among them. A good number of the Meches are government servants, teachers, doctors, nurses, drivers and business persons in West Bengal. Many have joined the military and paramilitary forces as well. They have shown a good deal of progress in the development of formal education, in comparison with the other tribes living in the plains of West Bengal. The community has even initiated a movement and asked the Government for the introduction of Bodo language as the medium of instruction in the primary schools of the area. The literary wing of the tribe, Bodo Sahitya Sabha, has taken up a project of organising training classes of Bodo language in these schools.

The Meches are generally patriarchal but have always shown respect to their women. There are several clans or *ari*s among the Meches of West Bengal—Narjeenary, Hazari, Basumatari, Iswarari, Mochhary, Borogaon (Borogaonri), Champramari and so on. The names of these subdivisions are used as their last names but are basically the synonyms for their exogamous clans. Some of the Meches are found to use last names such as Roy, Suba, Mandal, Boro, Gabur,

Thakur, Brahmma, Katham, Saiba and Karjee; these are not based upon their traditional clans but on socio-economic background. For example, the title, Suba, was given by the Bhutanese to some Mech zamindars who used to collect taxes in the Duars during the British period.

As among the Kachharis, Bathou is the chief deity of the Meches. They worship the *sijou* (euphorbia) tree, which they plant in the northeast corner of the courtyard of their house. Another important deity is Mainao, whom the Meches regard as the guardian of the paddy fields. Most of the Hindus in the tribe view Bathou and Mainao as Lord Shiva and Goddess Durga, respectively. They also have a series of river and regional deities such as Mahakal and Tistaburoi. The Christians observe Christian rituals and festivals.

The panoramic folk dances of the Meches—Bagurumba (dance for the spring fest); Baishagu-methay (for New Year); Dhal-Thungri-Gelenay (war dance) and Khera-Kheri—have been widely appreciated. The community is also known for its age-old cottage industry, eri-culture. The Mech women are traditionally skilled in the rearing of silkworms, spinning and weaving on their traditional home loom, called *chanchhali*. The industry is, however, fast disappearing with the rapid development

of the power loom-based cloth industry. Mech women now buy their traditional attire, *dwakhna*, from Bengali weavers.

In North Bengal, I have found the Meches migrating not only from villages to townships (the 5.3 acre Swrang Residential Complex, near Salugara, on the outskirts of Siliguri), but also from townships to villages (Balapara forest *busti* at the Bengal-Assam border in the Duars). *Swrang* in Bodo means 'light' and a band of Mech people have chosen this term for their exclusive residential estate. I visited this mini-Bodoland in 2017 and found 16 beautiful urban houses; a few were under construction. Almost all the residents had their own four-wheeler and two-wheeler vehicles parked on the street. The beautiful road and streetlight system was installed by Assam's Bodo Autonomous Council (BAC), which also has a multi-storeyed guesthouse-cum-office-cum-cultural centre here, known as the Upendra Nath Brahma Memorial Cultural Centre. Upendra Nath was the legendary leader of Assam's Bodo statehood movement. The Bodo people, from many rural Bodo hamlets of the

Duars, have built houses here; others have come from Khoardanga, Mahakalguri, Taleswrguri, Chekamari, Satali, Kathambari and so on. Everyone is affluent, salaried or employees of government departments. There are teachers and engineers as well.

I found a Bodo family at this residency with international links. The story begins with Padam Narjinary's migration to Siliguri from Nepal. Padam's wife, Dalima, was a Bodo from Assam. Their daughter, Priyadarshini, after scoring 90 per cent marks in Class X, trained in computer engineering in Siliguri and got married to a Bodo boy from Assam. Both of them went to the USA and became American citizens. Padam has two sons; one of them, a scholar of electronics, went to China and set up a small industry there and married a Chinese girl; they had a daughter who Padam took home with him and is now teaching her how to speak Nepali.

The entire forest-village of Balapara grew up with a band of Mech people from Kamakshyaguri during the 1960s. Kamakshyaguri was a semi-township that was rapidly getting urbanised. The beautiful paddy lands of the Meches were converted to National Highway No. 31. A group of Mech families shifted to the more backward Balapara in the lap of nature. It is 250 kilometres from Siliguri and there is no direct conveyance. After a five-hour road journey, one has to cross the river Gholani by private boat; this single boat is the lifeline of Balapara.

Rabhas and Their Quaint Customs

The Rabhas, one of the most colourful Indo-Mongoloid tribes of the Northeast, were once found mostly in the areas adjacent to Assam, in the undivided Jalpaiguri and Cooch Behar districts. They are now being seen in the districts of Uttar Dinajpur, Dakshin Dinajpur and Maldah. Though partially creeping into the fold of patriliny, the Rabhas are still regarded as a typical matrilineal tribe, like the Garos. They have been categorised according to anthropological features and are said to have a close affinity with the Garos, Kachharis, Meches and the Koches. The tribe has a few social sub-groups such as Rangdaniya-Rabha, Pati-Rabha and Koch-Rabha. The West Bengal Rabhas are, however, said to belong to the latter two.

The Rabhas in West Bengal are primarily agriculturists while some have resorted to jobs such as that of a labourer. Some are in business, others in service. A large number of the tribe are inhabitants of the forest-villages of North Bengal and have, therefore, been categorised as forest labourers. They also earn their livelihood partially

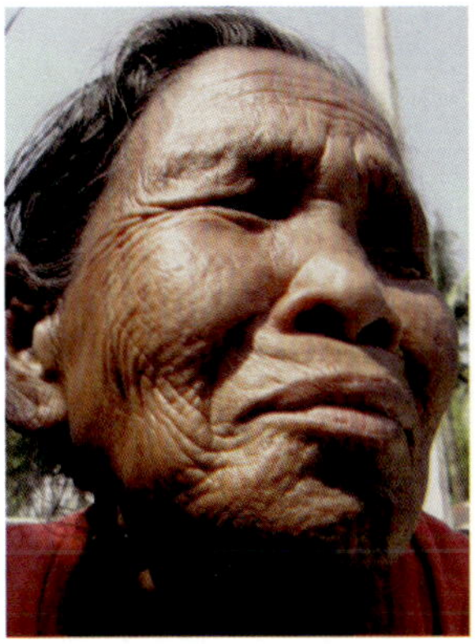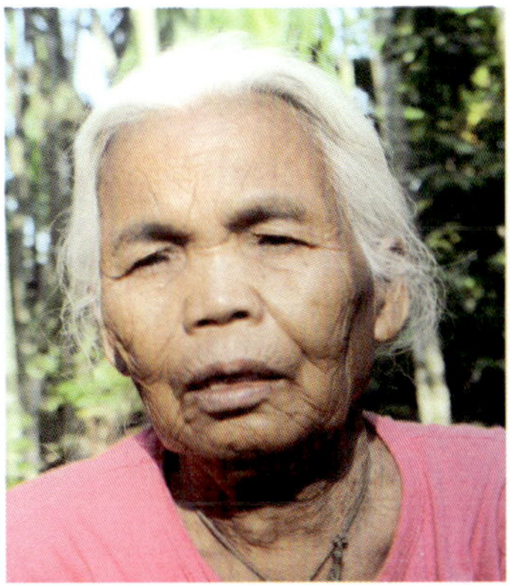

through agriculture and allied activities. The forest-dwelling Rabhas of Bengal make a beautiful local beer, *chakat*, with fermented maize, rice and other grains. Once I took an overdose of *chakat* at a Rabha house and became highly intoxicated; I could not go back home and had to spend the night at the *busti* itself.

The Rabhas speak a script-less dialect belonging to the Bodo group of the Sino-Tibetan language family. In Assam, they are working at developing their literature while, in West Bengal, the Rabhas have adopted the Rajbanshi way of communicating through Bengali. Many of them, mostly the Rabhas who live in the forest-villages, however, converse among themselves in their own Kocha-krow dialect.

The Rabhas (or the Koch-Rabhas) of West Bengal have their own *husuk*s (clans) and children reckon their descent through their mother's *husuk*. In general, the bridegroom goes to the bride's house after marriage. The Rabhas have a custom of inheriting property in favour of the youngest daughter. Among the Rabha clans, Banda, Chinchet, Kantram, Kencham, Pomroi, Uni and Moiji, have been found in the Duars. All the Rabha *husuk*s are, however, not totemistic in nature. Persons belonging to a totemistic clan observe many restrictions and prohibitions in connection with the totem objects.

The Rabhas of West Bengal are divided into two major groups—Christians and non-Christians. Among the latter, the majority practice the Rabha way of traditional Hinduism, which may be regarded as a form of animism; their principal deities are Rantuk and Basek. A sizeable number of the so-called Hindus have converted to a new and localised religion called Jonjogism (named after Jon Jogi Baba who came from Nepal to the Bengal Duars during the early 1950s). There is a Jon Jogi pagoda at the South Poro forest *busti*, near Alipurduar, where an annual festival is celebrated during Buddha Jayanti.

The Rabhas were included in the list of Scheduled Tribes for West Bengal in 1956. They are also a ST community in Assam. The total population of the community in West Bengal is 27,820, as per the census of 2011 (in Assam, the total Rabha population was 236,931, according to the census of 1991). In undivided Jalpaiguri, the 2011 census recorded 14,487 Rabhas. The district of Uttar Dinajpur and Cooch Behar have 5,199 and 3,801 Rabhas, respectively. They are also found in Meghalaya, where they have recently been declared as a Scheduled Tribe.

In West Bengal, the lesser-known Rabhas are gradually coming into the limelight for their performing arts, colourful folk songs and dances such as Naak-Cheng-Reni (fishing dance) and Handaboru (war dance). Like many other Indo-Mongoloid tribes, the Rabhas have a tradition of weaving. They call their typical loom *kountang*. Most of the women can weave traditional attires with this portable pit-loom. During social functions, the Rabha women wear *lufun*s (upper garments) and *kambang*s (lower garments) made by them.

I took photographs of Kharsang Rabha sometime in 2006 at his Gadadhar *busti* home and used one of these as the cover of an earlier book. A Bengali novelist, capitalising on that photograph, used it in one of his post-editorial articles for a Bengali daily before the 2010 assembly poll in West Bengal. The old man, who died around 2008, knew nothing about this. He was already a centenarian struggling with several old age-related ailments when I met him.

Kharsang Rabha's Gadadhar *busti* got electricity in 2012, after a long period of darkness. His house now accommodates two families and about a dozen people. His son, Bishu, was basically jobless, growing paddy in a small piece of land given by the forest department. He also takes up a casual labourer's job, when available.

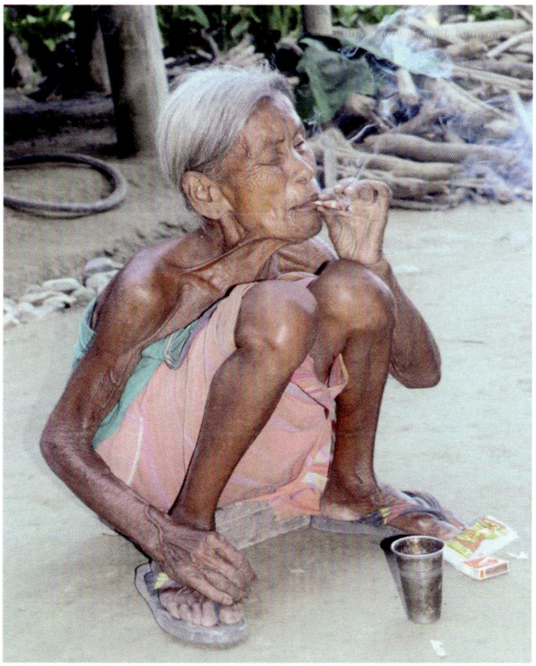

Bishu's wife gathered firewood for selling at the nearby Salsalabari market. Their daughter, Sorita, married at the age of probably 13, had already given birth to a girl child, Sonea. Six-year-old Sonea was attending a nearby primary school, a first for Kharsang's family.

Sherpas Scale Great Heights

Sometimes a community is known by the achievements of a single member of its clan. Tenzing Norgay is such a name in Indian history. His real name, however, was Namgyal Wangdi and he was given the name, 'Tenzing', by Nwang Tenzing Norbu, the then chief Buddhist priest of the famous Rangbuk Monastery. This legendary mountaineer was a son of the Sherpa tribe and was chosen by *Time* as one of the 100 influential persons of the 20th century. The Sherpas are internationally known for their expertise in high altitude mountaineering. On 29 May 1953, Tenzing climbed the peak of Mount Everest and the Sherpas gained a name in world history.

The story goes that Tenzing was once sold as a slave in his boyhood by his father as the family was suffering from acute economic poverty. The deal, however, did not materialise. He escaped and finally made his home in Darjeeling's Tungsung

busti. Tenzing was the eleventh among his brothers and sisters. His father, Ghangla Sherpa, was a Yak-man in the Kharta valley of Tibet. Tenzing loved his father dearly and later named his Darjeeling home 'Ghangla'. His mother was Dokomo Kinzom. The great Himalayan legend died at the age of 71. After Tenzing, Noang Gombu, another Sherpa, brought India's name high in the mountaineering fraternity. Gombu was a nephew of Tenzing who also hailed from the Kharta valley and made Tungsung *busti* his home. Two other Sherpas of Nepal, Apa Sherpa and Phurba Tashi, have made world history by climbing the Mount Everest 21 times.

The Sherpas are believed to belong to Indo-Mongoloid racial stock and it is said that they migrated to the Khumbu valley of Nepal from Tibet between the 13th and 14th centuries. Their original homeland was at Kham Dirke, the eastern province of Tibet. It has also been said that the Darjeeling Sherpas migrated to the eastern part of Nepal some 700 years ago because of the constant harassment by invading Mongolians. Their migration from Tibet is evident from the nomenclature of their community name, as *sher* means east and *pa* means man in the Tibetan language.

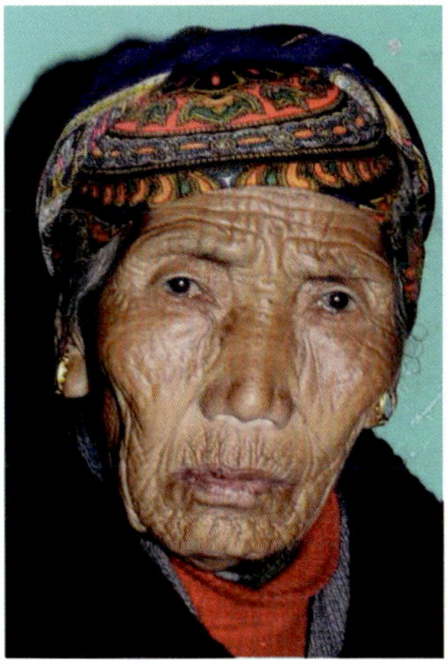

In West Bengal, the Sherpas are largely found in Darjeeling Sadar and Kalimpong. They also live in adjoining Sikkim.

No separate population figures for this community are available post-1951 for they have been clubbed with five other tribes as 'Bhutia'. However, in 1951, there were 8,998 ethnic Sherpas in West Bengal. In 1998, *The Statesman* reported that there were 30,000 Sherpas in India.

The community has its own language but most of the present generation Sherpas do not pursue that traditional speech of communication. In the Darjeeling hills, they largely converse in Nepali. The language of the Sherpas is only used by the older members of the tribe. The names of the days of the week—Monday: *Dawa*; Tuesday: *Mingma*; Wednesday: *Lhakpa*; Thursday: *Phurba*; Friday: *Passang*; Saturday: *Pemba* and Sunday: *Ningma*—are prefixed as the first names of babies. The Sherpa language has attained an official status in Sikkim and a few books have already been brought out, including *Sherpa Pratibimb* and *Sherpa Samachar Patra*, published by the Nepal Sherpa Student Forum and the Nepal Sherpa

Association, respectively. The first textbook in the Sherpa language, written by Thupten Lam Sherpa, was published by the Nepal Sherpa Association in 1992.

The Sherpas are religious-minded people who live a life of simplicity. The well-known Zang Dhog Pherli Nyingamapa Monastery, located in picturesque Durpindara, Kalimpong, attracts a large number of domestic and international tourists. This monastery was founded in 1954 by TN Sherpa, a monk and spiritual head. The 16th century Tek Bochay Monastery, decorated by the high Sherpa priest and monk-incarnate, Nawang Jangbo, in the Solokhombu area of eastern Nepal, is one of the oldest Sherpa monasteries.

Most of the Sherpas in the Darjeeling hills are Buddhists who follow Tantric Buddhism, also known as Lamaism, which is a combination of ancient Tibetan Bonism and the tenets of Buddhism. They mainly belong to the Nygma-pa or 'Red hat' sect. There is a very old Sherpa-Buddhist monastery in Darjeeling. The Sherpas follow the instructions of the *lama*s in matters pertaining to their socio-religious affairs.

Among the popular Sherpa folk dances are Syabru, Sili, Swargay and Nading, usually performed during festivals. The traditional festival of the Sherpas is Loshar, which marks the Tibetan New Year and heralds happiness and prosperity for all. Dumjay and Mani Rindu are also celebrated with great enthusiasm. During Dumjay, the Sherpas offer prayers to the gods and goddesses for seven days. Mani Rindu is a popular festival among the Sherpas in the Solokhumbi area.

These tribal people generally build beautifully designed, two-storeyed houses in the hilltops. The ground floors accommodate cattle and the rear part of the house is used for storing firewood and farm products; the family members live upstairs. The traditional male wears a *fagu*; the female garment is *mogo*.

Sherpa is a Scheduled Tribe in West Bengal. They have a number of exogamous septs or *ryui*s, which sometimes resemble the *gotro* divisions of the Hindu castes. Some of these septs are Dong-ba, Chukate, Mende, Chiwa and Haluri. Marriages are generally forbidden within the same *ryui*. The Sherpas in West Bengal have their own association, called Sherpa Buddhist Association, with its head office in Kalimpong. Many Sherpas are now taking up jobs in several professions including the police and administrative services. The people living in the remote villages in the hills are, however, still facing economic hardship and a major portion of the community is under distress. In Sreekhola, near the Rammam Hydel project in the district of Darjeeling, the Sherpas are seen to pursue the life of hard-core hill people.

Kusang Sherpa is a mountaineer who is widely known among the mountaineering fraternity for he has climbed the Mount Everest five times and created a record. Like Tenzing Norgay and Noam Gombu before him, he has been associated with Darjeeling's Himalayan Mountaineering Institute (HMI) as an instructor; he retired in June 2016. I have had long talks with Kusang about life and the Himalayas. Born in Darjeeling's Alubari lower *busti* on 15 February 1965, Kusang was taught up to primary level at a local school. Kusang's father was an agriculturist and Kusang is the eldest of nine brothers and sisters. In 1993, he got married in Sikkim; he has two sons and two daughters. His son, Passang Tenzing Sherpa, is also a mountaineer and works at HMI as an instructor.

Kusang climbed the world's highest peak first in 1993 from the South Ridge. In 1996, he did it from the North Ridge. His third attempt, from the South Ridge again, was in 1998. In 1999, Kusang joined an American team of mountaineers as its solitary Indian member and climbed the Everest through the very difficult Kangshung Face or East Face of China. In 2003, he went through the North Ridge and became a mountaineering legend. Apart from the Mount Everest, Kusang has also climbed the world's fifth highest peak, Makalu, in 2009, the first Indian to do so. He has received several awards for excellence in the field of mountaineering, trekking and adventure sports, including the Tenzing Norgay National Adventure Award in 2003; Tenzing Norgay Award (West Bengal) in 2003; 150 years of Sipahi Bidroha Celebration Award in 2007 and the Kanchenjungha Award for 2016 (Siliguri). He was also presented the Banga Bhushan in 2013 by the Government of West Bengal.

Rites and Rituals of the Tamangs

Everyone has heard the name of Subas Ghising, the chief architect of the Gorkha identity in the Darjeeling hills, but very few among the non-Nepali know that Ghising belonged to the Tamang community. People can identify the Tamangs by their surnames—Dong, Mokhtan, Nyasur, Golay, Bomjan, Gomden, Pakhrin, Waiba, Zimba, Yonzon and so on. There are several such *thor*s, which many use as their surnames, but, in general, they use Tamang.

The Tamangs are believed to have descended from the Indo-Mongoloid racial family. The term *tamang*, according to some people, was derived from the Tibetan word *tamak* or *ta+mang*, meaning horse-trader or horse-rider. They were part of the cavalry of the king of Tibet. It is also believed that they hailed from the border areas of Tibet and were known as Mulmi (in Tibetan, *mul* means border). The Tamangs, it is said, originated from a place in Nepal called Tagmaluijin. They were basically people living in high mountains who later travelled down to

Sikkim and Darjeeling. Many of the Tamangs are found in the Duars and Terai region of the Jalpaiguri (now bifurcated with the new district of Alipurduar) and Darjeeling (now bifurcated with the new Kalimpong district) districts. The tea garden inhabitants are plantation labourers while their counterparts in the villages thrive on agriculture. Many of the community members took up military and police jobs. Like other hill communities, the Tamangs are often found as motor drivers. A good number of educated Tamangs hold various government jobs and are teachers as well.

The Tamangs have their own speech. As in the case of other Himalayan languages, the Tamang language is also dying so most of them communicate in Nepali. Yet, I visited a Terai village where the community uses the Tamang language. They are good artisans and their bamboo craft is known in the Himalayas for its artistic beauty. Though a section of the Tamangs has converted to Christianity, the majority among the tribe are still Buddhists. This form of Buddhism is, however, said to be a typical amalgamation of Bonism (the most widespread tribal religion of the Bhutan and Nepal Himalaya region that existed prior to the spread of Buddhism) and Lamaism. Bonbo is their spiritual priest and one of the major religious ceremonies is Khepa Soom, which is held once a year on the eve of Dasain or Dussehra. They also celebrate Domang, Wang, Buddha Jayanti, among others. Jhankrism is practiced to appease the evil spirits; the man who conducts this rite is called a Jhankri. The community has its own custom for marking births, marriages and deaths. Their name-giving ceremony, Thapsang, Thansap-thui or Naurawn, is held usually after three days from the day of the birth of a child. A priest confers the name to the newborn baby on the basis of the calendar. The Tamangs observe the Kan Khyaba ceremony for giving rice to a child, generally at the age of six months. Marriages among the Tamangs are held under a very careful social order. They have their typical *rit* system where the bridegroom presents 12 different articles to the bride's parents. The number 12 is symbolic for the tribe as they used to have

12 basic social divisions. Chardom Saimunri is an important part of the rituals and no marriage is solemnised without observing this ceremony of oath-taking as well as the settlement of marriage. The Tamangs generally cremate their dead. The funeral service has two parts—Ngowa and Chewa (Ghewa) and used to last for 49 days, but it has now been shortened to 13 days. The Tamangs believe that the soul takes rebirth.

Like many other Himalayan tribes, the Tamangs have a panoramic socio-cultural life. Their folk dances and songs portray their history and social fabric. Among such folk dances, the most colourful one is, perhaps, the Bakpa where the participating artists wear wooden masks and wigs made of yak tails. Dances are performed generally in the night around a fire. Jungba is, however, done in the daytime and without any masks. Another interesting dance form of the tribe is Choi, which is performed to keep a dead body away from evil powers on the way to the crematorium. Domphu is usually carried out during marriages and on other

social occasions. The new year in Tamang society is called ‘Charlo’. The festival, Sonam Lochaar, is held during the month of Magh (January to February) and lasts for five days.

The Tamang community was declared a Scheduled Tribe in 2003 in West Bengal, prior to which it was given the status of an OBC. One of the largest social organisations of the tribe is the All India Tamang Buddhist Association, which has its headquarters in Darjeeling. The Tamang population in West Bengal, according to the census of 2011, was 146,203. The majority of Tamangs are found to live in Darjeeling, Kalimpong, Jalpaiguri and Alipurduar districts.

The Tibetan Touch

It is generally presumed in Bengal that the monks seen in the Buddhist monasteries, ranging from ages 5 to 100 years, are the Tibetans. It is said that these monks have no families and the monasteries are their entire world. The villages from where they come and the places where they usually go to are little known. I also believed that the monks, both the youths and the seniors, were spending their lives in exile in the monastaries. However, in Siliguri, at the foothills of the Himalayas, I saw the Tibetan monks, males and females, walking in rallies to protest against the treatment given to Tibetan refugees all over the world. Their religious leader, the Dalai Lama, often visits Siliguri's Salugara Buddhist monastery. I once came across a Tibetan civil officer in North Bengal, Passang Norbu Bhutia. I was told that this name was given to him as he was born on a Monday. Passang is now working as a bureaucrat in Kolkata. Bhutias are

actually known as Bhotes in Sikkim and the adjacent West Bengal hills, but many Bengalis refer to them as Bhutia. The Tibetans have their traditional handicraft enterprises in Darjeeling and parts of Sikkim. There is also an institute of Tibetology in Darjeeling. They use two types of scripts, U-Med and U-Chhen. One has the top line while the other does not. Their language belongs to the Tibeto-Burman family of languages. There is no specific population figure for this community because they have been clubbed with a few other tribal communities in West Bengal.

Tibetan tea, which is prepared with butter, salt and milk, is well-known, as is their home-made beer, *chhang*. Another interesting aspect of the Tibetan people is the dress of married women who wear a coloured apron, *pangden*. Like many other tribal groups, the Tibetans have their clans. A study conducted by the Archaelogical Survey of India in 1994 revealed that the clans included Andowa, Tsongpa, Thomowa, Drobthaba, Khampa and Lhasawa.

A Tibetan community council, known as *kyi-dug*, deals with the social problems of the people. The Tibetans are mainly Buddhists and are divided into four sects —Nyingma, Kagynd, Sakya and Gelug. They worship deities such as Gonsa, Gya-Nag-Ko, Chungyal, Ba-lang-dar, Ta-dar, Shal-Nga, Nyam-Nag-Ko, Pa-phyng, Do-solba, A-shangpa, Ma-shang-khyung, Dung and so on.

The Archaelogical Survey of India has identified Pang, Lhabsol, Losoong, Saga-Dawa, Kpayat-Dance and Losar (new year) as Tibetan festivals. Their folk dances, songs and plays are interesting and form an intrinsic part of their life. The folk musical instruments include *gyaling kangling radung, dungkar, lingbu, kharnga, nga, rolmo* and *silnyen dramnye*. The Tibetan people still depend on their traditional medical system and often many non-Tibetans also opt for this method of healing. The women are experts in embroidery on cloth and engraving artwork on silver and gold. The Tamangs, Yolmos and many Himalayan tribes hoist sacred flags around their houses. The main religious centre is Gomba where they worship the Buddha and Guru Rinpoche.

The Tibetans are mostly found in the hill areas of Bengal and in Sikkim where they are known as the Sikkimese Bhotias or Denzongpas. Actor Danny Denzongpa and the soccer player, Baichung Bhutia, are from Sikkimese Bhotia families. Though the main occupation of the Tibetans is agriculture in the mountains, many of them are government employees, traders and so on. They generally marry among themselves; however, inter-community marriages with the Sherpas, Tamangs and Lepchas also take place.

Unique Heritage of the Totos

The Indo-Mongoloid Totos are the most interesting tribe of West Bengal. They are known for their uniqueness in many socio-cultural facets and also for once being projected as a 'vanishing community'. This tribe can only be found in a tiny hilly village known as Totopara, in the valley of Tading hill, at the Indo-Bhutan border in Alipurduar district, North Bengal. Their existence was, perhaps, not known to the world of written literature before the beginning of the 19th century. It was Baboo Kishen Kant Bose who first wrote on the Totos in the English language in *Political Missions to Bootan* (1865). Bose was a British government employee who visited Bhutan in 1815. The tract known as Totopara was, at that time, under Bhutan.

In his monumental settlement report (1895), DHE Sunder wrote about the Totos and got a little less than 2,000 acres of land reserved for the tribe. During Sunder's time, this land was under a tract known as the Western Duars, which

was amalgamated to the Bengal district of Jalpaiguri in 1869. The district of Jalpaiguri, however, was subsequently bifurcated and the Toto country became a part of the district of Alipurduar in 2014. The village is situated between 750 feet and 1,500 feet above sea level.

The entire village was inhabited by the Totos in the past and the tribe has not been found anywhere else in the world so far. Though the name of this 'country' is still Totopara, the Totos comprise only 25 per cent of the population.Today, there are more than 70 per cent Nepali-speaking people who came here after India's independence, more specifically after the 1950 Indo-Nepal treaty. Under the changing circumstances, the Totos have become a minority in their homeland. At the end of December 2014, the headcount of Totos stood at 1,564, which spread across 337 families. This marginalisation of the tribe has drawn attention from various quarters and has also become a point of controversy as to how the non-Totos were allowed to make their home in this so-called Toto land.

In the east, towards Totopara, flows the river Torsha, originating from Bhutan, while in the northwest lies Tading hill and the river Hauri. The village is 30 kilometres from Madarihat and about 150 kilometres from Siliguri. Even though Totopara is now well-connected by road, it becomes a closed country during heavy rains.

Totopara, the silent, tiny tribal land begins where the Indian state of Bengal ends, at the Bhutan hills. I have visited Totopara many times since 1980 and each time I make a new discovery. As the tribal people are at the brink of their transformation into detribalisation, my story may reflect a contemporary situation. The first thing that comes to my mind when I experience this picturesque land is, 'All that glitters is not gold'! Most of the stories here are of either the personal struggles of the Totos, or the changing mosaic of Totopara. This is the land of the primitive Totos of the Duars, who have been living in this charming Indo-Bhutan frontier for at

least 10 generations. Both the Government of West Bengal and the Government of India view these people as an official Primitive Tribal Group (PTG). There are 72 PTGs spread over 15 states of India (five of these—Birhor, Dongaria Khond, Kolam, Koragu and Lodha—are, however, common for more than one state. Hence the actual number of PTGs is 67).

In order to know more about the Totos, one should first understand the historical implications of India's proximity to Bhutan, which lies just across the northern border of West Bengal. This is where the Totos came from. The Indo-Bhutan or the Bengal-Bhutan border was only annexed 150 years ago. Prior to that, though the region was officially under the Koch kingdom, it was occupied by the Bhutias. It was estimated that this occupancy lasted for 300 to 400 years. There were conflicts and wars between the Bhutias and the Koches. During this period, the Bhutias often took war captives from among the downhill communities and used them as slaves. From among these slaves emerged the Totos.

Totopara is one of my favourite destinations and I often make a trip there for no reason. When I visited the place in 2013, I spotted a new children's school, the brainchild of a London-based British lady, Lissa Davies and her NGO, Bright Eyes Global Action Project (BEGAP). Not only was the school exotic for the place, but Lissa's long pinkish hair and auburn complexion added an English touch to this country of relatively darker-skinned people. I was rather surprised to find such a British enterprise suddenly anchoring in Totopara, a place I had been visiting for the past 36 years. This news did not find place in the media. Lissa wrote in the project brochure that this was a dream of Bakul Toto and she had conceived the idea in 2009. So, in a sense, this English school was publicised as the demand of a modern Totopara. It was a new concept for the Totos, like a circus at a village fair. A group of Totos and other kids assembled there and Lissa and other teachers taught them using a novel approach. Lissa recruited a local Toto young man, Prakash, who had recently graduated and was seeking a government job. Her second recruit was a Mech lady, Mitali Narjeenary. In addition, there was Susanto Toto, teaching assistant and Poonam Toto, caretaker.

Lissa's boyfriend from Manchester was also a part of this venture. Besides, she had supporters for her project in Australia, France, the UK and Germany.

As a temporary arrangement, the playschool was housed in government premises. Lissa showed me a thatched house being constructed nearby where the school was expected to shift to very soon. The school house was being built like a Toto traditional dwelling, *na-kosha*. The school was named Chittaranjan Toto Education Centre (CTEC), after Chittaranjan Toto, who was the first Toto to complete the Madhyamik examination in 1979. I knew Chittaranjan's mother, Ningtangma Toto. The Toto scholar met with an untimely death, caused by malaria.

Lissa badly needed money to run the school but had not yet applied for permission from the Government. As far as I know, the school is still there at Totopara and they have even introduced a class on the Toto script that was developed by a Toto intellectual, Dhaniram Toto, in collaboration with a foreign linguist.

In 1997, for the first time in Toto history, four young Totos, including one girl, converted to Christianity under the auspices of a Nagaland-based Baptist church. Of these four, Sandesh and Sadhana announced that they were going to marry according to Christian rituals. The entire tribe mobilised against this wedding and there emerged an unprecedented law and order problem in Totopara. The ceremony could not be held and the main architect of this conversion, Reverend Lomango Chamo Lotha, who came to Totopara from Nagaland, had to leave Totopara within a week. This story made news in the Bengali daily *Aajkaal*, dated 15 January 1997.

In another incident, Bakul Toto, along with his friend Sandesh, went to a hideout on New Year's Eve. When the police took up the matter, Bakul issued a press statement that they had opted for Christianity of their own will. Bakul brought

a serious allegation of social corruption against the then *kaiji* (priest), Sachin Toto, and wrote, 'We, in protest of the bad deeds of some of the conservationists in our society, left the Toto religion. But, yes, we are still with the Toto culture. Faith in religion is the individual's fundamental right. None can blame anybody for a conversion.' This letter was sent to the Jalpaiguri police by post from the hideout. Following this, the situation in Totopara turned grave. From then on, Bakul Toto, who is now the secretary of the Toto Kalyan Samiti, came to be known as Totopara's Jishu (Jesus), a name coined by a media house in Kolkata. I admire him immensely and, in turn, Bakul has also said that he has a special regard for me as I was the newspaper reporter of the incident. Bakul did not marry a Toto; his wife is a Santal girl from Samuktala, where he had attended school. I am not sure if it is purely coincidental that his in-laws' religion is Christianity.

Sandesh is a young father now and the chief of the Totopara's Kohima Lutheran Baptist church. Sandesh's wife, Sadhana, is second in rank in the church hierarchy. I first saw the church operating on a Sunday at Totopara in 2013 and was told that it had 40 Toto members by then. With the Kohima Baptist church, the number of churches in Totopara rose to three. Of these, one is run by a very old Garo family

and the other by a section of the Nepali community. Recently I heard that a fourth church is emerging in Totopara's Yaibadara. As the Indo-Bhutan border is open, people visit this church from adjacent Bhutan.

There is an interesting story about Smita (name changed) Toto, the most progressive Toto girl of her times, who fell in love with a local schoolteacher from a neighbouring tribe. Smita was the first girl from the community to have passed the Madhyamik examination of the year and those around her had high aspirations for her. But, Smita's relationship with a non-Toto man became a curse. Though people did not raise their voices, an undercurrent started to brew about this love story as it was an extramarital relationship. It was also because the man was influential in Totopara—he belonged to an ally of the ruling political front and had been a respectable chief of a local body. A Nepali-speaking Indo-Mongoloid origin clergy, Kumar Tamang (name changed) came into Smita's life at this very crucial stage. He gave her emotional support and got her to convert to Christianity. Smita then started living with Kumar Tamang. This created a further furore in Totopara and her reputation went down further within the Toto community. In 2006, Smita got a teaching job at a primary school in Totopara. During my conversations with her, she expressed concern for the development of the Totos and was also outspoken

about the exploitation by middlemen in Totopara. She promised to write her autobiography one day.

None of these stories seem to have found a place in the works of those who wrote on the Totos. The tribal community has so far been the subject of researches whose focus has been its dwindling numbers and the apprehension of extinction. This may be so because the Totos are a conservative people and do not marry non-Totos. Their practice of community endogamy usually goes against the codes of other neighbouring societies. Incidents of death cases from tuberculosis among the Totos also drew people's attention to the assumption of a loss of population. My study of the year-wise Toto population, however, revealed that the fact that they are a dwindling tribe is not true. This community of 171 people in 1901 became 1,195 in 2001. It then rose to 1,564 in December 2014. In 1995, when the community gave birth to its 1,000th son, the event was celebrated by naming the child 'Hajare Toto' (thousandth Toto).

The Totos are certainly not 'the world's smallest tribal community', as mentioned by the media in Bengal. Other Indian tribes such as the Onge, the Great Andamanese of Bay Islands, the Kadaku and the Pando of Madhya Pradesh, the Cholanaikan of Kerala and the Toda and Kota have a population that is below 500.

A few years ago, the Kolkata-based Netaji Subhas Chandra Bose Cancer Research Institute announced that 14 per cent of unmarried Totos were carriers of the thalassemia virus (*The Hindu*, 29 January 2009, e-paper, www.hindu.com). The news report claimed that the Department of Biotechnology, under the Ministry of Science and Technology, Government of India, New Delhi, had sanctioned Rs. 30 lakh to the Institute for the Toto study. Further, according to the Director of the Institute, Dr Ashis Mukhopadhyay, 'There could be actually more carriers of the virus among the rest of the population, since the test was conducted only among unmarried Totos.' Given the high incidence of the thalassemia virus among the members of the tribe, he pointed out, that inbreeding increases the chances of children carrying the deadly virus. As per tradition, any Toto member marrying outside the tribe is ostracised, which makes matters more complicated, the story highlighted. The news report also stated that recent findings by the Indian Anthropological Survey reveal that the average lifespan of the Totos is 35 years. A satellite centre was supposed to be opened shortly at Totopara, to spread awareness among the tribals about the prevalence of the virus and to advise them not to marry immediate relatives and have blood tests done before they get married. The treatment of thalassemia patients was to be an integral part of the programme. This news report got me worried, but this worry did not echo in Totopara.

It is known that the Toto community is conservative about marriage with non-Totos. However, this rigidity appears to have partly faded over time. I collected 21 cases of inter-community marriages that took place during recent times, including Sanjit Toto, who had married a Nepali-speaking girl from the Newar community. Among my Toto friends, Ashok Toto also had an inter-community marriage.

The first Rajbanshi-Toto marriage took place in 2012 when Jhuma Toto married Shyamal Barman of Salsalabari. Jhuma is the daughter of my friend Bhakto Toto who is well-known in the region, as he is a Toto scholar and branch manager of the Uttarbanga Kshetriya Gramin Bank (UBKGB), Totopara. Rajbanshi is a Hinduised SC community of North Bengal with quite a large population. A marriage such as this seems unthinkable as the two cultures are totally different. Most of the inter-community marriages that took place among the Totos were with the Nepali-speaking communities such as the Tamangs, the Mangars, the Rais, the Limbus, the Newars and the Sarkis. It was apparent that largely people from the lower castes married the Totos. Here, too, there was an exception when a Toto girl, Youngtaima, married a Nepali Brahmin boy.

I am told that, under ordinary circumstances, migrating outside Totopara was beyond the Totos' imagination. Wherever they went, they would come back to Totopara before sunset. There are, of course, exceptions to this and many Totos have bought land outside Totopara. I developed a list of 20 such people during my trips to this area. Take the case of Lora Toto who bought seven acres of land in Ballalguri's Burja-dara in 1990 and shifted there. This new village is quite far from the river Hauri and is generally safe from the possibility of any river-borne calamity. One of Lora's sons, Nima, got a job in the army in Assam, which is what may have prompted Lora to shift from his ancestor's land. Nima married a Mech girl, Reshmi Karjee. Thus, Lora's family not only left Totopara, but also the Toto culture and has merged with a new one.

Among the early Toto emigrants is Sugrib Toto, a Gramin Bank employee at Totopara and the Toto society's *gappu* (head dealing with village and management matters). Sugrib bought 3.33 acres of land for Rs. 60,000 at Ballalguri and shifted his house there in 1996. Dirsa Toto also bought two acres of land there for Rs. 30,000.

This tribe has been living in Totopara for 10 generations or so. Dr BK Roy Burman estimated 'eight generations' in the 1950s. The author held that at least up to 1772, that is, up to the middle of the 18th century, there were slaves in the hill part of the Duars. Before that, the tribe emerged as war captives and slaves of Bhutan. These slaves were used as porters for various purposes in Bhutan. The Bhutia state machinery needed them for making a socio-economic and political bridge between the uphill and the southern plain land of the Duars. Eventually, the slaves entered Bhutan. This happened over a long period of time while wars continued between the Bhutias and the Koches. These captives-turned-slaves were gradually organised into working gangs by the Bhutias, in order to render slave labour. The Toto word for slave labour is *hui-hwa* and they ultimately formed a community. Totopara, being close to the Indo-Bhutan frontier, in the Bengal Duars, was under the virtual occupation of the Bhutias till the second Bhutan-Duars war that ended in 1864. From then to December 1868, it was with the British district of the Western Duars. In January 1869, it came under the Jalpaiguri district and, finally, in June 2014, Totopara became a part of the newly-formed Alipurduar district.

Dr Roy Burman claimed that the entire Toto community was an outcome of Bhutan's statecraft. As far as I know, his politically-sensitive thesis has not yet been contested. Until this view is challenged, the Totos will remain on record as a wonderful example of Bhutan's statecraft. The interpretation that often comes to my mind, instead, is 'Bhutan's hegemonic outburst'. I am not certain whether or not Bhutan's statecraft proved well for the Totos, but Bhutan definitely was instrumental in bringing about a social division among the tribe. Was it because the Bhutias had such dualism in their socio-political format? The authorities of Toto history agree that it was the Bhutias who crafted the *moiety* (primary social division in which a tribe is sometimes made up of two groups) of the Totos. Maybe, this dichotomisation was necessary to maintain Bhutan's supply line from the hills to the plains. Dr Roy Burman has provided many insights into this issue. The Toto community has always had a dichotomised social formation with two broad divisions—the Orangbeis and Wangtengbeis. The Orangbei group were the uphill dwellers, while the Wangtengbei people were believed to be lowlanders. At the time, Bhutan was spread across the hills as well as the plains of today's Duars. The ancestors of the Totos were used to maintaining links with the people from the plains and from Koch, the Mechs and the Rabhas and also with the uphill Bhutias.

Knowledge of this *moiety* division of the Totos takes us close to Bhutia politics in which the entire Toto community has been submerged. The 13 clans of the Totos are affiliated to one of the above two *moieties*. A survey conducted in 2003 by

the Cultural Research Institute of Kolkata reveals that 138 families of the Totos belonged to the Orangbei category, while 122 to the Wangtengbei. At that time, there were altogether 260 Toto families and the number has now risen to 337 (December 2014).

I have always found the Toto language tough to learn and was surprised when I came to know that the Totos do not call themselves 'Toto', but 'Tot-bee'. The ethnic name of their language (or dialect) is Diyaw-e-kya. The word Toto was given by the non-Totos. This appeared to me as a serious error of viewing a tribe with a hegemonic vision. Bhakto Toto declared this officially in 2011 in an article in the special Toto edition of a local Bengali magazine.

I was privileged to roam in the Diyaw-e-kya lexical galaxy and compile 1,100 words during one of my self-sponsored projects of compiling a lexicon of tribal speeches. However, this did not improve my situation regarding the language! During my encounters with the tribal people of North Bengal, I managed to learn smatterings of Bodo (Mech), Rabha, Kurukh (Oraon) and Sadri (the Adivasi lingua franca), but not Diyaw-e-kya. Also, I have not come across any non-Toto person of my time who knows the language.

The authorities of linguistic sciences have classified the language of the Totos (the dialect, in particular) as belonging to the Tibeto-Burman family of the Sub-Himalayan group. It is stated to be non-pronominalised. In non-pronominalised languages, the sentences are not formed by suffixing the personal pronouns to the verbs to denote not only the subject but also the direct and indirect objects. I found a sizeable part of the Toto vocabulary to be similar to that of the Dhimals, but later realised that the sentence formations are different, as Dhimal happens to be a pronominalised language. It was also fascinating to learn that the original source-speech, from which the Toto and its friendly languages have developed, was rooted in Southwest China's Yang-tze-Kiang and the Ho-ang-Ho basins.

Pujagaon is a hilly village in the northern part of Totopara, whose picturesque landscape, drowsiness and silence give it sanctity. The river Torsha (*Mu-tee* for the Totos) is not very far from here. On crossing it, one reaches the colourful Bhutia city of Phuntsholing. The Totos call this place Baduri. They have their own names for other hamlets in Totopara as well. In Pujagaon, there is a sacred house called the *dhem-sha*. One can compare it with a temple or a pagoda. In Toto, *sha* means house. They call their home *nako-sha*. The *dhem-sha* had a thatched roof, wooden floors and bamboo walls in the recent past. I was privileged to see its older version. Now, the Government of West Bengal has made it into a *pucca* house and has also erected a brick boundary wall. No trip of mine to Totopara gets its sanctity until I visit the Pujagaon *dhem-sha*. I find it to be calm and quiet, exuding indigenous purity. There are no images or idols of Toto deities, or any altars for worshipping. One has to imagine and feel that here live Ishpa and Sainja, the main Toto deities. Traditionally, the Budhubei clan has been the caretaker of the *dhem-sha*, which is probably why its members live uphill and were once very close to the Bhutia conservatives. Two sacred *bakung*s (drums) are permanently hung from the roof of the *dhem-sha*. Dhaniram Toto informed that they were named *chigaimu* and *mugaimu*. Some see these two drums as Mahakal and Mahakali, which could

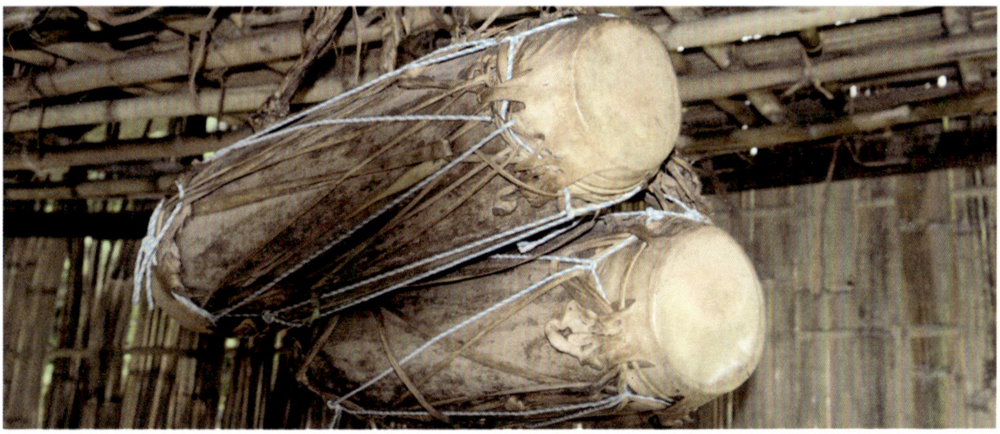

well be a Nepali interpretation. According to Dr Roy Burman, '*Moiety* division has nothing to do with marriages. But during the Mayu festival [Mayu puja is held in the winter months when oranges break and the Totos celebrate two main festivals, Omchu puja and Mayu puja] the symbolic marriage between a son and a daughter of Wangtebei and Orangbei, respectively, takes place. The son and the daughter are symbolised by two drums.' This leads me to believe that the two drums at the *dhem-sha* are the turning point in Toto history as they symbolise creation and the basic social dualism of their culture.

I was initially hesitant to go to the *dhem-sha*, as entry of non-Totos was restricted. Once, in 2013, I finally managed to enter the sacred house and take pictures of the drums. I was accompanied by Sandesh's elder son, Clement, who encouraged me to go in silently and quickly take the photographs. Dr Roy Burman narrates a great story about these two drums in his article, *The Drama of Two Drums: Mayu Festival of the Totos*, which is regarded as an exclusive account of the history of the drums. The surreal *dhem-sha* and its illuminating drums engulfed my memories of the Toto land and kept me mesmerised. The ritual that the Totos have not yet forgotten is clan worshipping, which is done every two or three years. This is when married women and their children go to the ancestral homes to participate in the prayers. Another popular ritual is totem worshipping. The community has 13 Toto clan objects spread across 13 different places in Totopara. This appears to me the best and finest evidence of the tribe's legacy. Among the objects they devised for this purpose are stones and the remnants of trees, mostly mango trees. Each clan member comes to the shrine spot and pays homage to their ancestors, sacrificing hens, pigs, cocks and even cows, according to prescribed ritualistic norms.

Between September and November 2013, I got to hear five stories from Totopara, each one of them was tragic. Seventeen-year-old Wangdi died in an accident in Sikkim, where the young boy had gone for work. Rikash, 19, also met an untimely death in a Bhutan dam site accident while crossing a turbulent river with stone slabs on his head. Rikash worked there under a contractor. These incidents raised many questions about employment opportunities for Toto labourers. Two young Totos died of jaundice and another succumbed to tuberculosis. These deaths also raise serious questions as to how we nurture our primitive people.

The main crisis of the Totos, however, is not their dwindling numbers, but their marginalisation in their own land. The tiny community has already been reduced to a minority in demographic terms. More than 70 per cent of Totopara's population presently consists of non-Totos and more than two-thirds of their land in Totopara is occupied by them. The Toto language is now heard at a very low octave, signifying their dropping confidence. Whatever be the contemporary predicaments, I have reason to believe that the plight of the Totos had its roots in the closure of the Second Bhutan-Duars war of 1864 and the annexation of the Duars in 1865. After the end of Bhutanese rule in the Duars, the Totos were seen to initiate their settled life

at Totopara. Perhaps, they found some peace there, at the bank of the river Hauri, after a prolonged spell of war captivity. This was the beginning of their orange-growing life. At this juncture, there was an influx of people from the outside world into Totoland, which became an international orange mart. I had the privilege to witness the colourful orange market in Totopara even during the early 1990s. Totopara was also a significant ginger and betel nut market. It was, however, the orange that attracted outsiders to a mono-ethnic Totopara. As Dr Roy Burman says, 'Previously Totopara used to send out its antennae, through which the existence of the larger world was felt; now the world invaded Totopara.' Along the way came the Nepali who further invaded the area and laid the foundation stone of a new Totopara.

In 1951, the Totopara Welfare Centre was established under the auspices of the Tribal Welfare Department, Government of West Bengal. However, in 1954, the first teacher-cum-organiser, Jogendranath Sarkar, was murdered. He was vocal in protesting the encroachment of the area by non-Totos. This incident came as a blow to both the Toto community as well as the Government of West Bengal. Meanwhile, in 1956, the Totos were incorporated as a Scheduled Tribe for the state of West

Bengal and were clubbed under the broad head of Bhutia (Scheduled Castes and Scheduled Tribes [Modification] Order, 1956, dated 29 October 1956).

The entire Totopara land of 1,991.59 acres in Mouza was in the name of Dhanapati Toto, the chief at that time. Dhanapati paid an annual tax of Rs. 150 for this land to the Government of West Bengal. As the influx of the Nepali people shadowed Totopara and the Totos could not bring the entire land under cultivation, the Government of West Bengal took no time to declare them as lazy and viewed their land under Section 44 (2a) of The West Bengal Land Acquisition Act, 1953. Under this proviso, the Government vests land that was found unutilised. The primitive Totos were then on the verge of their transformation from a *jhum* cultivation to a settled one. They required some more time to come out of their deep-rooted apathy towards settled farming, which, unfortunately, the Government did not take into account.

In 1969, the Government of West Bengal vested 1,644.76 acres (85 per cent) of Dhanapati Toto's 1,991.59 acres of land in the name of land reform. This issue has not yet been resolved. The 100-acre Kuapani forest, used by the Totos, was also taken away from them by the Forest Department later in 1992. The Totos, by this time, had come to understand the romance of an open Totopara and the magic of India's pluri-cultural mosaic yet they became a minority in their own land. Totopara's politics centred round the non-Totos.

On 8 June 1994, a delegation consisting of four MLAs, three RSP leaders and four Toto leaders (Muktaram Toto, Jiten Toto, Gouri Toto and Sanjit Toto) met the Chief Minister of West Bengal in Kolkata and sought land restoration. On 11 March 1996, once again, the Totos sent a memorandum to the Chief Minister and the Governor of West Bengal as well as to the Prime Minister and the President of India. All in vain.

In the meantime, the rapid spread of formal education among the Totos has given birth to a new predicament, namely, a huge employment crisis. The Totos have already produced 100 matriculates, which include 31 Higher Secondary students. Of these, eight have become graduates and, of those graduates, one boy has done his masters and another is pursuing his postgraduate course. Each year, there are new matriculates and new graduates. Already, 35 to 40 young Totos have got salaried jobs in various fields and the number of job-seekers is increasing rapidly. At least 66 Toto boys and girls are pursuing their education outside Totopara. Of these, Satya Toto is in Nagaland. He was brought there to study by a Christian missionary organisation.

The community's 150 years of freedom from slavery brought in a new mosaic in their life. A series of visits over a prolonged period of time to the Tuesday *hat* at Totopara gives a glimpse of the change. This *hat* has got an international character now. Here, along with Indians of non-Toto origins, one finds Nepali and Bhutanese people. Totopara's change began with 'Radio Nepal', which almost all the young Totos listen to. It broadcasts Hindi film songs, Nepali hit songs and more. Totopara quickly became a consumer's hub. Then came television sets, cell phones, the internet, banks, electricity, gas, motorcycles, *pucca* houses, soaps and serials. The hospital, buses, the library, hostels and high schools have added a new wave to the tribal land's assimilation process. With this came *churidar*s, jeans, frozen rohu, trout and hilsa. Chinese food, Mika's songs and Bachchan, too, became the heartbeat of Totopara. The Government ensured salaried jobs for the Totos and, recently, rice at Rs. 2 per kilogram. The tribe has English schools, Mahindra and Maruti vehicles and Royal Stag, McDowell and rum from Bhutan. This is the new Totopara, no longer the monochromic Totopara of the past. Bhabesh Toto has opened a Totopara rest house for tourists, while Bakul dreams of a resort on the banks of the river Hauri. The Totos have found their own guitar and church and Totopara now glitters.

Yet, the Toto has to sell his trees, jackfruits, ginger, bamboo and betel nuts. A Toto has to send his children outside for formal education in order to qualify for a job. They may get a job if they pass the Madhyamik, because they are Totos. The romance of getting a government job has started to suffer setbacks and the unemployment toll is on the rise. Bakul, a wonderful boy who dreams of new things, is still without a job.

Dhaniram beautifully renders typical Toto folktales into Bengali. He told me the story of Hipsa and Padua, the two small hills of Totopara. Padua was the maternal uncle of Hipsa. The two hills often fought with each other and contested their height. Hipsa once conspired to kill Padua so he invited him to a duel. The two had to excavate a pond within a night. The first attempt went in vain as the sun rose before the excavation was complete. The second attempt near Dhumchigaon was successful and a heavenly blue waterbody emerged. The pond was so picturesque that Padua kept his eyes glued on it. Hipsa was waiting for this absentmindedness of Padua and cut down his head with a chopper. But god's favourite, Padua, did not finish. Though he lost his head, two eyes grew on his chest and Padua was reborn with a new look. This folklore explains how the Padua hill became sacred for the Totos. The people believe that worshipping the Padua hill with a red cock for sacrifice cures headaches.

For the Totos, each and every stream in their country is a deity. The river Torsha flows from the north to the south through Bhutan, India and Bangladesh. Totopara's 'Toto country' is situated on the right bank of this river at the Indo-Bhutan border. This river is their *mu-tee* (*tee* meaning water) and they worship it. The Totos worship at least 15 such water bodies as their deities. The Dating-tee and the Goe-tee are given the highest regard. The river Hauri at the entrance of Totopara is their Hauri-kung-ning-tee. The god attached to this river is worshipped with a cock sacrifice. The Totos believe that this river god causes eye trouble, vertigo, headache and high fever to its offenders. The river Ji-tee even has children, according to the Totos. The tribe has given names to these kid rivers as well. Ji-tee's son is Ma-bei and the

daughter is Chem-bei. The Totos bring down their sacred drums from the *dhem-sha* once a year for bathing in the sacred Goe-tee at the time of Mayu puja.

Most of the Totos suffered from a skin disease called yaws in the past and considered it a blessing of their god, Ishpa. They believe that their women would have eloped if they had not had this disease in their community. Madi-pai-po-wa is the name-giving ceremony among Toto society. It is held at the age of five, seven, nine or 11 days and the baby is given local beer, *iu*, on that day. The Totos do not celebrate marriages and these are confirmed only once the woman conceives. In the past, they had youth dormitories, known as *niangko-sha*, away from their houses. Here, an unmarried boy could live with an unmarried girl for a couple of days. It was virtually an institution where aspiring youths could select their life partners themselves. *Niangko-sha*, however, no longer exists.

The members of the tribe have their own dresses, *angdung* and *bachha* for males and *mera, bijung, tumba* and *pari* for females. These traditional dresses are, however, not in use today. The Toto terms for their traditional ornaments are *iring, tishe, kei* and *narshi*. The women use typical bamboo combs, which they call *bida*.

Unlike the Hindu Bengalis, the year commences among the Totos with the Bengali month of Sravan (July-August). The first month is called Kati-mashe. Accordingly, the Bengali month of Bhadro is Agaai-mashe for the Totos. The 12-month-long Toto year concludes with Badoi-mashe in June-July. The tribe reckons its new year on the eleventh day after the new moon in Kati-mashe, which is celebrated with Mahakal puja.

One of the most important traditional institutions that the Totos could not dissolve is *latchi-jangwa*, their highest village council. A *latchi-jangwa* session can be held at any time, when required. The council functions from the *dhem-sha* at Pujagaon and the *kaiji* is the head of this village council. *Sangai-laumi* (penance) is the provision for a social offence. In this forum, the pronouncement of a judgment is delivered by the *kaiji*. In the face of the detribalisation of Totopara and the change in society, Suchana Toto's vision for a contemporary Totopara has undergone a change as well. She does not welcome outsiders now and is a little suspicious of Toto seekers. Bhakto, Sachin, Bakul and Ashok grew up in Totopara. While Bhakto became a bank manager, Sachin is a branch postmaster. Bakul and Ashok went for business. Ashok was the first car-owner among the Totos; I know Bakul also dreams of a car. Bhabesh, Dhaniram, Sanjit and Rita have government jobs. Except for Sanjit, all of them are fortunate to be posted in Totopara and enjoy their freedom,

plus draw a handsome monthly salary. Sandesh and Sadhana have their Kohima Baptist Church enterprise. Their son stays in Siliguri and studies in a Christian missionary school.

The quest for modern education and aspirations for job opportunities constitute the dream of today's Totopara. The debates and discourses that animate the community are riveted on two options—holding on unflinchingly to the mores of the past and moulding them sufficiently to adapt to the evolving ethos of the marching time. Totopara seems to be an agitated country where these two options, which do not apparently rhyme with each other, are being weighed in the deeper recesses of their collective psyche. Yet, a new Totopara is emerging in the midst of this subjective churning that goes on in the backdrop, almost imperceptibly.

Yolmo's Man of Peace

One Sunday morning, I decided to go to Champasari, at the outskirts of Siliguri, in search of Dorjey Yolmo, a centenarian man from the great Yolmo tribe. I had first heard about him from a friend who was a press photographer. I had also heard that the traditional occupation of the Yolmos was paper-making. Dorjey Yolmo appeared as a surviving progeny of the great paper-makers of the past; today, they are also known as Kagatays.

I met Dorjey a couple of times. He told me that his old homeland was situated in Nepal's Yolmo province and that his forefathers hailed from that Himalayan valley. He moved to Alubari village at the outskirts of Darjeeling's Jorebunglow after his retirement from the British Army. He later shifted to Champasari where he now lives with his elder son, Phurba, and his family. There are, however, no written records of this journey. Phurba appeared to be well-versed on the paper-making tradition and explained that their community name, Kagatay, was derived from the word *kagaz* (paper). There is a valid controversy as to whether the Yolmos and the Kagatays are the same community or not. The Government of West Bengal, in 2003, in its 'Ethnographic Notes on the Scheduled Tribes of West Bengal' corroborated that Kagatay is also known as Yolmo.

Dorjey is probably the oldest Yolmo of the Darjeeling hills and also of the downhill terrains. He was a designated 'colour sergeant' of the British Army's Gorkha regiment. In fact,

the British Army pays Rs. 40,700 every month as pension to this veteran, who had fought during the Second World War. This money goes straight to his bank account and Dorjey often distributes a part of it among the children in the locality.

According to the official record in his red book, issued by the British Army, he was born in 1927, though Phurba believes he is much older. Dorjey retired from service in October 1966 after 20 years of army life at Kuala Lumpur, Singapore and the UK. Dorjey had to declare himself as a Tamang because the British Army authorities did not know much about the Yolmos and were, instead, familiar with Tamangs, Lepchas and Subbas (Limbus) and regarded them as constituents of the Gorkha people.

He is an old man, with hearing and speech problems and failing eyesight. Yet he walks easily around his courtyard with the help of a stick. Dorjey still remembers Netaji Subhas Chandra Bose, whom he saw in person. Phurba, who has retired, a decade ago, from the Sashastra Seema Bal (SSB), an Indian paramilitary force, now looks after his father. Another son of Dorjey's, Lakpa, was also with the British Army. He retired in 1969 and lives in Nepal. Two of Dorjey's granddaughters, Passanglamu and Passang, have studied at Darjeeling schools.

The Yolmos have five exogamous clans in their society—Dhong-ba, Seng-ba, Solben, Chya-ba and Sorpa. People belonging to the same clan cannot marry each other. Dorjey belongs to the Dhong-ba clan and Phurba's wife is from the Solben clan. Phurba informed me that their tribe was the architect of Makdhoj Gumba, a heritage Buddhist monastery at Darjeeling's Alubari. I had heard of many such monasteries and even visited more than a dozen of them across the

Sikkim-Darjeeling-Bhutan hills but was unaware of this monastery. I knew that in different places in the Himalayas, indigenous people such as the Lepchas, Sherpas and Tamangs built Buddhist monasteries of their own. The Lepcha monastery of Kalimpong, the Sherpas at Sonada and Darjeeling and the Drukpa monastery of Bhutan's Phuntsholing stand testimony to these people's connections with Himalayan Buddhism for centuries.

I saw a 10-foot-long coloured cloth flag, which the Yolmos call *lungdar*, permanently hoisted on the roof of Dorjey's home. It indicates that this is a Yolmo house. The flag has a couple of multi-coloured strips, which, according to Phurba, symbolise the different *prahar*s (parts) of the day and night. The Tamangs and a few Tibet-originating hill communities also hoist similar religious flags on the rooftop, but the hymns printed in Tibetan scripts vary from community to community. Dorjey's family is Buddhist by faith; they have their *lama* who presides over various social ceremonies. 'Our death-pollution lasts for 49 days. This is the lengthiest ritual,' said Phurba.

I heard the Yolmo language for the first time in Dorjey's house. According to linguists, it is a dialect of a larger Tibeto-Burman family of languages. On my request, Phurba gave me a set of sentences as they are spoken in the Yolmo language.

During one of my recent visits to Dorje's house, I found Passang missing and was told by Phurba that she has gone to Hong Kong where she has taken up the job of a housemaid. Her employer is a Chinese engineer whose wife is a doctor. She will be allowed to visit her home every two years.

Time moves on, but the people belonging to this community of traditional ancestor-worshippers still visit Dorjey on the eve of Nepali Dussehra (at the end of Durga puja) every year to pay their homage to the old man and seek his blessings. Indeed, Dorjey has become an icon of peace across the terrains of Darjeeling.

PART 2

The Proto-Australoids and Others

ASUR
BAIGA
BEDIA
BHUMIJ
BIRHOR
BIRJIA
CHERO
CHIK BARAIK
GORAIT
HO
KARMALI
KHARIA
KHARWAR
KISAN
KORA
KORWA
LODHA
LOHARA
MAHALI
MALPAHARIA
MUNDA
NAGESIA
ORAON
PARHAIYA
RAJGOR
SABAR
SANTAL
SAURIA PAHARIA

These Asurs are Not Demons!

Listening to the superhit 'Mahisasuramardini' on the All India Radio, Kolkata, has been a ritual since my childhood. This is a radio-ballad, compiled with Sanskrit rhymes and Bengali songs, on Goddess Durga's victory after the battle with Mahisasura, the buffalo demon-king, as narrated in the *Puranas*. This beautiful musical melodrama is broadcast at the dawn of the day of 'Mahalaya', which is generally observed on the new moon day before Durga puja. With television gaining popularity, it has also become a much-viewed morning show. It prompted us to believe that Goddess Durga is the saviour of humankind whereas the Asurs or the demons are the evil powers. We thus grew up with the notion that the Asurs are dangerous for they challenged the gods.

Things changed during my upbringing as an inhabitant of the Duars. I started deciphering its codes of conduct and my childhood notions took a new form. I was growing up amid local tribal countrymen and was gradually coming to learn generic terms of referring to my neighbouring communities. There appeared some

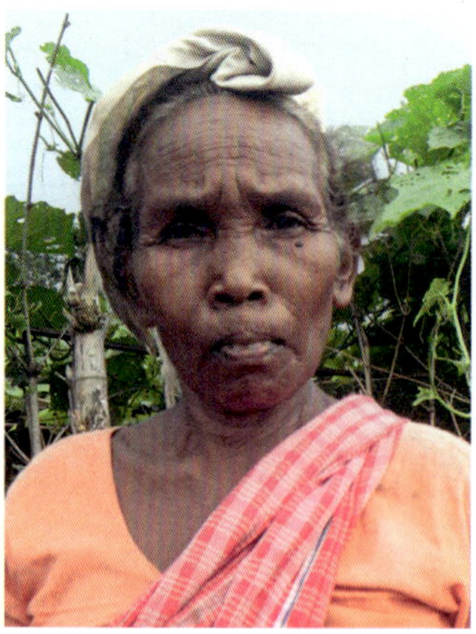

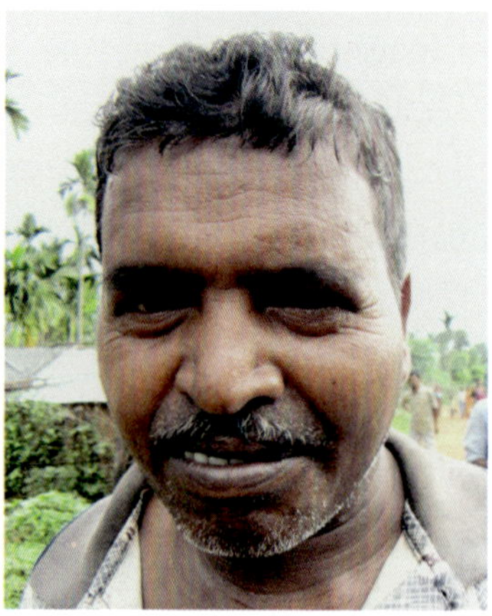

people who were actually known as the Asurs. Their curly hair, high cheekbones and relatively darker complexion were similar to the Mundas. I came to know that these people are the progenies of the earlier Proto-Australoids of India.

I first shot an Asur lady, Fulmani, at the East Garam *busti*, on the outskirts of Alipurduar's Damanpur forest. The Asurs, Kharias and Oraons live in this area. The old lady's hairstyle was as huge as an ocean wave! She was winnowing some homegrown pulses in the courtyard and there were heaps of cow dung and melted clay powder stored there. On my arrival, a band of children suddenly assembled around her, making Fulmani look like a village grandmother. A pet dog also came for this photoshoot, which was witnessed by pigs, small and big, tied in a small pigshed. A few poultry birds appeared and quickly vanished. Fulmani, too, retreated to her solitary world as soon as I had finished taking the photographs. And though Fulmani has now passed away, I will always remember her ethnic beauty.

As far as I can remember, this incident took place in 1985, my fourth year as a tribal inspector of the Government of West Bengal. Later, at the Gudamdabri forest *busti*, there appeared a few Asur families with whom I had worked. I found their counterparts at the Majherdabri Tea Garden nearby. I later undertook a socio-economic field study on these Asurs at the Garam *busti*. By now I had understand that the Asurs are a tribal community, not demons. I started locating the Asur people from anthropological works and also came across them in Siliguri-Terai's Naxalbari and Matigara blocks. I often met the Asurs at the Carron Tea Estate near Malbazar but got genuinely excited when I heard about an Asur working in the city. He used to come to Siliguri from a nearby village and return home exhausted after having cleared the city's waste. He works for the municipal corporation and nobody knew about his anthropological legacy. I met this aged Asur a couple of times.

I first saw Sukra Asur on a sunny day, taking a bath using water from a privately-bored ringwell at his homestead. I met him at his village, Jaldumur, at the outskirts of Siliguri. He has an illustrious Proto-Australoid tribal face and physique. He has not heard of the Qutb Minar, which is believed to have been built by iron-melting Asur artisans. He knows nothing about Mahisasura's battle with Goddess Durga and it is futile to talk to him about the Indus Valley civilisation of Harappa in which the Asurs were supposed to have a stake. He does not know his mother tongue, Asuri. His Asur identity is only confined to his father, Etoya (probably born on Sunday, the Etowar day for the Adivasis). The name 'Sukra' was given by his parents because he was born on a Friday. His clan is Topo, which means his forefathers hailed from a bird.

Etoya Asur, an immigrant from Ranchi, was an ill-fated plantation labourer at the Jaypur Tea Garden, near Belakoba. He left the garden and came to Hatiadanga village, near Siliguri's eastern bypass road and started cultivation as a sharecropper.

Sukra was born at their old Hatiadanga village home. The Asur boy became a road construction labourer and was granted a permanent *khalashi* (labourer) status. He married an Asur woman, Birshi, from the Daina Tea Garden, near Banarhat. She was from the Beng clan and was born on Bistibar (Thursday), hence her name; it would have been Birsha in the case of a male. She works in a tea garden nearby and gets Rs. 95 a day.

Sukra has been working for the municipality for the last 39 years. He started the job of clearing the waterways of the city at a daily wage of Rs. 5 and later became a regular employee. His salary rose to Rs. 247 per month. In 2015, he was earning Rs. 21,000.

He does not know how to write his name and, therefore, gives his left thumb impression when asked for his signature. As a government employee, he is entitled to a monthly pension. At the close of my short Sunday interview, Sukra shared, 'During my early days as a gang-*khalashi*, people abstained from taking water from us as our work was considered to be an unclean occupation.' He also said that though some children do go to school, they are not regular, 'maybe the classes and the school environment do not give them pleasure'. This reaction on tribal schooling took me back to Sukra's boyhood, 50 years ago, when he had opted to work at the road construction sites instead of going to school.

In March 2016, I met Sukra once again and found him superannuated from his government job. He was constructing a *pucca* dwelling house in his own homestead; it almost appeared that he was reconstructing his identity. Sukra sends willing Asur boys to the Siliguri city's civic body for work; a few are now working in the waste management department. I presented a 15 x 12-inch printout of his image that I had captured the last time I had met him, to which he responded, 'Well, this is good. We should preserve such senior family member's photographs at home! I saw people doing it in Siliguri city.'

Even before my discovery of Siliguri's Sukra Asur, I had come to know that the Asurs are an indigenous tribal community of India. They comprise one of the most marginal groups of people among the communities, castes and tribes living in West Bengal. In the states of Bihar, Odisha, Jharkhand and Chhatisgarh, the Asur population is somewhat larger than West Bengal. The Asurs are seldom found in towns, except for a few lesser-known rural hamlets of this state. In the census of 2011, their population in West Bengal was only 3,864, a considerable decrease from 1991 when there were 4,864 ethnic Asurs. It has been found that 91.34 per cent of the Asurs still live in the almost inaccessible tea gardens and forest-villages of the Terai and Duars region in its Sub-Himalayan foothills where the Bengali or the mainstream gentry has very little to do with the tribe. Their mobilisation in the rural belts during 2001 to 2011 has significantly grown. In 2001, 87.01 per cent of Bengal's Asur population was rural; it grew to 91.34 per cent in 2011.

In earlier literature, the Asurs were also referred to as the Agorias and the Lohras. The Agorias, Birjias, Kolh-Asurs and Paharia-Asurs were reported to be the sub-tribes of the Asurs. It was stated that the Asurs had three economic and territorial sub-groups—the Saikias, Birjhias and Jati-Asurs. The Aiyens, Minjs, Mendhaks, among others, are said to be their totemistic clans. According to some accounts, the Asurs were found to use Mahato as their surname in the past, which has now been replaced by the name of their community. The Asurs have been identified by anthropologists as an offshoot of the Mundas; some even saw cultural similarities among the Asurs and the Lohras. They are said to have subsequently emerged as an independent community. However, the Asurs (demons), as described in the *Rig Veda* and the *Atharva Veda*, are believed to be the ancestors of the Asurs of the present day. According to some scholars, it is this community that had set up the Indus Valley civilisation but was pushed out of the area towards the eastern region by the powerful Aryan-speaking people. Later, in Ranchi, the Asurs fought with the Mundas, who proved stronger and that is the reason why they had to move further towards the hills for survival. It has been said that the melting of iron was the traditional occupation of the Asurs and Delhi's Qutb Minar was built by these Asur artisans.

Though the Asurs have their own Austro-Asiatic dialect, they seldom speak it in West Bengal. In the Duars and Terai region of North Bengal, they converse in a corrupt version of Bengali and Hindi while Sadri (a popular language in tea gardens and many tribal-dominated places of the Terai-Duars region) has, for all practical reasons, become the essential medium of communication. But, yes, I saw some senior Asurs in Carron who can speak their dialect, Asuri.

Those belonging to the present generation of the Asurs living in North Bengal do not pursue their traditional cultural events but some of the older members remember them as a matter of their ethnic identity. The Asurs consider Pat-Deota as their chief deity while Mahadaniya, Sarna and Devi Mai are also worshipped. They venerate evil spirits such as Darha, Nashan and Mua. Among the major cultural fests are Sarhul, Hariyari, Sohrai, Fagu and Sendra. The Asurs of the Duars celebrate Gram puja (worship of the village deity), Fagua (festival of colours in the spring) and Deothan puja.

According to a survey that I had conducted in 1987–88, some of the names of the clans of the Asurs are Baghwar, Barowa (wild cat), Beng/Bengwar, Indwar, Tirkey (bird), Toppo (bird), Kerketta and Soma. Among them, Indwar, Tirkey, Kerketa and

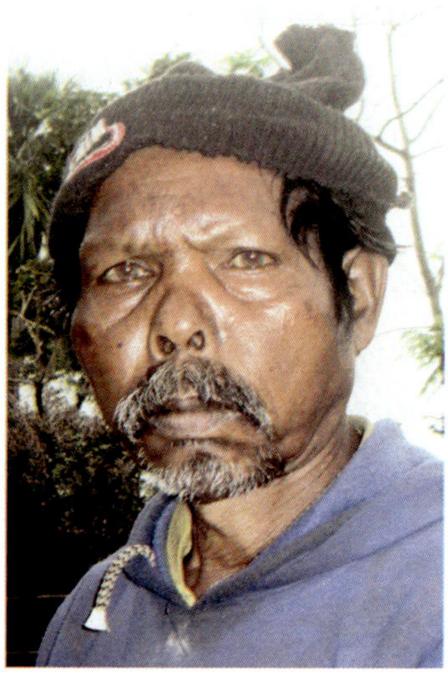

Toppo are common Duar tribes, originating from Chota Nagpur, mainly among the Oraons. One of my knowledgeable Oraon friends once told me, 'All these totemistic clans had been borrowed from the Oraons. Many people did that and the Asurs are also no exception.'

The Asurs pray for a daughter as their first child, which reflects an interesting psycho-cultural attitude of the community. Given the backdrop of a dominating patrilineal social format, this preference for a girl did seem rather unbelievable but I found it to be empirically valid during my trips across the Asur villages in the Duars. The Asurs here also permit post-marital cohabitation, even without a ceremonial marriage. In such cases, the marriage ceremony of the parents takes place together with those of their son's or daughter's for the children's marriage receives social sanction only after that of their parents. In the Terai-Duars, mass wedding ceremonies are conducted for the poor tribal people. A few social organisations have voluntarily come up with this project at a subsidised price, if not free of cost.

The Asurs mostly convert to Christianity and customise the faith in their own way. Yet, there is every possibility of coming across non-converted Asurs, whom we generally call the Hindu Asur. In the Carron Tea Estate, 90 families (out of 101) are now Christian converts. In Garam, too, most of the Asurs are Christians. In an interview for *The Indian Express*, after the Mahisasur controversy of 2016, one Asur woman of Carron, aged about 38 years, strongly denied their link with Mahisasura. The young Asur lady also referred to a few other non-Asur surnames. For me, this is the best example of how the Asur people in the Bengal-Duars, perhaps in other parts of the country as well, have been coming out from their *puranic* identity of being the progenies of demons.

I was looking for a student who was studying at an undergraduate level among the Asur settlements I visited, but could not find even one. Not a single village shop I saw was an Asur enterprise. In government offices, even in the private transport sectors, there appeared to be no Asurs as employees.

During my last visit to Garam, I talked to Pukli Asur, Fulmani's daughter. Sancharua, Fulmani's son, was there as well, but he remained silent. I took my wife to the Carron Tea Estate and introduced her to the happiest person of the world, Sukhu bura. Nestled in the Himalayan foothills, the tea estate, with its own multi-shaped valleys, is indeed picturesque. It seems that god planted the tea bushes here and this is god's own country. I met an Asur lady, Rampeyari, at the beautiful Belgacchi Tea Estate when she was returning from work. At Carron, I saw Lalita, Anita and Taramani wearing colourful clothes and carrying something in their head-baskets. They did not speak to me for they were rushing to the weekly market at Lukshan. I remained silent for a couple of minutes, watching them leave. I will never forget the footsteps they left behind, between the green tea bushes.

Baigas, the Earth People

The Baigas believe that they are the descendants of mother earth. Legend also says that the community descended from a man called Nanga Baiga. As among the Parhaiyas, the term *baiga* means priest or *panda* and the Baigas are also known as village-priests and medicine-men. According to British ethnographer and colonial administrator HH Risley, the Baigas were experts in witchcraft and sorcery *(The Tribes and Castes of Bengal*, 1891). They were said to be master propitiators of the local deities and priests for the Gond tribe. They were mainly found in the Mandla and Balaghat districts of the then Madhya Pradesh and, in smaller numbers, in the Seoni, Chhindwara, Bilashpur, Shadol and Durg districts. In Madhya Pradesh, the Baigas speak the local dialect, Parshi *bhasha* or Gavahi *bhasha*, a corrupt form of Hindi. They also converse in Baigani, a dialect of the Chhattisgarh language, which belongs to the central group of the Indo-Aryan family of languages. They can be identified by their scanty dress and tangled hair (*girda*).

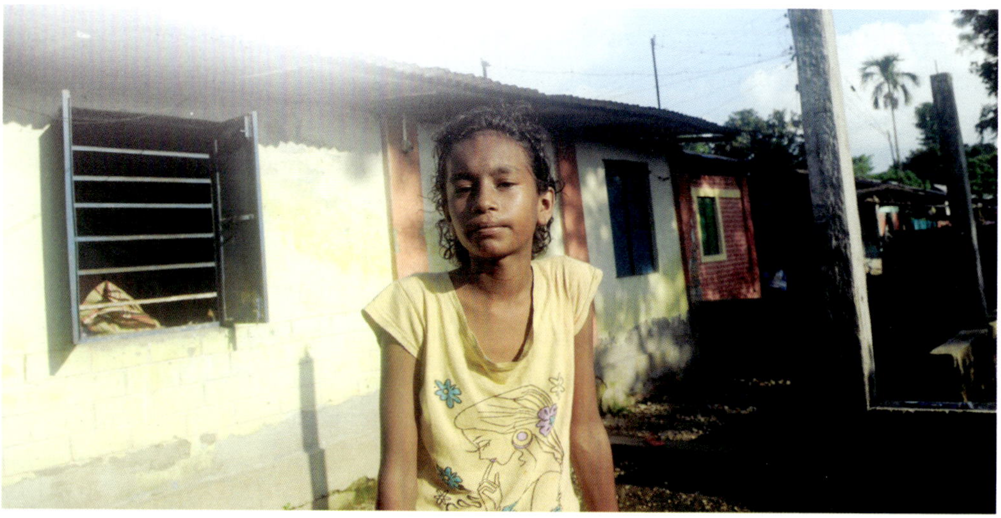

In September 2016, I finally managed to locate a few Baigas in the Fulbari Tea Estate in Khoribari, near Batashi. The people referred to as the Baigas at this tea estate, however, knew very little about their community and seemed to only use the term as their surname. I met Krishna Baiga who was 59 years old, but looked so much more. Krishna's elder brother, Ram, 71, now retired, said that they were given Rs. 17 per week as wages during their early days in the plantations. I met his wife, Cheria, at their tea garden home (labourer quarter). Krishna informed that his father, Samai Baiga, came to this tea estate in 1958 from the Kadopani area of the Muni Tea Estate. Their forefathers were inhabitants of Nangrigaon village of the Shadol district. Both the brothers said that their language was Baigani. During my discussion, I learnt some of the names of their clans—Dhukia (the totem of this clan is Charondhukia, which is believed to be a bird), Boloria, Parsoa, Singartha, Belgaiha, Padhnaria, Mosuria and Gurha. The Fulbari Baigas have gone in for inter-caste marriages as their population is very small and they have been living in a mixed culture among multi-ethnic communities. There have been marriages with the Oraon, Munda, Gond, Nagesia and Rajbanshi communities. In fact, I found six communities in 10 Baiga families. These inter-caste marriages could probably be the reason for the loss of ethnic identity among this tribe.

The Baiga population of West Bengal has shown an increase; according to the census figures of 1991, they numbered 7,624; in 2001, they grew to 11,681 and, in 2011, the number stood at 13,423. The latest census enumeration reveals that the majority of the Bengal Baigas live in the district of Paschim Medinipur (12,845 or 95.69 per cent).

The Growth of the Bedias

The Bedias is a tribal community of Bengal, largely found in Uttar and Dakshin Dinajpur in North Bengal and in North and South 24 Parganas in South Bengal. They saw a phenomenal growth in the span of a decade. In 1991, there were 44,875 Bedias in West Bengal; this number rose to 88,772, according to the

2011 census projections. Owing to the resemblance between both communities, the Bedias are often confused with the Kurmis, particularly in North Bengal. This creates political controversy because the Bedias are recognised as a Scheduled Tribe community while the Kurmis are not. The Bedias are more inclined towards the tribal way of life whereas the Kurmi culture is found to be closer to the Hindu style. Risley wrote, 'Bedia ... a small agricultural Dravidian tribe of Chota Nagpur, supposed to be *Masiaut bhai*, or cousins through the maternal aunt, of the Kurmis.' Risley also stated that the Bedias are the twelfth sept of the Santals; the clan is supposed to have been left in Champa and has long been separated from the parent tribe.

It has been perceived by some authors that the Bedias were originally the inhabitants of a hill in the Hazaribagh district of the then Bihar, known as Mohdipahar. The story goes that the Bedia people had descended from the union of a Vedbanshi prince with a Munda girl. There is one more view about their emergence as a separate community that believes that some of the Kurmis were outcasts and came to be known as the Bedias or the wandering Kurmis. The Bedia community referred to here, according to authorities such as Risley, was different from the Bediyas, the generic name of a number of vagrant gypsy-like groups. In North Bengal's Duars, I have found in the Dheklapara Tea Estate's Sona Line, the Cherra/Chidra (squirrel), Kachua (tortoise) and Sundi (flower) clans living among the Bedias, which were common with Risley's list. The Bedias are not very different from the Adivasi communities originating from Chota Nagpur.

The Historic Bhumij Tribe

The tribe, Bhumij, is said to be an offshoot of the Mundas of Ranchi. Their language has an affinity with Mundari. The Bhumij people of Bengal are largely found in the two southern districts of Purulia and Paschim Medinipur in West Bengal though many of them have spread over other districts such as Bankura, North 24 Parganas, Nadia, Bardhaman and Hugli. Bhumij is a Scheduled Tribe community in West Bengal since 1956. According to the census of 2011, the Bhumij population of West Bengal was 376,296 (it was 291,808 in 1991) and their share in the state's ST population was 7.10 per cent.

A section of the Bhumijs of West Bengal consists of Hindus; most of them worship their traditional tribal deities such as Sing-Bonga (chief deity of the Mundas), Dharam Thakur, Jahir Buru and Panchbahini. In the month of Kartik in the Bengali calendar (October-November), they pray to Garai-Thakur for the growth of their livestock. To please the deity, the Bhumijs used to sacrifice buffaloes, but now they offer fowl instead; this practice is called Kara-kata. In the Duars, the community worships Gram-Thakur, Taribari and other traditional gods.

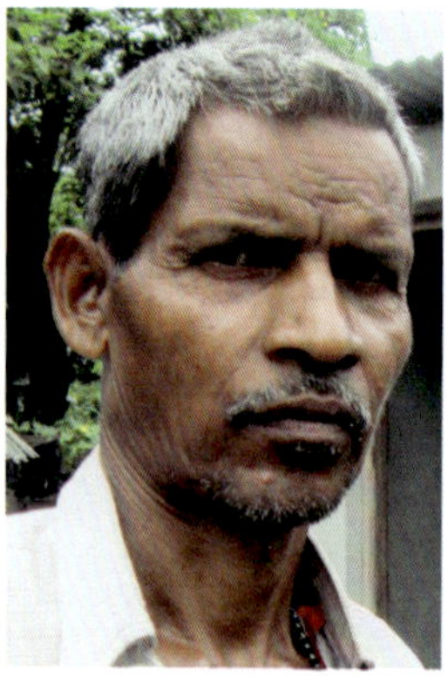

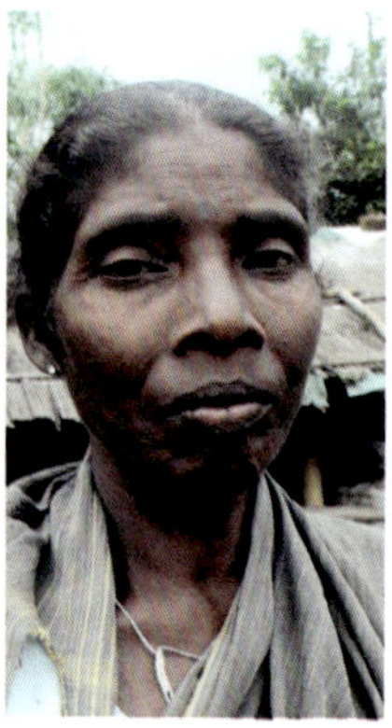

The various Bhumij clans are Ubursandil, Gulgu, Hembrom, Jugi, Baghra, Kauri, Nag, Chalki, Kachchyap, Saral, Khatughgushyama, Hemla and Tesa. These are exogamous and totemistic. In the Duars, the Bhumijs also have a clan named 'Samad'. The Bhumijs had, in the past, funeral sites at separate places for the different groups.

The tribe is known for the historic Bhumij Rebellion against the British, the Ganganarayani Hangama of 1832–33, which took place in Manbhum (present Purulia) under the leadership of Ganga Narain Singh. I visited the Bhumijs in the Terai and the Duars region. The photographs of the Bhumijs were taken at the Dagapur Tea Estate's Daknikata labourer line, near the Champasari area, at the outskirts of Siliguri.

Birhors, the Jungle People

Though small in number, Birhor is an interesting tribal community of Bengal. Edward Tuite Dalton, popularly known in the anthropological world as Dalton, narrated a folktale from the Hazaribagh region about the emergence of the tribe in 1872. He wrote, 'The Birhors affirm that they and the Kharwars are of the same race descended from the sun. They came, seven brothers, to this country from Khairagarh (in the Kaimur hills); four went to the east, and three brothers remained in the Ramgarh district. One day, when the three brothers were going out to fight against the chiefs of the country, the headdress of one of them was entangled in a tree. He deemed it a bad omen, and remained behind in the jungle. His two brothers went without him and gained a victory over the chiefs, and returning found their brother employed in cutting the bark of the *chob* creeper. They derided him, calling him the *birhor* or *chob* cutter. He replied that he would rather remain a *birhor* and reign in the jungles than associate with such haughty

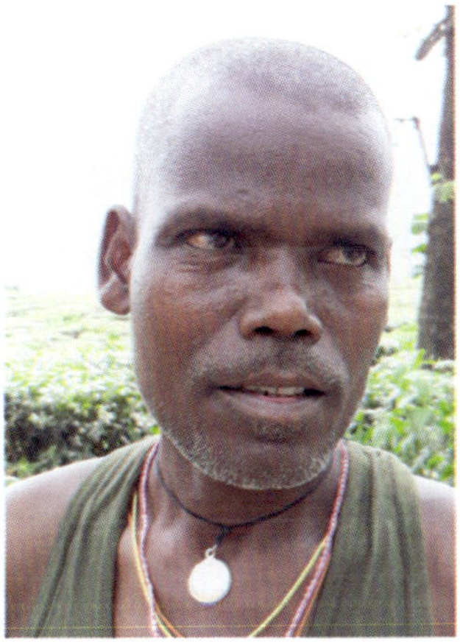
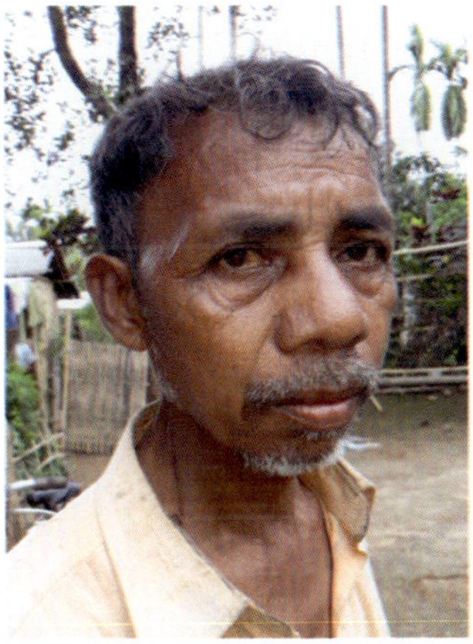
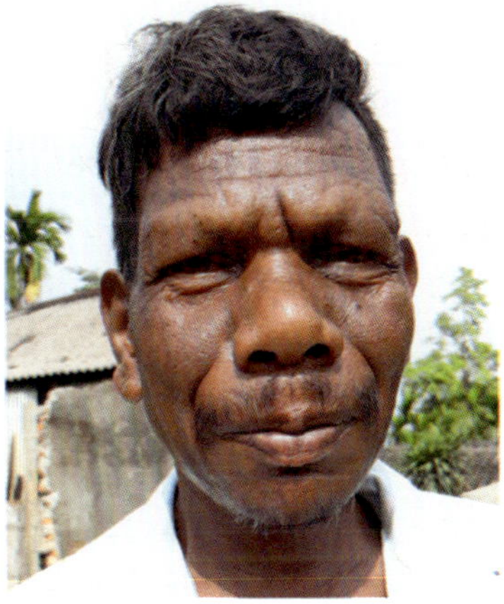

brothers. Thus originated the Birhors, lords of the jungles. The other two brothers became Rajas of the country called Ramgarh.'

The Birhors are still found in the forest belts of the districts of Purulia and Bankura and are known as rope-makers and hunters. In Purulia, a good section of the community engages itself in making ropes from a vine called *chihorlata* in Bengali. Forests play a vital role in the life of a Birhor. Since they did not take up farming till recently, forests remained the hub of their economy, society and culture. It is also believed that the term *birhor* was derived from *bir*, the Mundari word for forest while *hor* means man—hence, the 'people of the forests'. Outside Bengal, they are found in Ranchi, Gumlah and the Hazaribagh districts of the Chota Nagpur plateau of Bihar. They also live in Madhya Pradesh and Odisha.

The Birhors were known as a nomadic tribe in the past but they have settled down now. They are considered a part of the Proto-Austroloid family because of their anthropological features. The language of the tribe has been identified with that of the Mundas and Santals. However, those observations were mostly from Bihar and that, too, in the past. In Purulia, the Birhors have a language of their own

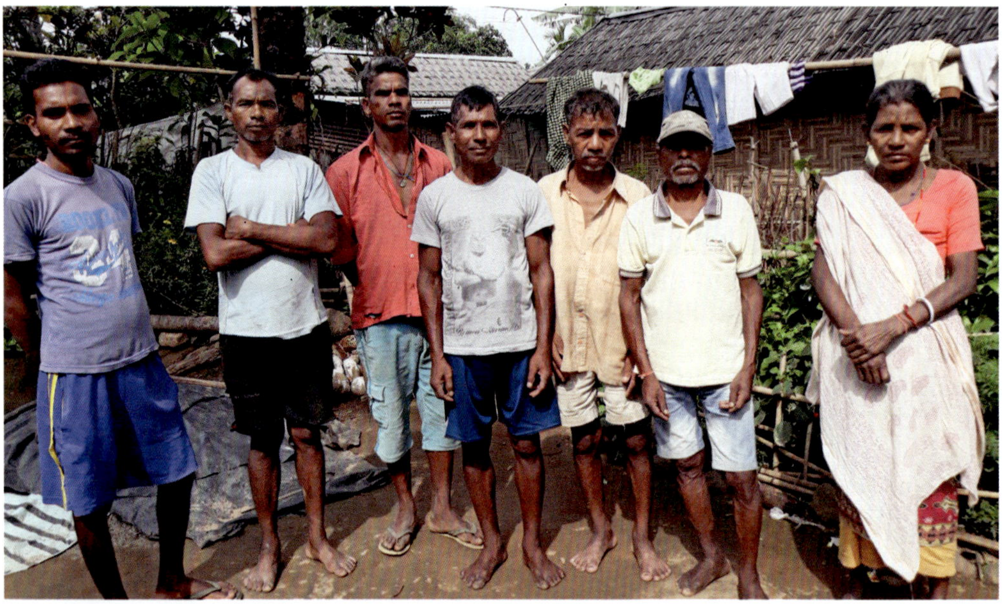

called Birhori, which seems to have a Bengali influence. The Birhors of Purulia are close to the Saṇtals and have developed a linguistic relation with them. The Birhari speech is a language without a script and has been classified as a speech of the Mundari group of the Austro-Asiatic language family.

In Purulia, they use 'Shikari' as their last name. The Birhors are further divided into clans such as Jagsaria, Sawren, Murmu, Induar, Hembrom and so on. The majority of these clans are similar to the Santals. In 1991, only about 21.79 per cent of the Birhors of West Bengal were declared literate. Up to the eighties, there was only one Birhor person who had passed the Higher Secondary examination while there were six others who had reportedly completed matriculation. In the 2011 census, there were 2,241 Birhors in Bengal (855 in 1991). But, according to a section of anthropologists, the Birhor population of this state does not exceed 500. Since the tribe was habitually semi-nomadic, their settlement was a priority and hence the Government of West Bengal set up a Birhor colony in a village known as Bhupatipally in the district of Purulia in the late sixties.

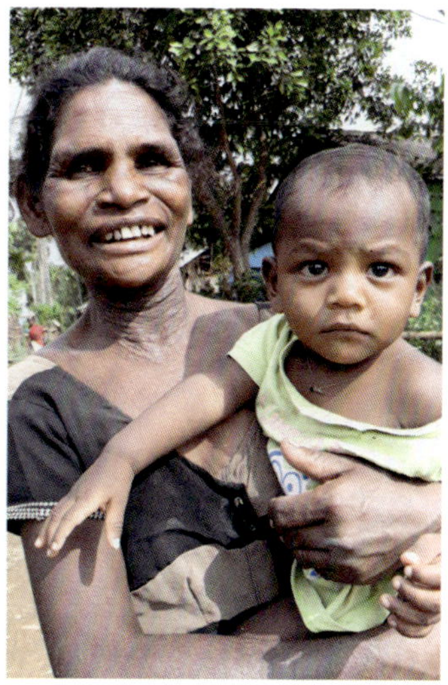

In West Bengal, the Birhors worship Banhi, the deity of the jungle. A one-foot-long wooden stick painted red on the upper portion symbolises this deity. Lugu (named after the highest mountain of Ramgarh) is their saviour, similar to Marang Buru of the Mundas. Many Birhors consider Biku and Biru-Bonga as their mountain god. They worship Burikmai and Dudhmai; the latter is represented by the ironhead of an arrow. They also worship Lord Hanuman, the monkey god and believe that he will save them from evil spirits and attacks of wild animals from both the east and the west, which is why they keep two Hanuman symbols on both sides of their houses. In North Bengal, people in general do not talk about the Birhors. I found no one in the area speaking about this community during the last 37 years of my tenure as a tribal welfare worker in the region. However, many members of the Birhor community reside in North Bengal and are one of the major primitive tribal groups like the Totos. It is unfortunate that we have been unaware of their existence.

A few years ago, I found a Birhor family at Chalsa in the Duars. A man there showed me his Birhor certificate. His name is Ganesh Birhor. A retired primary school teacher, he told me that his father was an employee of the state forest department and somehow his family had migrated to the Duars. He did not know much about their culture except for the meaning of the term, Birhor—*bir* meaning jungle or forest and *hor*, man. His interpretation was similar to the views of the anthropologists. According to him, not more than a dozen Birhor families could be found in the Duars as, owing to intercaste marriages, people ended up losing their Birhor identity.

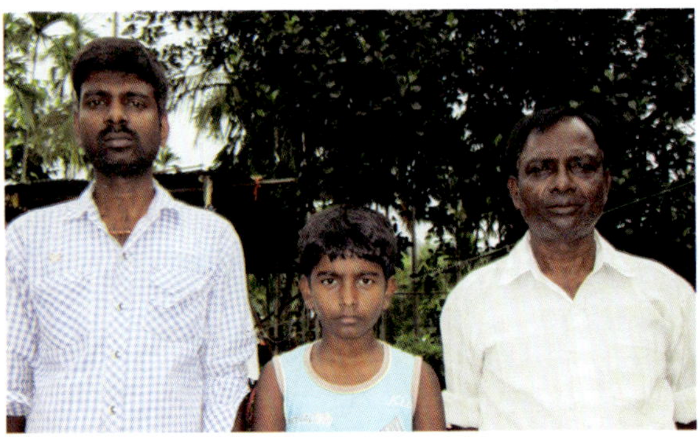

I saw Ganesh's married daughter at his house in Chalsa and wanted to take her picture. However, he was hesitant to comply as the girl was married to a Rajbanshi (a pre-dominating Hindu Scheduled Caste community of North Bengal) boy and her photograph, if showcased in the media as a Birhor, would downsize her status. Instead, he allowed me to take a group photograph of him with his elder son and grandson. Six years after my encounter with Ganesh, I explored the existence of 58 Birhor families at the Nagessuri Tea Estate in the Metteli block of the Jalpaiguri district. In Nagessuri, there is a pucca line, a hamlet of labourers, in the remotest corner of the tea gardens of North Bengal. Here live more than 200 families and each member of the Birhor community uses surnames similar to those of the Santals. A few of them also have tribal certificates mentioning their subcaste as Santal. They use clan names such as Hembrom, Hansda, Murmu, Kisku and so on, which are also the surnames of the Santals. But a few of the seniors seemed to be well-versed with the Birhori dialect and spoke Birhori at home. I met Shyam Baskey, Mangra Baskey, Salkhan Murmu and Ramesh Majhi and they all declared that they are Birhors but out of compulsion introduce themselves as Santals. 'The Birhor community is not recognised or taken into consideration, hence the Santal identity,' said Salkhan Murmu, a senior Birhor man of the pucca line. Among the women, I met Basanti Kisku, Duleri Majhi and Purungi Majhi and they, too, use Santal surnames.

The Birhors are popularly divided into two broad social groups—those who migrate are known as Uthlu or Bhulaiya and the section of the tribe that prefers a settled life are known as Jaghi Birhors. One of my Nagessuri informants said that they belong to the Jaghi sect. A few of them, however, still remember their traditional occupation of rope making.

Meeting the Birjias

In the Austro-Asiatic language, the term *bir* often means jungle or forest and hence Birjia or Brijjia came to mean 'fish of the jungle'. According to a Birjia folktale, they originated from a scarecrow and had migrated from the Sarguja district of undivided Madhya Pradesh to the jungles and hills of the Chota Nagpur plateau in undivided Bihar. From there they spread across Bengal and elsewhere.

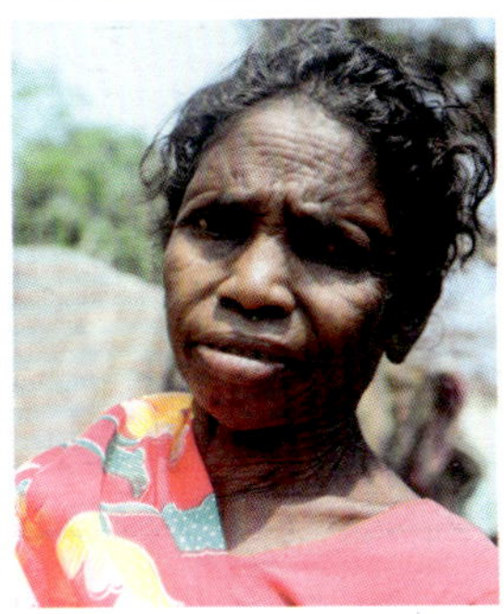

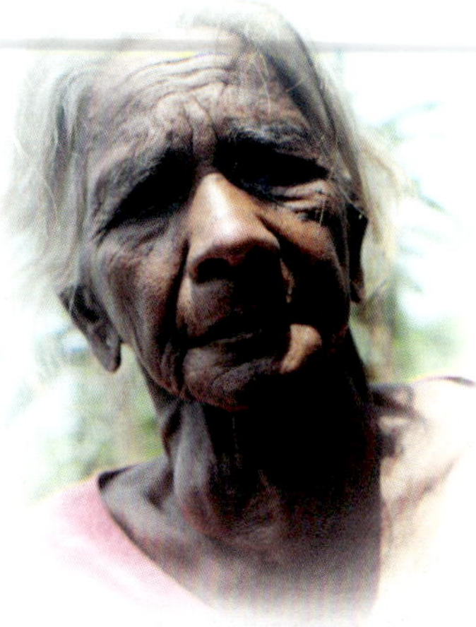

The Birjias are divided into two major social groups—Telia and Sinduria. In the 2011 census, 1,123 Birjias were found in West Bengal; 58 per cent of them were living in the district of Darjeeling. I met some people of this tribe at the Jagirjote village, near Khoribari, 50 kilometres from Siliguri. The Birjias speak their own language at Jagirjote.

The Low Profile Cheros

According to the *People of India,* National Series, Volume III (1994), brought out by the Anthropological Survey of India, 'The word *chero* is probably derived from *chera*, a snake. They trace their origin to Sage Chyavana and are also known as Chero and Cheru. They are concentrated in Palamou, but are also distributed in the Ranchi, Sahabad, Champaran and Monghyr districts. The Chero live in the hills and forests, which have a warm climate, low humidity and moderate rainfall.' In the Bihar report, including the Jharkhand Series, it was said that the Cheros were also known as Charwas. In Palamou, they are known as Barahazari.

The study revealed that the Cheros had an early link with the Kharwars: 'It is alleged that when Bhagawant Rai first seized the *pargana* [a group of villages or a subdivision of a district in India], he was either accompanied or joined afterwards by an army composed of Cheros and Kharwars numbering 12,000 and 18,000 men, respectively, and that the two tribes were afterwards distinguished as Barahazari Chero and Atharahazari Kharwars.' It was also stated, 'The social status of the Cheros was very high even in the Mughal period. They were given the rank of a Mansabdar in Akbar's court. Their children are given the sacred thread by a Brahmin priest at the time of marriage.'

After a long search, I came across the Chero people in the Duars, though in very few numbers. I found them at the Songachi Tea Estate, near Malbazar, in the district of Jalpaiguri. Three Chero men, Rambrij, Jogeswar and Karam,

first came from Palamou of the then Bihar to this tea garden. In 2017, there were 35 Cheros.

The Cheros of the Duars do not know much about their heritage and culture. The people became silent when I narrated the story of Barahazari and Atharahazari to them. I visited the place for the last time in January 2017 and found only six families; Ajit, Bahadur and Diplal were the senior Cheros here. They are the sons of the original inhabitants and it appeared from our discussions that they belong to the Morwa branch of the Barahazari Cheros. The tribe is mainly divided into two groups, namely, Barahazari and Atharahazari. Each of these has sub-groups, one of which is Morwa and the Songachi Cheros belong to it. The Chero term for clan is *pariya* and I found most of them belong to the Chowon clan. I could not trace their counterparts during my journey, possibly because of their low-profile existence, but the 2011 census shows that West Bengal is home to 5,477 Cheros. The census also traced 1,047 and 841 Cheros in the Jalpaiguri and Darjeeling districts, respectively. According to the census, the Chero population is increasing. In 1991, there were 2,238 Cheros in this state. The Chero women of Songachi told me that they themselves were in search of other Cheros for matrimonial reasons. Owing to the non-availability of people of their own caste, they had to go to Bihar in search of spouses for their children. This is the problem that the Cheros of the Bengal Duars are also facing. I have been told that there are college-going students among the Cheros at Songachi, but could not meet them.

The Elusive Chik-Baraiks

The Chik-Baraiks are one of the little-known tribes of West Bengal. They are popularly believed to be Madhesia or Adivasi, originating from Bihar. Their population in West Bengal was 21,376 in 2011. The district of Jalpaiguri was found to be a big home of the tribe with 14,263 people, according to the census of 2011. Districts such as Darjeeling and Nadia also have a sizeable Chik-Baraik population. The people of this tribe migrated to West Bengal and other parts of the eastern region, mainly from their ancestral home in Chota Nagpur. They are a tribe of the Proto-Australoid racial stock. The Chik-Baraik people, however, speak an Indo-Aryan language, the Nagpuri. A large number adopted Sadri, Bengali and Hindi while migrating from Bihar to Bengal. In some parts of West Bengal, they also speak Panchpargania, an Indo-Aryan language.

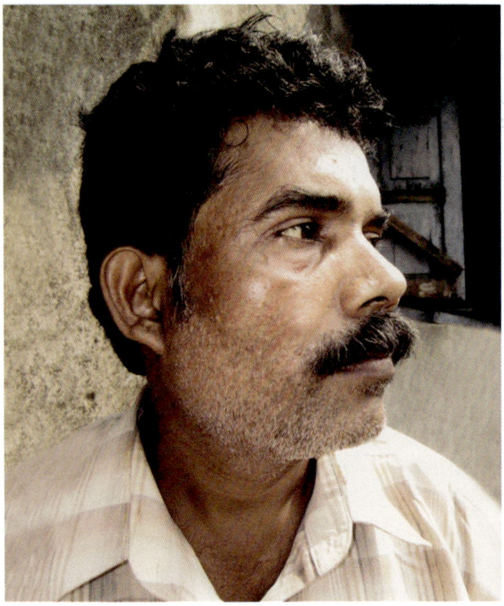

Most of the present generation Chik-Baraiks of West Bengal cannot remember tales of their origin, yet, it is believed that they originated from a scarecrow brought to life by Lord Shiva. The Chik-Baraiks were weavers in the past. Their society was divided into several groups, namely, the Sut-Bansi, Gura-Baraik, Paihka, Das-Baraik and so on. They also had totemistic clans such as Induar, Norangi, Barha, Basera, Baxi, Sona, Bhal, Harin, Bati, Surma, Tajan, Keora, Ketri, Kacchap and Mubara. They use Ganjhu as a title and Baraik as a surname. In the Duars, this community is divided into separate clans such as Bag, Bakla, Barbhuinya, Kohot, Kunthi, Loha and Pradip. Among their festivals in the Duar region in North Bengal is the Fagua Go puja. The Chik-Baraiks of West Bengal bury the dead and observe austerity for 10 to 12 days.

Data reveals that, in 1981, 99.07 per cent of the members of the tribe, in Bengal, were Hindus and the remaining were Christians. In the Darjeeling and Jalpaiguri districts, the majority of the Chik-Baraiks are tea garden labourers while a section of them are peasants. A small portion of the people are also government servants, teachers and businessmen.

The Goraits Move On

A very small number of Goraits are found in West Bengal (2,498 in 2011). Their low-profile existence proves to be the main obstacle in locating them in the multi-ethnic tribal galaxy of Bengal. Moreover, the members of this community have mingled in the general lifestyle of the Adivasis. It is, therefore, difficult to identify them. After two decades of working among the tribals of North Bengal, I finally found them in early 2000 at a labourer colony in the Siliguri terai; they were working at the Zabra Tea Estate, near Naxalbari. In West Bengal, they are found in relatively large numbers (2,025) at the Purulia district.

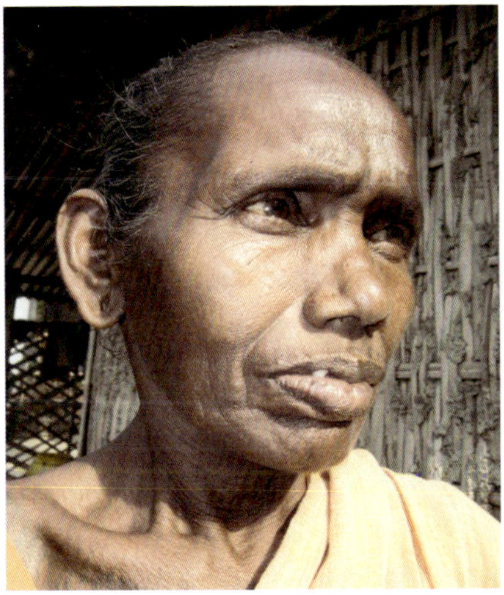

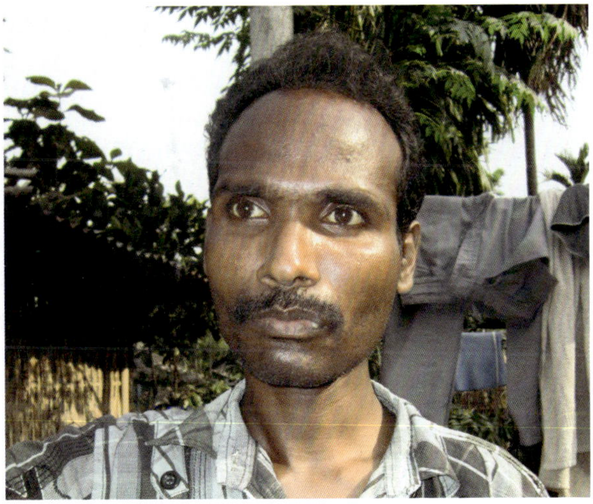

The Goraits are said to be a tribe of the Chota Nagpur plateau from where many of the Proto-Australoid and Dravidian tribes migrated to West Bengal. They have their totemistic clans, namely, Khalkho, Indwar, Topowar, Kerketta, Dhan and Sontirkey. Among this tribe (women, in particular), especially those belonging to the Sontirkey clan, are not allowed to wear gold ornaments. I met Sohagi Gorait at the Zabra Tea Estate's Purna Dhura who confirmed this. I found a Gorait girl, Ananti, at the tea estate, who had already graduated from NBU. Her brother, Amit and her younger sister were also doing well in their studies. Ananti's grandfather, Agnu Gorait, was a tea garden labourer.

The Goraits are traditionally drum-beaters and used to receive an annual payment from the villagers for performing in ceremonies, rituals and festivals. The Gorait people, as seen in Bengal, however, do not pursue this occupation any more. In North Bengal, they work as labourers in tea plantations and speak Sadri.

The Beautiful Hos

The Ho people were once known as Kol and Larka Kol and were mainly the inhabitants of the Kolhan area of the Singhbhum district of undivided Bihar. They are also known as Kolha. In Odisha, this tribe was found in Cuttack, Kalahandi, Dhenkanal, Keonjhar and Mayurbhanj. They were also living in Madhya Pradesh. As the community spread from the original homeland of Singhbhum, a section of the Hos came to West Bengal.

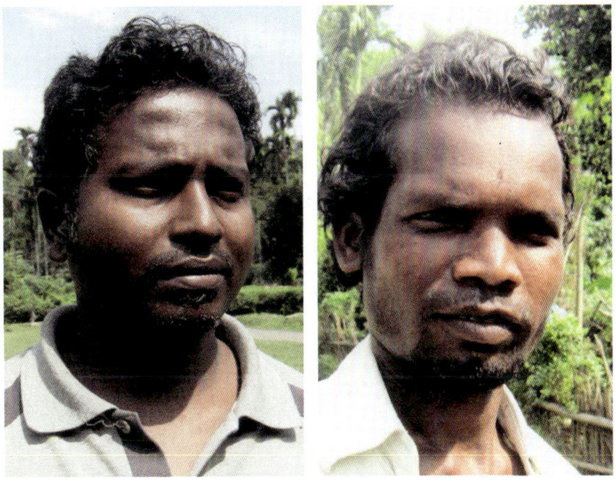

While I was in search of the Hos and a few other lesser-known tribes in the Terai-Duars's galaxy for my documentation project, a friend informed me about a Ho girl who was doing her Masters in NBU. Her name was Gouri Kolmunda and she was from the remote Zurrantee Tea Estate of the Duars. This came as a real surprise and I wanted to know about the journey of this girl. How did she manage the load of such sudden urbanism?

To reach NBU from Zurrantee, one has to get to Chalsa by a shared jeep. It is a zig-zag journey of an hour, even more. From Chalsa, there is a Siliguri-bound bus; it takes about two hours or more to reach the Mittal bus stand at Siliguri's Second Mile. A shared auto to Sevoke More and, finally, another bus or an auto for the Shiv mandir takes one towards the university. Walking down the NBU campus road is, however, charming. There are many private lodges and paying guest houses available here.

It was in 2000, when I bought a Ho-English dictionary, that my interest in the Hos grew. Published by Xavier Ho Publications of Chaibasa, Bihar, this 390-page hard-bound volume cost me just Rs. 35 for a very old copy. A Ranchi-linked tribal bookselling team of Kolkata had displayed it, among many other tribal titles, at the Kolkata Book Fair. This lexicon proved to be a breakthrough in my knowledge of the Hos and I came to understand that their language is really different from the Mundas. I also gathered that the Ho community happens to be a separate ethnic community altogether. The dialects of the Hos and the Mundas are different even though their origin is from the same source, Sing-Bonga and Ote-Baram.

As I had heard about the existence of the Hos in the Duars through the census report, I was determined to look for them. In 2013, it seemed that I had found my Ho country! One of my Oraon friends, Ganga Beck, an energetic young man, was my guide in locating this tribe. I requested him to accompany me for my first Zurrantee trip as he had a motorcycle. He is also known to have done good work on the tribals. While planning for this trip, Ganga had once casually mentioned that his wife, Basanti, happens to be a Ho and I could start the Ho expedition from his home at Malbazar. Needless to say, I was at Ganga's home without any delay.

So it was that, at an Oraon home, I first saw a Ho woman, Basanti Soy-aa. She was well-conversant in Bengali and her conduct was that of a Bengali middle-class family. Basanti gladly gave me a small list of patrilineal Ho *killi*s (clan names), including Soy-aa, which was her clan. As I wrote all this down in the Bengali script, Basanti made the necessary spelling corrections for generating phonetic clarity into my notes as far as possible. She said that she was brought up at the Denguajhar Tea Estate on the outskirts of the Bengali-dominated Jalpaiguri town. She was a fair-complexioned lady, which was unusual for an Australoid.

As I had grown up in the Duars, my upbringing was different from the Kolkata-dominated Bengali mindset. This land has many geo-political frontiers and its internal cultural plurality did, inevitably, affect my mindscape. There is Assam in the east, echoing Bhutan in the north; China and Japan influencing Nepal; the famous *desi* Bihar in the northwest and the great 1971-branded Bangladesh in the south. Under this backdrop, I learnt to believe that a tribal boy should always marry a girl from his own community but from another clan. Thus, the customary law of clan-exogamy prevails. Under the rule, a tribal girl will always

opt for her bridegroom from her own tribe, an Oraon with an Oraon, a Munda with a Munda and so on. Basanti, however, chose to marry an Oraon boy, Ganga, in what is undoubtedly a special case of an inter-caste marriage where a Proto-Australoid girl bonded with a Dravidian-speaking boy. Ganga explained that this had happened because of their old connection at the Denguajhar Tea Estate.

My quest for gathering more information on the Hos led me to the Zurrantee Tea Estate in Bhutan's countryside. To reach Zurrantee, I had to cross Meteli bazaar and the Nagessuri Tea Garden. The road was totally damaged at that time. People visit this remote tea estate for many reasons, but most commonly for doing business. Though its nearest township is Meteli, the major business is done in Malbazar, an enclave of at least 3,000 Adivasi people. Among the most frequent Zurrantee visitors are trade unionists-cum-political activists. High-profile tourists are a new class of visitors to this region. The tea garden management has, for this purpose, converted the director's bungalow, which is on a hilltop, into a unique resort with its own transportation service to bring tourists from the airport. Those from the civil service form another kind of visitors. As the tea gardens are now under the orbit of the statutory panchayat system, often the government staff comes here for official purposes. A vegetable vendor whom I spoke to is a daily visitor from Dhupguri.

On reaching Zurrantee's Damuline, in the lap of the Indo-Bhutanese landscape, it seemed that for the first time the people here were receiving a person with an interest in their community. This is the place where Ganga's wife's relatives live

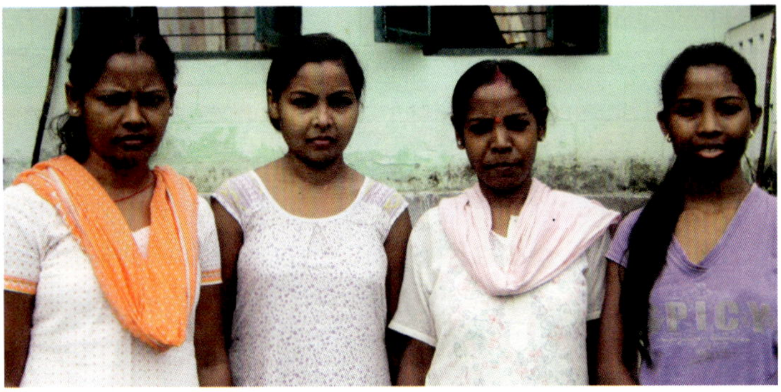

and so I got a special welcome. Soon I found Gouri's house, where her father, Tupa, explained the Ho tragedy of amalgamating with the Munda culture. Among the people assembled at Tupa's house, there was a young boy who works at the Malbazar Block Development Office (BDO). According to him, many Ho boys and girls obtained their tribal certificate as Mundas because the office was not aware of the Hos but are familiar with the Munda community. The Hos did not find anything wrong with this. To me, this Mundaisation of the Hos is equivalent to a crime as it would ruin the history of this tribe in the Duars and there would officially be no Hos in the Malbazar region.

In this Zurrantee countryside there are very few Hos unlike the Santals, Oraons, Mundas or the Boro-Rabha-Toto people. Of the 23,483 Hos of West Bengal, only 3,760 (about 16 per cent) were counted from the Darjeeling and Jalpaiguri districts in the 2011 census. Under most circumstances they assert their identity with the Mundas. Many of them use Kol-Munda as their surnames, hence to outsiders like me they are referred to as the Mundas.

For several reasons, the Hos have had an identity crisis and most of them in the Duars and the Terai have been on the verge of a suicidal amalgamation with the Mundas. This branch of the Hos is, therefore, very special to me. This tribe was once known as Laraku-Kol in Singhbhum. I took up the story of their predicament with Suhas, the tribal inspector at the Sub Divisional Office (SDO) in Malbazar, and requested him to correct their wrong tribal certificates, if possible. After two years, when I reviewed the matter, I found that nothing had changed. Recently, however, the local BDO office organised a special camp for issuing certificates to the Hos of the Zurrantee Tea Garden area under my initiative.

When I first visited Zurrantee's Ho country, I remember being extremely impressed by the work done by Dalton in his *Descriptive Ethnology of Bengal* (1872). I shared some of his thoughts on the Hos, which he had observed 150 years ago. The Hos are fairer-skinned compared to the other Proto-Australoid tribes in the country and their beauty has been referred to by most of the scholars who wrote about them. The picturesque Zurrantee on the bank of the river Neora-khola provided a great opportunity to photograph several Hos who were exceptionally beautiful and fair-complexioned. Natho Kolmunda, the chief of this tea garden, had a robust tribal figure and his photograph portrays a true Ho leader. According to Kartik Chandra Bawanda, a man from the Ho community of the Medinipur district of West Bengal, the reason for this fair complexion of the Hos, especially the girls, was due to their Jain connection in Singhbhum, which was once dominated by the Mathura *gowala*s (cow-keepers) and others from the Aryan race.

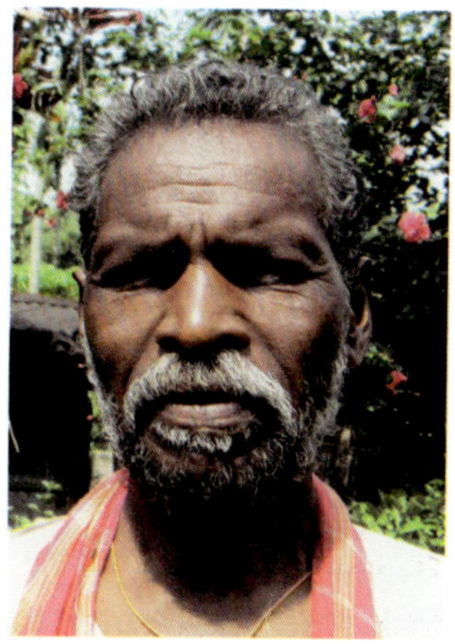

The Hos are an interesting tribe but they are unaware of their history; I found their story of origin in anthropological literature. It is interesting that the Mundas also have the same story. Yet, there are differences in the dialect. 'Ho', 'hore', or 'horo' mean man in their language. 'Hor' means man in Santali, too. In Mundari, 'horo' signifies a man. When describing this tribe, Risley said in 1891, '...the word is used in their language to distinguish human beings from brutes'. As for the close proximity of the Hos with the Kols, or more particularly the Mundas, all the earlier works said that the Hos belong to the same family history as the Mundas. Though Singhbhum was once a Ho country, they claimed that their ancestors were from Chota Nagpur. This is why the Sing-Bonga and Ote-Boram are their common chief deities. Ote-Boram is also stated to be another name for Sing-Bonga or the sun god and Sing-Bonga is often called Sim-Bonga. Sim in Ho means fowl. Hence, Bonga is often described as the fowl god.

An old British account on the Hos reads, 'The Hos have a tradition concerning the creation of the world and the origin of the human race. Ote-Boram and Sing-Bonga were self-created; they made the earth with rocks and water and they clothed it with grass and trees and then created animals, first; those that man domesticates and afterwards wild beasts. When all was thus prepared for the abode of man, a boy and girl were created, and Sing-Bonga placed them in a cave at the bottom of a great ravine.' One may assume the proximity of the term, Singhbhum, with this great Sing-Bonga.

Finding the boy and the girl to be too innocent to give hope of progeny, the story unfolds, he (Sing-Bonga) instructed them in the art of making *illi*, rice beer, which excites the passions, and thus the world became peopled. When the first parents had produced 12 boys and 12 girls, Sing-Bonga prepared a feast of the flesh of buffaloes, bullocks, goats, sheep, pigs and fowl, along with vegetables. He made the brothers and sisters pair off and told each pair to take what they most relished and depart. The first and second pairs took the flesh of the bullocks and buffaloes and thus originated the Kols (Hos) and the Bhumijs (Matkums); the next took the vegetables only, and are the progenitors of the Brahmans and Kshatriyas; others took goats and fish, and from them came the Sudras. One pair took shellfish and became the Bhuiyas; two pairs took pigs and became the Santals. One pair got nothing; seeing which the earlier pairs gave them their superfluity and from them spring the Ghasis, who toil not, but live by preying on others.

This Ho folktale enchanted me and I felt that I had found a real Ho country at Zurrantee's Damuline after 200 years. Modern-day anthropologists should visit this region in order to survey the changing psyche of the Hos. There is a beautiful tourist resort on a hilltop at the Zurrantee Tea Garden.

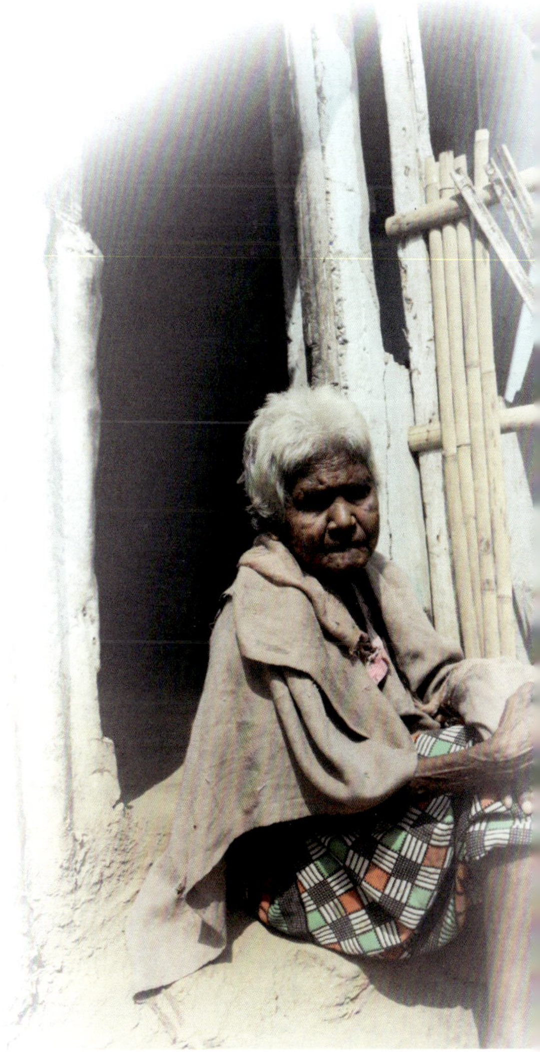

My Ho informers at Zurrantee gave me a list of Ho clans: Husuk for the Rabhas; Aris for the Boros (Meches) and Thors among the Nepalis. The Hos from the tea garden were particular in identifying them with their clans. Everyone was prompt in responding, even neighbours came forward to help me with the clan names. Here is a list though I am not sure about the spellings: Purti, Hasa, Hembrom, Mundri, Bandra, Korah, Hansdah, Deogam, Saweya (Soy-aa), Garpai (Gaypai), Sundi, Kud-da, Buri-uli, Mun-dui-yaa and Darai. I was delighted to find eight among these as Ho clans mentioned by Dalton (1872) and

Risley (1891). Ten of these clans have also been found in a list provided by Bawanda. The magic of these people is such that once you get to know them you would be forever faithful to them.

Another interesting aspect of the Hos is their uniqueness in naming male children. One of them was called Kapten (captain) Mankimunda. Kapten had migrated to the Zurrantee Duars from Odisha's Mayurbhanj and was extremely proud of his identity as a Ho. Dalton observes in the *Descriptive Ethnology of Bengal*: 'The Hos have a pleasing custom of introducing into their families the names or titles of persons they like, irrespective of creed or race. Thus Major, Captain, Tickell, Doctor have became common names in the Kolhan. The names thus introduced will probably remain in the Kolhan for ages. The writer of an article that appeared not long ago in the *Calcutta Quarterly Review* appears to be under the impression that this custom of naming Kol children after officers had been introduced by the missionaries. The missionaries have had nothing to do with it. It is a spontaneous act of goodwill on the part of unconverted Hos.'

My Ho dictionary had ignited in me the desire to know more about this beautiful community, with its diversity of languages and people. It helped me make several speeches. I recently heard that the All India Ho Language Action Committee, Ho Bhasa Sikhsa Parsat, Odisha, Ho Samaj Yuba Mahasabha, Jharkhand and the Ho Kala Sangam, Chaibasa, have asked that the Ho language be included in the eighth schedule of the Indian Constitution. I have also heard that a Ho script, *Varangchiti*, has emerged and is helping to promote the Ho linguistic movement in Bihar, Jharkhand and Odisha. The propagators of this script claim that it is Guru Lako Badra who gave rebirth to it.

The Hos at Singbhum, Mayurbhanj, Chaibasa and Chota Nagpur celebrate seven major festivals. These include Magh Parab or Desauli Bonga, which, according to Dalton, 'is held in the month of Magh, or January, when the granaries are full of grain, and the people, to use their own expression, full of delivery. They (the Hos) have a strange notion that at this period, men and women are so overcharged with vicious propensities, that it is absolutely necessary for the safety of the persons to let off steam by allowing, for a time, full vent to the passions.'

'The festival,' continues Dalton, 'opens with a sacrifice to Desauli of three fowls—a cock and two hens, one of which must be black, and offered with some flowers of the *palas* trees (*Butea frondosha*), bread made from rice-flour, and *sesamum* (sesame) seed. The sacrifice and offerings are made by the village priest, if there be one, or if not, by any elder of the village who possesses the necessary legendary lore, and he prays that during the year they are about to enter on, they and their children may be preserved from all misfortune and sickness, and that they have seasonable rain and good crops. Prayer is also made in some places for the souls of the departed. At this period an evil spirit is supposed to infest the locality, and to get rid of it, the men, women and children go in procession round and through every part of the village, with sticks in their hands as if beating for game, singing a wild chant and vociferating violently till they feel assured that the bad spirit must have fled; and they make noise enough to frighten a legion. These religious ceremonies over, the people give themselves up to feasting, drinking immoderately of rice-beer till they are in the state of wild ebriety most suitable for the process of letting off steam.'

The next in the order of Ho festivals is Bah Bonga. It is said to be similar to that of Sarhul of the Mundas or Baha-parab of the Santals. 'Baha' means flower and the festival takes place when the *sal* tree (in Mundari, *sal* is called *sarjum*) is in full bloom, during March or April. I know a few Santal women who are named

Bahamuni, which is also the name of the third wife of the legendary Naxalite, Jungle Santal. 'The boys and girls collect baskets full of flowers, make garlands of them, weave them in their hair and decorate their houses with them. Each house makes an offering of these flowers and sacrifices a cock. The people dance for a couple of days and nights incessantly and refresh themselves meanwhile with beer,' notes Dalton.

The third Ho fest is Damurai, which was once celebrated in May, during the time of sowing the first crop. It is said that, through Damurai, the Ho people honour their ancestors and other spirits. They believe that if Damurai is not properly propitiated, the deity will prevent the seeds from germinating. Hero-Bonga is another festival that is celebrated in June. The Mundaris call it Harihar and the people propitiate Desauli and Jahir-Burhi to bless their crops. In the Mundari villages, every householder plants a branch of the *bhelwa* in his field and contributes to the general offering, which is made by the priest in the sacred grove—a fowl, a pitcher of beer and a handful of rice. This is followed in July with another festival, Bha-towli-Bonga. 'Each cultivator sacrifices a fowl, and after some mysterious rites, a wing is stripped off and inserted in the cleft of a bamboo and stuck up in the rice-field and dung-heap. If this is omitted, it is supposed that the rice will not come to maturity. It appears more like a charm than a sacrifice,' writes Dalton.

Jum-nama is the sixth festival when the first fruits of the harvest are offered to Sing-Bonga together with a white cock in August. And then there is the Kalam-Bonga festival, which is when rice straw is taken from the paddy-threshing places, *kalam*, to be stacked.

I was fascinated by the way in which a Ho wedding is conducted. The ceremony is held after a prolonged process of negotiation and, while the rituals are kept to the minimum, the pre-wedding inter-family settlement is a lengthy process. On

the appointed day, the bride is taken to the place where there are dances, songs and feasts amid *illi* drinking. According to Dalton, 'The turning point in the rite is when the bride and groom pledge each other. A cup of beer is given to each; the groom pours some of the contents of his cup into the bride's cup, and she returns the compliment. Drinking the liquor thus blended, they become of one *kili*, that is, the bride is admitted into her husband's tribe, and they become one.'

According to the census of 2011, the Ho population of West Bengal is increasing; the figure rose from 11,640 in 1991 to 23,483. The district of Paschim Medinipur has the largest Ho population in West Bengal, with 14,656 (62 per cent) ethnic Hos. Yet the voice of this community remains low as its share in the total tribal population of the state is a mere 0.44 per cent.

The Traditional Karmalis

The Karmalis believe that they originated from Lord Vishwakarma, the Hindu god of architecture. The community is known for its traditional occupation of making iron utensils and implements and the practice of ancestor worshipping. Their population in West Bengal was 2,466 in 2011. This tribe has some exogamous totemic clans such as Kavethoyar (Kayathoyar), Sonowar and Belowar.

Birshu Kashi came to Bagdogra, near Siliguri, at the age of 15 in search of a job. His forefathers were from Jharkhand's Dumarla village in the Gumla district. In September 2013, when he was 55 years, I took his photograph outside his house at Pahargoomiah Tea Estate's Damdama division's Baraline. Birshu said that when he came from Jharkhand, he took shelter at Chhottu Kashi's house and agreed to work at his master's residence. Later, he got a labourer's job at Pahargoomiah. Chhottu got Birsha married to his younger daughter, Jugantee and Birshu was allotted a quarter at Pahargoomiah's Baraline. His new life began there. Birshu and Jugantee have four children, Subhas, Babita, Durgi and Gauri. Subhas got his Bachelor's degree and took up a job at Bagdogra Airport's terminal as a ground porter. In the meantime, he obtained a Scheduled Tribe certificate stating that he belongs to the Karmali community. His parents, however, did not know anything about the Karmali culture. Birshu Kashi works in the tea plantation and his wife keeps animal husbandry—cows, goats and pigs. Birshu's children state that one day they will definitely take their parents to their ancestral home in Jharkhand.

When I met Birshu and his wife, the next day was Karam Puja. There was some sudden rain in the afternoon and Juganti excitedly declared that it was Karam Devta's rain. In the Pahargoomiah Tea Estate, there is a perpetual crisis of water and there is only a solitary ringwell in Birshu's labour line, so this rain was indeed a welcome gift from the gods.

Legends of the Kharias

According to some scholars, the word *kharia* is derived from the Oriya *khar-khar*. The Kharias believe that they are the descendants of the Kol tribe. *Kharia* is derived from *kher*, which, in Proto-Kol language, means bird (goose). One of the mythological beliefs of this tribe corroborates this argument where it is said that the ancestors of the Kharias hatched from the two eggs of a *kher*.

The Kharias were found largely in the forests of Madhya Pradesh, Bihar, Odisha and West Bengal. There are three major sub-groups—the Hill Kharias, the Dudh Kharias and the Dhelki Kharias. The Hill Kharias live in the Simlipal hills of Mayurbhanj in Odisha as well as in the Dhalbhum region of Bihar. They are also found in the districts of Medinipur, Bakura and Purulia on the West Bengal-Bihar border. The western counterparts of these Hill Kharias are known as the Dudh Kharias and the Dhelki Kharias. The former are found in large numbers in the hilly regions of Ranchi, Madhya Pradesh and in Sambalpur in Odisha while the Dhelkis

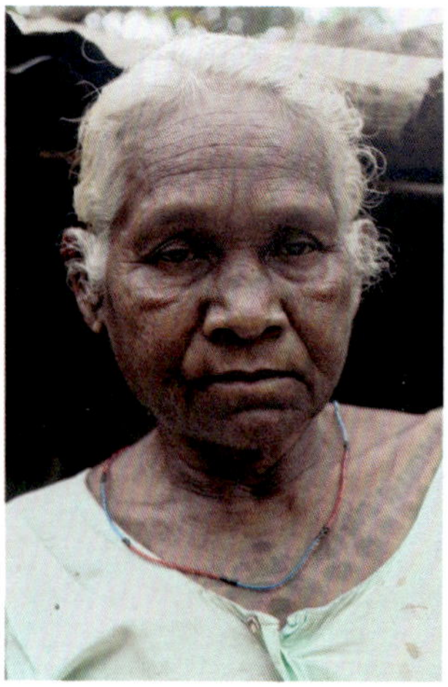

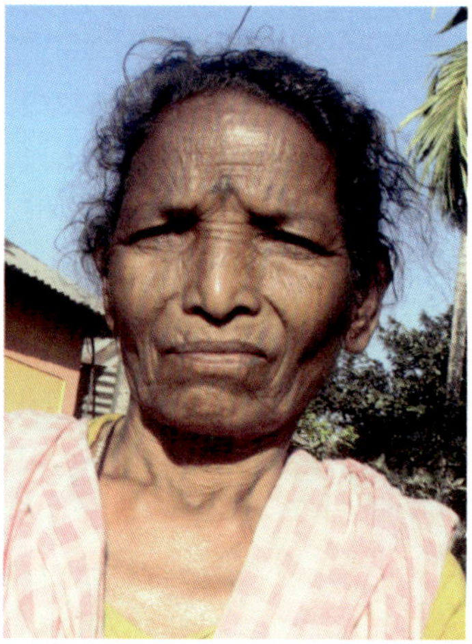

have settled in Gangpur, Odisha and in Rampur, Madhya Pradesh. A group of the Kharias migrated to the tea gardens of North Bengal a few decades ago.

They have a number of clans that are totemistic and follow a patriarchal lineage. The clans of the Hill Kharias include Gulgu, Hembrom and Bhuinya. The Dudh Kharias are divided into several clans—Dungdung, Kulu, Samad, Bilung, Soreng, Kiro and Topo. The Dhelki Kharias, too, belong to several clans such as Soren, Samad, Topno, Charha, Hansda and so on. In a recent study conducted in the Kumargram police station area of the district of Jalpaiguri, it was found that some Dhelki Kharias belong to the Mura, Soren, Samad, Bage, Barliha, Charhut, Hansda, Dungdung, Aind, Mail or Kiro and Topno clans while the Dudh Kharias belonged to the Dungdung, Kulu, Samad or Kerketta, Bilung, Soreng, Ba, Tete or Hoin, Toppo and Kiro clans. Among the Kharias of the Duars, the study identified clans such as Dhanowar, Indwaar, Kerketta, Soreng and Tirkey.

The Kharias have their own legends and folktales regarding their origin. One of the stories maintains that they are the descendants of the older brother of the Mundas. Once upon a time, the story unfolds, a Nagbanshi king reached Chota Nagpur along with his elder brother. Since the younger one knew horse riding, he became the king. He once escaped being bitten by a snake and hence his successors were named Nagbanshi. Chota Nagpur was named after this king. The Kharias or the Kherias are grouped in West Bengal together with the Lodhas, who are, however, not accepted by a section of the authorities. In classical literature, the Kharias were referred to as Savara, Nishada and Lubdhak (Lodha). In West Bengal, the Kharias or Kherias were mentioned along with the Lodhas as a single group in the list of Scheduled Tribes as they have a similar lifestyle, but there

 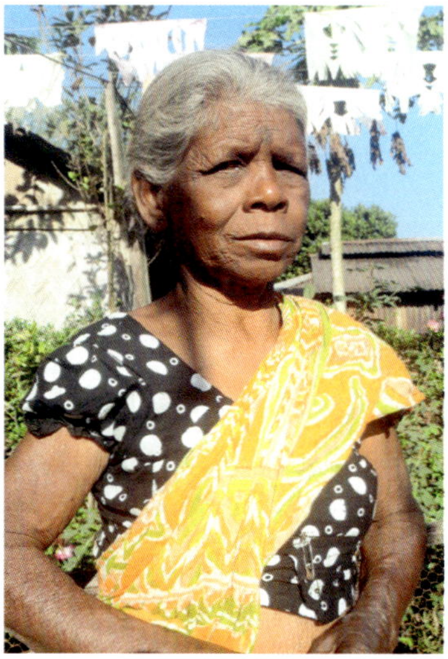 

are differences of opinion. Dr Amal Kumar Das (1962) observed, 'Though in the list of Scheduled Tribes, Kheria has been indicated to be a synonym of Lodha, our investigation revealed that everywhere they are regarded as different communities. Some Lodhas claim themselves to be Kherias, while others claim that they belong to the Sabars, but no Kheria admits that the Lodhas belong to their ethnic group. The difference between these two is also known to the general population.'

This controversy remains unresolved. A 1992 report (MK Chowdhury and others) reveals that the Kharias and the Lodha communities are grouped under a single category in the list of Scheduled Tribes (1976) by the Government of India: 'The reason for placing the two groups in a same category is not very clear, but it may have so happened for both the communities identify themselves as Savara and both of them have had criminal stigma attached to them. Even then, whether these two communities are the same or different ethnic groups remains a question to many social scientists; this needs further research to probe into their actual identity ...' Dhirendranath Baskey (1987) concurs. He states that the Kharias and

the Lodhas are not the same because the clans, religious rites and cultural beliefs and practices of the people signify their differences.

The justification of categorising the two tribes under a single head has been partially supported by Dr Suhrid Bhowmik (1980) under a linguistic perspective. His observation is that some tribal people of the Austro-Asiatic group in India are known as the Kharias. I am of the view that the name, Kharia, is an occupational one. That is why some Dravidian people, with the same occupation, entered this group, calling themselves the Oraon-Kharias.

The Kharias speak a script-less dialect known as Kharia that is said to be a branch of the Mundari speech family of the Austric group of languages. A large section of the tribe cannot speak its mother tongue and has adopted regional languages such as Bengali, Hindi, Oriya and Sadri. In the Manbhum (Purulia) area, their dialect is called Kharia-thar and has a strong resemblance to Bengali. According to the language of the Dudh and Dhelki groups of the Kharias, the word for a priest is *pahan*; however, for the Hill Kharias it is *dihuri*. Both the posts of *dihuri* and *pahan* are hereditary. The Kharias who practice the traditional rites of religious beliefs tend to categorise themselves as Hindus while those following the Christian ways are 'Mission Kharias'. The majority of the Dudh Kharias and the Dhelki Kharias are Christians. The so-called Hindu Kharias worship various deities; Giring or Bero is the chief among them. Regarded as the sun god, Giring is also called Thakur and is worshipped during almost all their festivals. The Kharias have a custom of offering five animals in a lifetime for satisfying the sun god. The animal sacrifice starts with a fowl and ends with a buffalo; a pig, a white goat and a sheep are sacrificed in the middle. The village deity of the Kharias is Garam Thakur. They worship Dharam Devta in every household and also venerate a series of evil spirits. The Jalpaiguri Kharias are found to observe Noya Khari puja in November-December to celebrate the harvesting of paddy and Goyal Puja for the growth and well-being of their

domestic animals during Kali puja. They also celebrate Fagua, Sal puja and Bara Pahari or Dongi puja; the latter is celebrated once in a decade.

It is difficult to give an exact number of the Kharia population because of their clubbing with the Lodhas in West Bengal. Yet, the combined population of the Lodhas and the Kharias/Kherias in the state in 2011 was 108,707; this figure is gradually increasing. The tribe is mainly found in the districts of Paschim Medinipur (51,772) and Jalpaiguri (34,481).

The History of the Kharwars

The People of India, National Series, Volume III (Anthropological Survey of India, 1994) states that the Kharwars once resided in the Sone valley. The legend goes that they came to Palamau from Khari Jhar and hence were known as the Kharwars. This tribe has six endogamous groups, which are Surajbanshi, Daulatbandi, Parbandi, Kheri (Chero Kharwar), Bhogti or Ganju and Manjhia. These groups are further divided into a number of exogamous totemic clans such as Nag, Aiyen and Kerketta. The Kharwars consider themselves to be Kshatriyas; they often identify with Attarah Hazari and claim descent from the Surajbanshi Rajput. This story was also common in the case of the Cheros and it claims a possible historical link between the Kharwars and the Cheros. The Kharwars appoint a priest (*baiga*) either from the Munda or their own community. The priest officiates over the Sarhul and Karma rituals and protects the people from evil spirits.

In West Bengal, the majority (51 per cent) of the Kharwars are found in the Malda district in North Bengal. Of the 20,270 Kharwars, 10,438 have been

living in Malda, according to the census of 2011. The Kharwars dominated the areas of Malda that were earlier attached to the Bhagalpur division along with the Purnea and Katihar districts of Bihar. In Risley's *The Tribes and Castes of Bengal* more than 50 septs are mentioned among the Kharwars and, apparently, in West Bengal they used titles such as Bhakat, Bhogta, Das, Gaunju, Kapri, Mahato, Mandar, Manjhi, Ohdar, Panjiara and Pradhan. In North Bengal's tea plantations, however, they use Kherwar or Kharwar as their surname today. They work as tea plantation labourers and live in the labourer colonies of the gardens. They use Sadri as the language of communication and many among them are Hindus and Christian converts.

The Many Names of the Kisans

The Kisans are a Proto-Australoid tribe that inhabits Odisha, Bihar, Madhya Pradesh and West Bengal and is, at times, said to be an offshoot of the Oraon tribe. Chota Nagpur was their early homeland. The word *kisan* means farmer and the community was named after their occupation. Some say that the Kisans called themselves Kunhar and their language was Kun-boli, which is known to be similar to Kurukh, the speech of the Oraons of the Dravidian language family. In North Bengal today, they speak Sadri, the most popular language of the region. In Bihar, the Kisans are also known as Nageswar or Nagesia. A section of this tribe in the tea gardens of Darjeeling is known as the Nagesias. The Kisans were also known as Kuda, Koda and Mirdha in different areas.

According to the 2011 census in West Bengal, the Kisans have been found in the districts of Maldah, Darjeeling and Nadia in large numbers. They are also living in Uttar Dinajpur, Murshidabad and Jalpaiguri where they work in the plantations

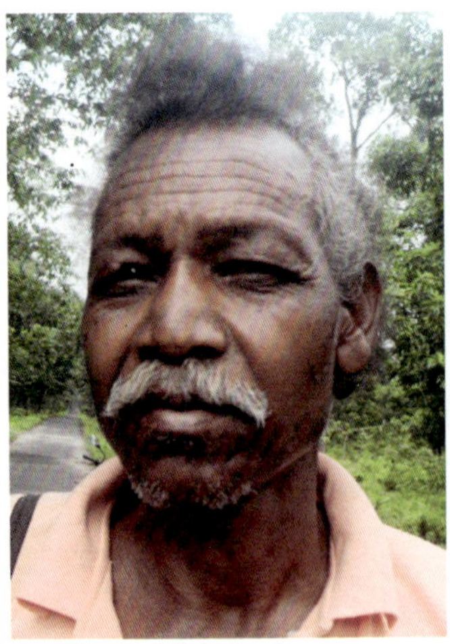

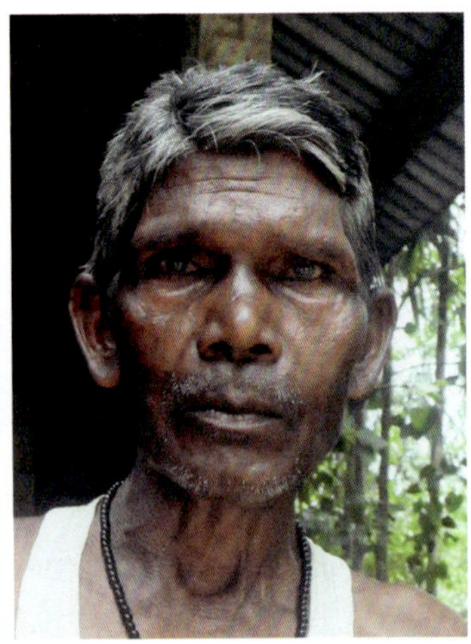

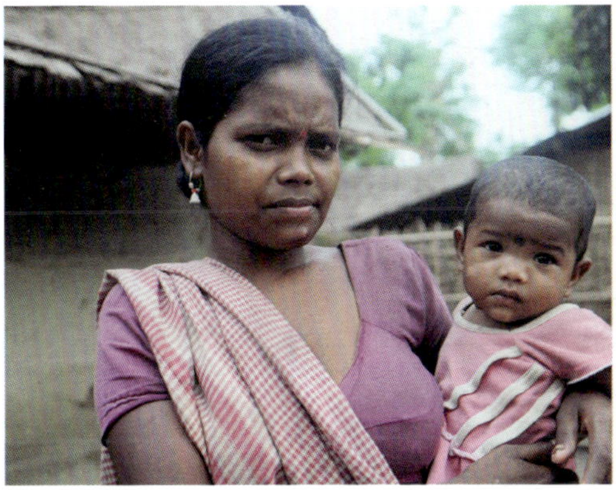

as tea garden labourers. They are generally agriculturists. The Kisan population in West Bengal was 98,434 in 2011; this was an increase from 40,535 in 2001. They are divided into four social sub-groups of Sinduria, Telia, Dehria and Agaria. Apart from this, there are clans, popularly called by their titles, which include Lakra, Toppo, Baxla, Kujur, Minz, Ekka, Tigga, Xess, Xaxa, Panna, Beck, Khale, Pala, Bada/Bara and Majhi. Most of these clans have their respective totemistic objects. For instance, the people belonging to the Lakra clan usually do not kill or harm the tiger. Similarly, those in the Toppo clan originated from a

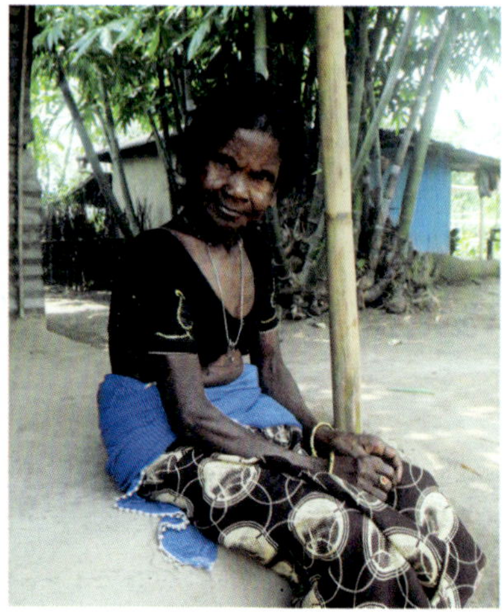

kind of fish, therefore the killing or eating of fish is restricted for them. Further divisions of the clans, including Khudi, are generally adaptations of the names of ancestral places.

The traditional village chief is known as *sian* and the priest is called *kalo*. However, a *kalo* does not necessarily preside over all socio-religious functions. There are people known as *mati*s who perform magico-religious rites. The Kisans celebrate the Ganga Utsav (festival of the river Ganges) in the Bengali month of Kartik or Magh on the banks of the rivers close to their village. Traditionally fond of dancing, Nadu-yatra was once a major social festival of this tribe.

Koras, the Earth Diggers

The Koras are a little-known tribe in West Bengal. A community of earth diggers, they are no longer associated with their traditional occupation. In 1891, Risley pointed out their occupation as earth workers and, in SC Roy's monumental book, *The Oraons of Chota Nagpur* (1915), there is mention of their skill in raising embankments, mud walls and so on. Though in today's Kora society, their social divisions do not play a primary role, they had four endogamous social groups—Modi or Mudi Kora, Kurmi Kora, Nagbangshi Murali Kora and Dhangar or Orang Kora. It has also been said that the Koras have seven sub-castes, that is, Dhalo, Malo, Sikharia, Badamia, Sonarekha, Jhetia and Guri-Baura. These emerged on

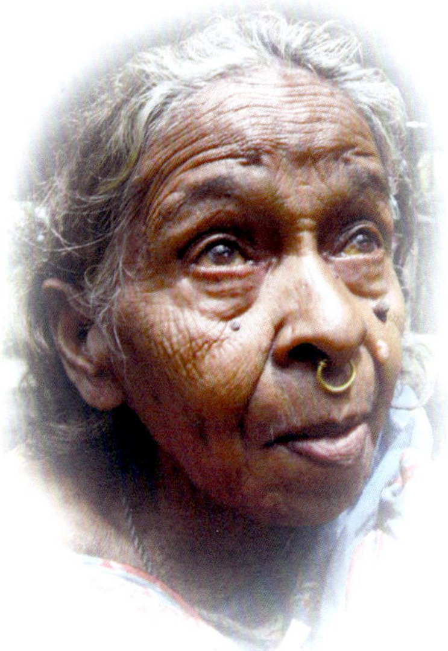

the basis of those belonging to their original homeland. For instance, the Dhalo sub-caste people claim that they came from Dhalbhum, the eastern *pargana* of old Singhbhum; the Malos say that they are from Manbhum and the Sikharias from a place between the rivers Damodar and Barakar, bound on the east by the Samet Sikhar or Parashnath hill. Similarly, the Sonarekha people believe that their homeland was somewhere near the river Subarnarekha.

Basically from the Chota Nagpur region, the Koras claim that their forefathers came to Bengal from Odisha's Koraput. In North Bengal's Lataguri I met some people of this tribe who live in a forest-village, Bichabhanga, and were from Odisha. In Bichabhanga, Madhu Kora, an enthusiastic collector of folklore, became my friend. Madhu has recently come to be known in North Bengal for exhibiting the Kora folk dance. Those worthy of mention among the Kora clans are Samar (fish), Nagdu (bird), Sapu (kite), Lodham (squirrel) and Tundu (a kind of tuber). The importance of these clans is that they are exogamous and totemistic in nature. In reality, however, this clan regulation has lost its glory.

In West Bengal, there were 159,404 Koras in 2011. In Bardhaman alone, there were 37,315 members of this tribe who once migrated to the colliery areas and Purulia had 33,266. The Koras are also found in Paschim Medinipur (29,115), Birbhum (14,980), Bankura (13,204), Hugli (12,345), Maldah (7,105) and South 24 Parganas (1,701).

This community has some interesting linguistic behaviours. Dr AK Das observed in his work, *The Koras and Some Little Known Communities of West Bengal* (1964): 'The mother tongue of these Koras differs from area to area. In Purulia district they speak a dialect, which is reported to be akin to Kurukh (Oraon) language. In Midnapore district, on the other hand, the Kora dialect is very much akin to the Santali language. In the western fringe of the Burdwan district, the Kora dialect is reported to bear some resemblance to the Oraon language. In central Burdwan, it is akin to Santali and, in Burdwan, it is reported to be a cruder variant of Bengali. In Murshidabad it is reported to be akin to Mundari.'

Das was of the opinion that 'The people, who are known as Koras in different areas, have been derived from heterogeneous origins. Kora seems to be a generic name, signifying the occupation of earth digging. It is not unlikely that the common generic name, Kora, has come to be associated with sections of different tribes in different areas, on their taking up the occupation of earth digging as the means of livelihood.'

The Changing Culture of the Korwas

The popular belief about this community is that the term *korwa* has been derived from a tree known as *kodera*. There is a second view that says that the term came from a word, *dodowa*, which means earth digging. The people are also reportedly known as Dihariya or Kisan-Korwa. They were mainly inhabitants of the then Madhya Pradesh, from where a section of them came to undivided Bihar, Odisha and West Bengal. In West Bengal's Siliguri-Terai, I found members of this tribe who stated that they had migrated from Bihar's Ranchi as labourers in forest-villages and tea gardens. The Korwas have their exogamous clans such as Samadhavar, Edigwar, Ganu, Hansdwar, Banda, Sanouani and Murriwar. In Siliguri-Terai's Kalabari forest *busti*, the Korwa people have been found to belong to three of these clans—Hansdwar, Murriwar and Ganuar. Their community deities are Dulha-deo, Andhari-mata, Dargia-thakur, Thakur-deo and Murki-mata.

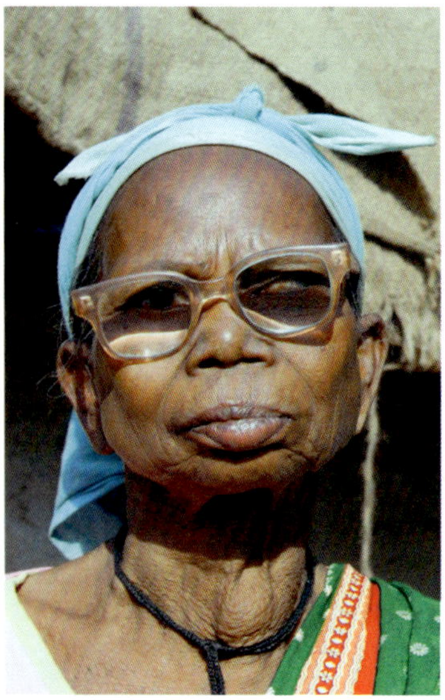

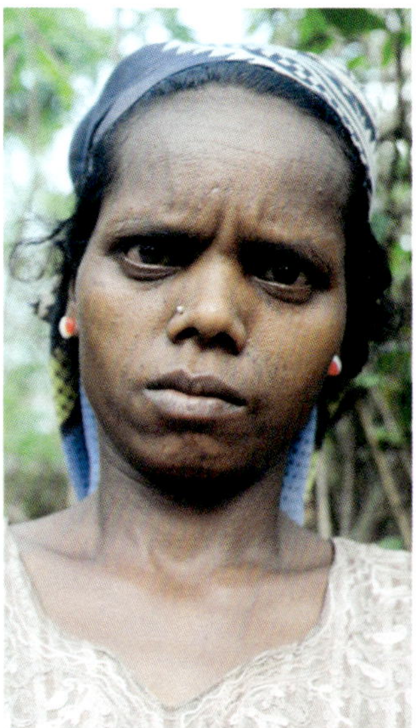

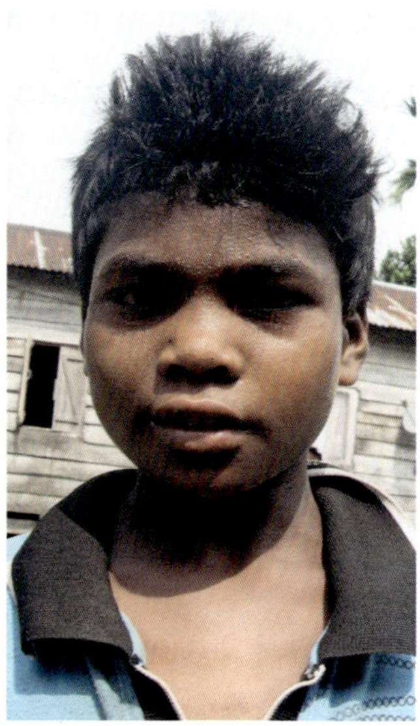

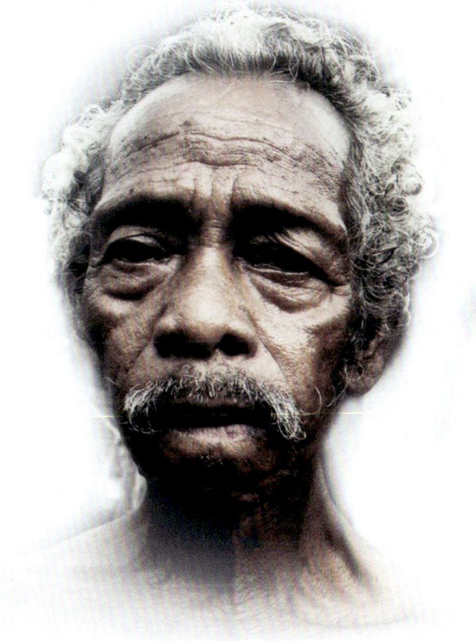

Among the festivals observed by this tribe are Karam, Nava, Charchera and Haryali, though, in reality, most of them have forgotten these traditional cultural practices. Karam puja, Holi and Kali puja are part of today's culture. They also participate in mainstream festivals such as Dussehra and Holi. The Christian segment of the Korwas does not really participate in these festivals and goes to church instead. For them, Christmas and Good Friday are important.

The total Korwa population of West Bengal in 2011 stood at 2,912. Jalpaiguri came up with a relatively high concentration of 959 Korwas, followed by Darjeeling (659 ethnic Korwas). Districts such as North 24 Parganas and Paschim Medinipur also had a Korwa population of 469 and 419, respectively.

Lodhas, the Hunting Tribe

The Lodhas were known as a tribe that was prone to criminal activities during the British era. Though this stigma was removed from the community in 1952 by the enactment of a law by the Government of India, which recognised them as a denotified tribe (DNT), some people still speak of the alleged atrocities they suffered. The Government, however, declared the Lodhas a primitive tribe community (PTC), considering their socio-economic status and other backwardness. There are 72 PTCs spread over 15 states of India today and the Government allots special funds for their development. Five of these—the Birhors, the Dongarias Khonds, the Kolams, the Koragus and the Lodhas—are, however, common for more than one state. Hence the actual number of PTCs would be 67.

The term *lodha* is derived from the Sanskrit word, *lubdhaka*, meaning hunter. The Lodhas can be seen catching fowl by using traps in the forests even today. The tribe, though inhabited in West Bengal since a long time, had an earlier homeland in Madhya Pradesh, according to a section of historians. They have proximity to a Madhya Pradesh-based peasant tribe, Lodh, Nodh or Lodhi. A section of the Bengal-Lodhas also identifies itself with the Sabar community in West Bengal, known for their mythological link with the Ramayana story of *Sabarir Pratiksha*. In West Bengal, the Lodhas are mainly found in the western part of the Medinipur district. They also live in Mayurbhanj and Baleswar of Odisha and in some forest areas of Bihar. There is no official population figure for this tribe in West Bengal as they are clubbed with the Kharia/Kheria community. It has, however, been estimated that there are about 20,000 Lodhas living in West Bengal. According to anthropologists, the Lodhas belong to the Proto-Australoid race and use the local tongues, Bengali in West Bengal and Oriya in Odisha. They are divided into clans, though this seldom plays a role in their day-to-day life. It does become important, however, when a marriage takes place. The clans have totemistic objects and there are taboos in respect of the totems. These clans include the Bhatias, Mallicks, Hayeks, Baghs and Aris, among others. The Bhaktas accommodate a majority among these groups.

The priest of the Lodhas is called *dihiri* or *dehri*. Their main deity is Baram who is believed to be a goddess riding a wild tiger. The Lodhas celebrate Baram puja at the Baram-than in the forests on the last day of the Bengali months of Poush and Choitra. The other goddesses that the Lodhas believe in are the three-eyed Chandi and Sitala. They also worship various evil spirits such as Jugini, Kundara and Pretsini. The Gunins or Ojhas perform magico-religious rites. Among the folk dances of the community, the Chang is the one where only men can participate. The musical instruments used in this dance are known as *changu* or *changul*. The Government of West Bengal has taken up special development projects at Dholkut, Daharpur, Kukai and Dhanshol to educate the Lodhas. In 1967, Bidisha, a non-governmental organisation, was established near Kharagpur in Medinipur for the welfare of the Lodhas as a private initiative by Professor PK Bhowmick. Yet, educational development among the Lodhas has not made much progress. Their socio-economic plight has not improved either. The suicide of one of the promising Lodha women, Chuni Kotal, had brought media attention to the tribe in Kolkata. She committed suicide while she was studying at the university. Chuni Kotal's case was taken up by Mahasveta Devi and an upper caste university professor of the Vidyasagar University of Bengal was believed responsible for the suicide. Though the professor was spared from the case, Chuni Kotal's untimely death signified many aspects of frustration that had risen in her life.

Lodha is one of few tribal communities of Bengal and the only tribe appearing in this book whom I never encountered. Yet, as the community is an integral part of tribal Bengal, I felt it necessary to write something about them.

The Skilful Loharas

It is said that the Loharas derived their name from the word *loha*, meaning iron and, therefore, presumed that they were traditionally blacksmiths. Like in other tribes, the Loharas have some exogamous clans—Kacchua, Ser, Bail and Suar. Some, whom I know in the Duars, use the surname, Baghwar. According to Risley, Lohara, Lohra and Asur are the names of a single community. As working with iron was the identity of these people, it is believed that the community is composed of several generic tribes. In the course of time they emerged as a full-fledged ethnic community. Reports state that the Bengal Loharas are basically two migrant groups from the then Bihar; one is the people whom the tea planters brought as workers and let them settle in the North Bengal tea belts and the other is the group who were brought for indigo cultivation and settled in the district of Nadia in South Bengal. According to the census of 2011, the total Lohara population of West Bengal was 24,783 in 2011. They are found in the district of Jalpaiguri in larger numbers (7,360). The other districts where a sizeable Lohara population is living are Purulia (3,664), North 24 Parganas (3,359), Nadia (3,097), Dakshin Dinajpur (2,136), South 24 Parganas (1,211), Uttar Dinajpur (1,106) and Paschim Medinipur (883). In North Bengal, many of the Loharas use Lohar as their community name and also as their surname.

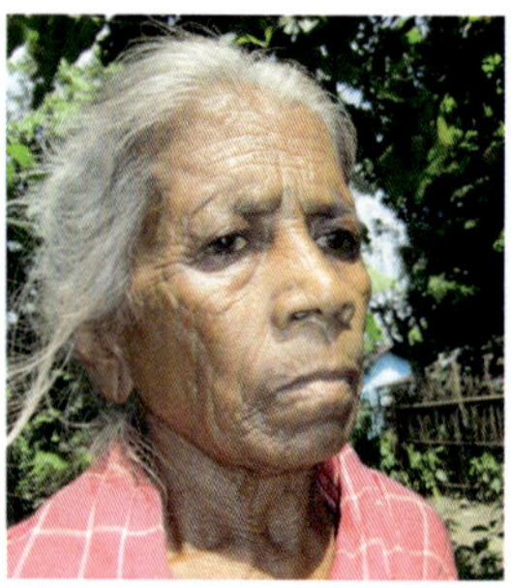

The Creative Mahalis

The Mahalis are one of the Proto-Australoid racial tribes of West Bengal and are spread mainly over the tea gardens of the Jalpaiguri and Darjeeling districts. According to the census of 2011, there are about 81,594 Mahalis in the state of which the district of Jalpaiguri has 26,904. They are also found in the South Bengal districts of Paschim Medinipur, Purulia, North 24 Parganas, Bardhaman and others. The Mahali community is said to be a composition of a number of heterogeneous offshoots from different tribes. As for the Mahalis of West Bengal, they are reportedly the descendants of the Santal, Munda, Oraon and Kol communities. It has been stated that, in West Bengal, the Mahalis were brought by the British indigo planters.

Various bamboo-based crafts such as basket-making were the traditional occupations of the ancestors of the present Mahalis. It was this trade that

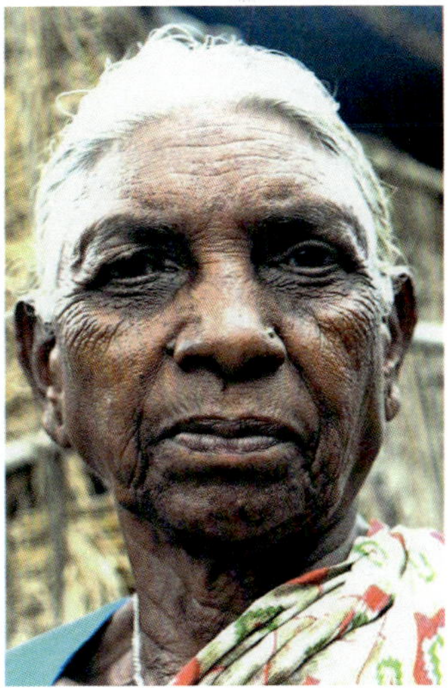

once made them outcasts from their parental stock and was also responsible for forming a homogenous social group under the common genetic name of the Mahalis or Mahlis. According to some researchers, the former is their popular name in West Bengal while the latter corresponds to their Bihar counterparts. The term *mahali* was derived from the Santali word *mat*, meaning bamboo.

The Mahalis of West Bengal have four broad social divisions—the Mahalis (believed to be the offshoots of the Santals); the Mahali-Mundas; the Oraon-Mahalis and the Kol-Mahalis. In the past, they also had social divisions such as the Bansfore-Mahalis; the Pator-Mahalis; the Sulunki-Mahalis; the Tanti-Mahalis and the Mahali-Mundas. According to earlier reports, the Bansfore-Mahalis were the bamboo-based craftsmen. The Pators used to depend mainly on agriculture and partially on their craft. The Sulunki-Mahalis were said to be palanquin-bearers. Nothing is, however, known about the Munda-Mahalis.

The language of the Mahalis belonged to the Mundaris in the past. The regional Bengali and Sadri (Sadri is a most popular lingua franca for the Chota Nagpur originating tribes living in the North Bengal tea gardens) were adopted by them later. Owing to their ethnic resemblance with the Santals and the Mundas, most of the Mahali clans have similar habits to those tribes, which happen to be exogamous and totemistic. The Mahalis observe both the Hindu and traditional festivals such as Karam, Sarhul and so on, while they worship Sing-Bonga (sun god), Orah-Bonga (family deity) and Dharam Deota (deity of harvest), among others. There are Christian Mahalis as well.

The Traditions of the Malpaharias

The Malpaharias of West Bengal are found in the districts of Murshidabad, Nadia, Bardhaman and Malda and in certain tea gardens of Jalpaiguri and Darjeeling. They are, however, also living in small numbers in some of the villages of North Bengal. According to the 2011 census, the Malpaharia population in West Bengal was 44,538, of which 14,064 were found in Murshidabad and 9,182 in Nadia. They live in all the seven districts of North Bengal. It is believed that the Malpaharias, who are of Proto-Australoid descent, migrated here from the Rajmahal hills and the Dumka areas of the Santal Parganas of Bihar.

Linguistically, the Malpaharias belong to the Dravidian speech family. But, in reality, the majority of the community in West Bengal speaks either the modified form of regional Bengali or Sadri. The word *mal* is believed to have been derived from the Dravidian word *moloi*, meaning hill. This is probably because the Malpaharias are from the Rajmahal hills. They are also considered to be close to two other tribes of the Rajmahal hills, the Sauria Paharias and the Kumarbhog Paharias. According to another belief, the Malpaharias call themselves Male, meaning 'man' in their own speech, which is often identified as Dravidian Malto.

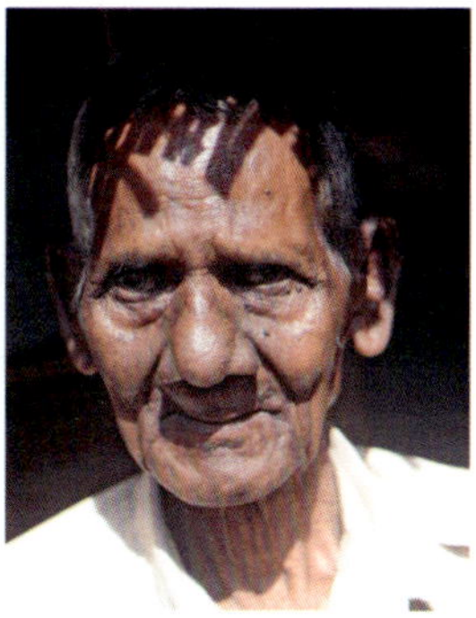
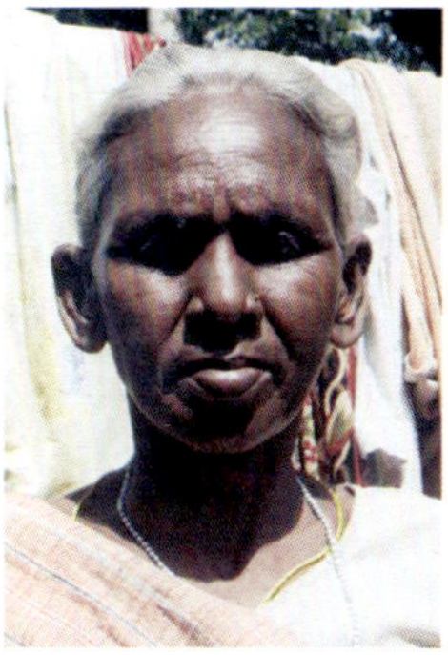

Unlike the Santals, the Oraons and the Mundas, the present generation of the Malpaharias of West Bengal are well aware of their origin and tradition. Yet, only a section of them could refer to a legend that states that they are the progeny of Lord Rama. According to this legend, when Sita was kidnapped by Ravana in Dandakaranya, Rama and Lakshmana set out in search of her. They travelled from one place to another and finally, exhausted, they decided to rest. While doing so they were profusely sweating and, out of this sweat some *mayla* or dirt came out from Rama's body. From this dirt, a man and a woman were created to provide company to Rama in his loneliness. As this couple was born of *mayla*, they eventually came to be known as Malpaharias.

The sun god is regarded by the Malpaharias as their supreme deity. They perform Ram Rami puja, Gowal puja, Pati puja, Manasha puja, Gao Devta puja, among others. Some Hindu deities such as Goddess Durga and Lord Mahadev are also worshipped by them. In the Duars, the Malpaharias observe Jaldevta puja, Dasami puja, Fagua, Masani, Bura Tkakur puja, Bakasur puja, Kalasur puja, Gai Devta, Morpa and so on.

In West Bengal, the Malpaharias have surnames such as Malpahari, Malgiri and Rajmol. The subdivisions among the community are called Knoms or Khunts; these are Deheri, Pujhar/Prijhar, Leya, Grijhi, Sing, Manjhi, Ahiri or Dhanuki and Pator. Though the Khunts are not exogamous, the Malpaharias still prefer to marry outside the Khunts, which speaks for their past exogamy.

The Iconic Mundas

The Mundas are one of the widely-known aboriginal communities of India that once inspired Rev SJ John Hoffmann to compile a 14-volume book, *Encyclopedia Mundarica*, printed in 1930. Another book on the tribe, *The Mundas and Their Country*, by Sarat Chandra Roy (1912), also provides a lot of information on the tribe. I managed to buy its 1995 reprint for Rs. 250 from a stall at the Kolkata Book Fair. This book had a 400-page story on the Kolarian Mundas. According to Dalton, this Kol tribe was said to be the descendants of Raja Kola.

Dalton's book, *Descriptive Ethnology of Bengal* (1872) and Risley's *Tribes and Castes of Bengal* also provided me with many stories on this fascinating Indian tribe. It was really amazing to read in Dalton's account that Chota Nagpur, which has been the main homeland of the Mundas, was known as Dandak forest in the past. Dandakaranya is where Lord Rama lived for 14 years in exile. This forest was said to be situated between the two great Indian rivers, Godavari and Narmada, and was once Munda country. Dalton found a link with King Yayati of the *Mahabharata* and said that, according to the *Harivamsha* (regarded as an annexure to the *Mahabharata*), he once ruled the northern part of the peninsula

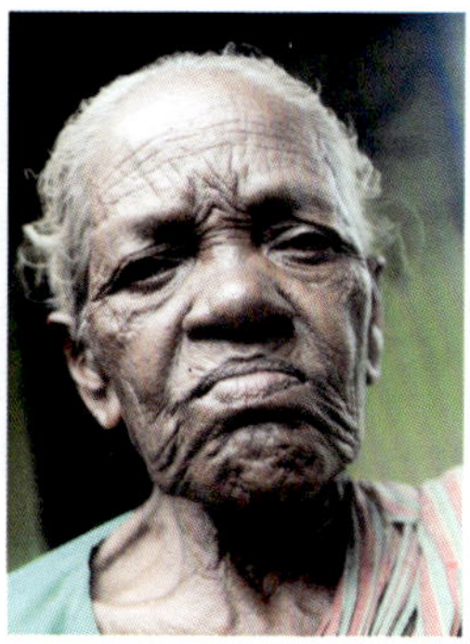

and his descendants are called Kols or Kolers. It is from them that India was once known as Kolaria. Dalton also mentions that the Kol people were in Magadha when Gautam Buddha was born. This was evident from the Bodh Gaya sculptures, which portray not Aryan but Turanian or Kol features.

From this history of the Mundas, the legendary freedom fighter of India, Birsa Munda, comes to mind. Birsa Munda or Bhagawan Birsa or Dharti Aba is an all-time cult figure of tribal India. He is widely known for his leadership of Ulgulan or the historic Munda rebellion of 1899–1900. Birsa was the son of Sugana Munda of the Purti clan of the Mundas. He was born in a village near Ranchi and died at the age of 25 in a British-Indian jail in 1900. I quote from Kumar Suresh Singh in this context: 'Centuries ago, the ancestors of Birsa, who belonged to the Purti clan, in the course of their wanderings in search of a homeland for themselves, came upon a river called Domdagara in the vicinity of Chutia, a suburb of modern Ranchi. It was inundated. They saw a log of wood floating down the current of the river, caught hold of it and crossed over to the other bank where they examined it, saw a hole in it and found a mouse (*chutu*) inside it. They took it as a good omen and to it they ascribed their escape and good luck. The land where they reached and settled down was called Chutia and their branch of the Purti clan, Chutia-Purti.' This appeared to me as a beautiful example of an emergence of a tribal clan. The genesis of the term 'Chota Nagpur' also has a beautiful story that the celebrated anthropologist and IAS officer Kumar Suresh Singh cited: 'The leaders who led them to their new homeland were the two brothers, Chutu Haram and Nagu. A sub-clan with its legends and history grew up around the episode. Subsequently, *chutu* was corrupted into *chutia* and later still into *chota*, and *nagu* into *nag*, as their folklore suggests.'

I came across a National Book Trust book on the great Munda leader, Birsa Munda, by Kumar Suresh Singh (2002), which provided interesting insights into the Mundas. Former President KR Narayanan spoke on Birsa Munda and his life in 1998; this speech is indeed a huge honour for an indigenous tribal leader of India:

> I am happy to associate myself with the unveiling of the statue of Shri Birsa Munda, a legendary figure in the history of our struggle for freedom. He is well-known as an early advocate and exponent of tribal rights and as an indomitable fighter against foreign rule and oppression. One of the lesser-known aspects of our fight against British rule is that tribal uprising constituted an important part of the defiance of the colonial regime. Birsa Munda is an outstanding representative of one such movement in the last 19th century in the Chota Nagpur region, who initiated a unique phase of our freedom struggle, which decisively influenced its course and subsequently made us deeply conscious of tribal issues vis-à-vis nation-building.
>
> Birsa Munda rose from the lowest rank of peasants to mobilise people against the appropriation of tribal land and the disintegration of their way of life, economy and culture by the colonial system. He fought against the predatory tendencies in the name of modernisation and the oppressive Zamindari system, invoking the spirit of a tribal order characterised by simplicity, absence of tyranny and living in harmony with nature.

He used the myths and symbols of his society and culture and became a rallying point for people to rise against foreign rule, oppression and injustice. His movement was also infused with the spirit of religious reform, social justice and cultural regeneration. He fought against the British rule, suffered imprisonment and subsequently became a martyr. Through his struggle, he became a cult figure, a part of the folklore and was even deified by the people as 'Dharti Abba' or 'Birsa Bhagwan'. The Bihar Regiment of the Indian Army invokes his name in one of their battle cries.

Birsa Munda's struggle was suppressed by the British authorities. But it did not go in vain. His fight for the right of the people for forest resources, land and preservation of their distinct identity was subsequently recognised when the then British Government, through a series of measures, guaranteed tribals rights to reclaim their land and empowered officials to forcefully evict the occupation of tribal land by others. The Chota Nagpur Tenancy Act of 1908, which partially protected the rights of tribals, is considered as an important outcome of Birsa Munda's fight.

The arduous fight of Birsa Munda against British rule and its ramifications found articulations in the large context of our struggle for independence when Surendranath Banerjee took up the issue in the Legislative Council and many other leading newspapers of the period editorially supported its cause. The impact of this movement was significant enough that even the British Government that suppressed it, recognised its gravity. This was reflected in the secret report of the then Lt. Governor who wrote, 'The disturbance may have quietened but Simla requires to be constantly reminded that it is sitting on a powder magazine.'

The popularity, intensity and relevance of the movement launched by Birsa Munda was so widespread that all the mainstream political groups supported it and eulogised its contributions to arouse the common people to stand against the mighty British empire. Acknowledging his crucial role, the Indian National Congress and the Forward Block observed Birsa Day in 1940 with great enthusiasm. Paying tribute to Birsa Munda, the Indian National Congress named the main gate of its Ramgarh Session in 1940 as Birsa Gate and published stories of his eventful life, which were circulated among the delegates.

The awakening triggered by Birsa Munda found its manifestation in the formation of the Kisan Sabha by many tribal groups, which later joined this struggle for freedom. Many followers of Birsa Munda who took pride in calling themselves 'Birsaites' joined the nationalist movement for independence and were greatly influenced by Mahatma Gandhi. Historians have asserted that the campaigns of Indian National Congress in Chota Nagpur would not have been successful without Birsa Munda's agitation.

As we survey the remarkable life and deeds of Birsa Munda, we are struck by the spontaneity of people's action. One important feature was that Birsa Munda's movement attracted a large number of women who suffered imprisonment, faced police bullets and embraced death. The then British Government was perplexed by the willing and large-scale participation of women in the agitation launched by Birsa.

Birsa Munda stood out as an early protagonist of tribal rights, a pioneer in mobilising women for the cause of freedom and as an irrepressible fighter for justice and human dignity. His movement launched in late 19th century has significance for our own times. Today, our tribals, in all parts of our country, are fighting for their inalienable rights to land, forest resources and cultural identity. In all such fights, we find an echo of Birsa Munda's striving. Today, our tribal brothers and sisters are heroically standing against the forces of so-called modernisation, which run antithetical to their lifestyle, and understanding of nature and culture. They resist the alarming deterioration of environment as they are the protectors and preservers of 'Jal, Jungle and Jantu' and draw our attention to the need for re-examining our concepts of development and progress. They underline the need for truly sustainable development projects.

Since the days of our struggle for independence, we have taken steps to guarantee the rights of our tribal brothers and sisters. Our Constitution, the fundamental law of the land, stipulates the provisions for their uplift. The unveiling of the statue of Birsa Munda is national recognition of the role of tribals in the freedom struggle and of the importance of preserving their identity and their traditional culture while improving their living conditions and integrating them emotionally into the mainstream of national life. Jai Hind.

The Journal of Parliamentary Information, Vol. XLIV, No. 4, December 1998, pp. 400-2

The Mundas comprise the third largest tribal community (in Bihar, Jharkhand and Odisha, they form quite a large part of the population) and, according to the 2011 census, there are 366,386 Mundas in West Bengal. Almost one-third (28.53 per cent) of these Bengal Mundas are the inhabitants of the Jalpaiguri, Alipurduar and Darjeeling districts. Many of them are found in North and South 24 Parganas and Medinipur (undivided) districts. The tribe is ordinarily an agricultural community and once they had their own traditional land tenure system. They migrated to West Bengal from their original homeland of Chota Nagpur about two centuries ago, as labourers. In the Jalpaiguri and Darjeeling plains, the Mundas are largely found in the tea gardens. They took up agriculture in the villages and work as forest labourers in some forest-villages of the Terai Duars.

The name Munda was derived from the Sanskrit word *munda* meaning head. The term was used to mean head or chief of the village in Bengal. But the Mundas call themselves 'Horo-ko' meaning 'man'. They are also known as Muras or Horohon. The Horo surname seen among the Mundas may have originated from the term *horohon*. Considering their physical features and background, researchers are of the opinion that the Mundas have a good deal of affinity with the Santals, the Hos and the Kherias. According to a popular Munda legend, they are the progeny of the 12 human creatures created by their traditional god, Sing-Bonga. It is relevant to note here that the Santals also call themselves Hor and that, too, means 'man'.

The Mundas believe that Sing-Bonga (sun god, also known as Pat-Sarna) and Otebaram, their traditional gods, once directed a young male and a female to stay inside a hill cave together and asked them to produce human beings. Since they had no knowledge of sexual interaction, they were given a lesson on how to prepare *hanria* or *pachai*, the indigenous beer. Once the couple imbibed it, they produced 12 pairs of males and females. Later, it was found that they belonged to different tribes such as the Santals, Kols as well as Mundas. Among the Mundas there are a number of totemistic clans. Risley provides an exhaustive list of about 350 such clans in his book; the Bhengras, Gondlis, Jirhuls, Kerkettas, Bulums and Horos are just some examples.

The tribe also worships Marang-Buru, the mountain god. There is no visible object for worshipping Marang-Buru and sacrifices are offered at the top of the mountain or in a holy place in the jungles of Chota Nagpur. This deity is said to be responsible for the rain and he has to be appealed to with the sacrifice of a buffalo to get rid of droughts. Similarly, Ikir-Bonga is the god for all water bodies such as tanks, streams and wells. Another water-body-related deity is Garah-era, who is very pertinent in Chota Nagpur as she is the goddess of rivers and the hilly streams that are widely prevalent there.

Besides these, there are a series of minor deities or spirits who wander across the terraced paddy fields and often become instrumental in spreading diseases among men. The Mundas call these spirits Nage or Naga-era. While Ikir-Bonga

 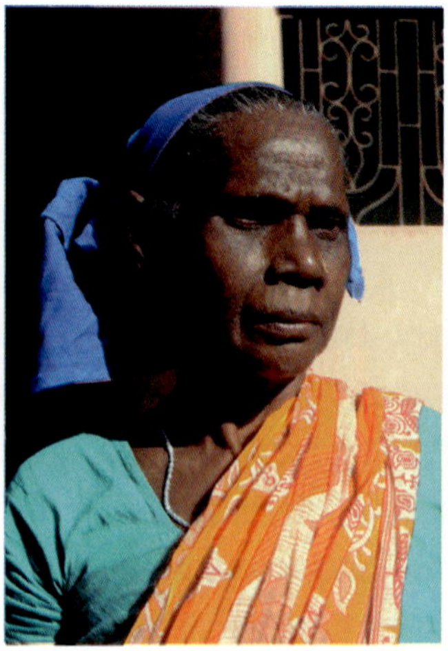 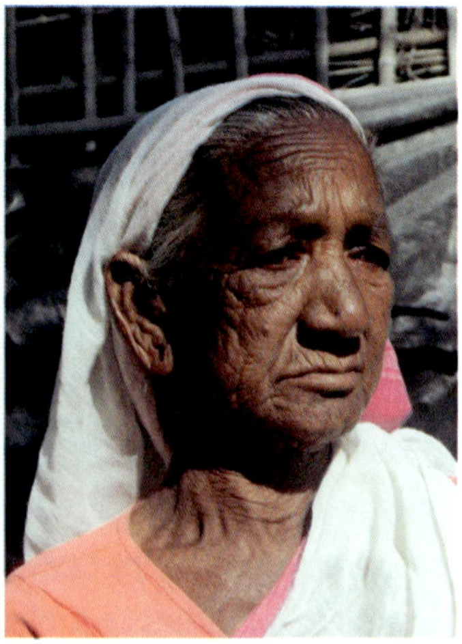

is worshipped with white goats and black or brown cocks, Nage is propitiated with eggs and turmeric. The Mundas worship Deswali or Kara-Sarna as their deity of the village. Kara-Sarna lives in the *sarna* (the sacred forest grove) with his wife, Jahir-Burhi or Sarhul-Sarna. According to Risley, every village has its own Deswali who also governs crops and is, therefore, worshipped during the agricultural festivals with *kara*s or he-buffaloes. His wife, however, does not like buffaloes and is, therefore, generally offered fowl.

The Munda festivals, Risley elaborates, include Sarhul or Sarjum-Baba, the spring festival that corresponds to the Baha or Baha-Bonga of the Santals and Hos. This is in March-April, when the *sal* tree is in bloom. Kadleta or Batauli is celebrated in Ashar (June-July) at the commencement of the rainy season. The Mundas believe that if they omit the Kadleta festival, the rice may not grow fully. Nana or Jom-Nana is the festival of new rice, which is observed during the harvesting period of Ashwin (September-October). During this festival, a white cock is sacrificed to Sing-Bonga together with the first fruit of the harvest. Kharia puja or Kalamsing and the Maghe-parab are the winter harvest festivals. In the Duars, I have been told by my Munda friends, they observe Taribari, Fagua, Gram puja, Mahakal mela, Surya puja, Marangmu and Singmua. They also worship cattle.

Regarding marriage customs, Dalton points out in his *Descriptive Ethnology of Bengal* (1872), that the Mundas had a tradition of marrying the bride to a *mahua* tree and the bridegroom to a mango. This practice, however, has been abandoned. Mundari, which is the dialect of the Mundas, belongs to the Austro-Asiatic speech family. It has no script yet. Most of the Mundas living in West Bengal speak

Sadri, Bengali or Hindi. I did, however, see some Mundas speaking in Mundari on a few occasions. Many literary works on Mundari have been undertaken in Bihar in the Roman and Devnagri scripts. The Ranchi University has developed a beautiful treasure of tribal studies under the leadership of the celebrated scholar Ram Dayal Munda, who was the Vice-Chancellor of the University and an internationally acclaimed intellectual on tribal India. He is also well-regarded for his role in advancing the Jharkhand statehood movement in Bihar and that of the international indigenous people's rights as well.

Seinka Munda of the Ord-Terai Tea Estate does not bother about the serious stories on Munda history; he is only concerned with his own life struggles. He is a Munda who migrated to West Bengal's tea country and I met him near Bengdubi military city at the Indo-Nepal border of West Bengal. He was a retired tea plantation worker then and was busy repairing his house. His spectacular physique, burnt-copper coloured skin and white hair attracted me on a bright autumn Sunday. Sabita Kujur, someone whom I had known for many years, introduced me to the old man. He did not care much for his life and when I tried to photograph Seinka, it seemed that many things were left unseen. He was an extremely low-profile man and looked shaky when conversing with a stranger.

During my second trip to his home, I was told about Seinka's death and this time I met his two widows. During his working life in the plantations, Seinka was the headman of a gang of tea garden labourers. His job was to command one of the Adivasi labour brigades of the tea garden. After his retirement, Seinka looked after his domestic affairs and was sincere to animal husbandry at his home. One day in December 2011, when returning home, he was caught by a huge swarm of bees. Brutally stung by the violent bees, he died on his way to the hospital. The two widows remembered their husband as a hockey player of Topkara-Kamda village, near Ranchi, from where he had migrated to this new country. Seinka's polygamy was not because of his higher status among the labourers, but because his first wife, Hiramuni, could not give birth to a child. Seinka's second wife gave birth to his two surviving daughters.

Another well-known Munda, Shanti Munda, regarded as an eye-witness of the historic Naxalbari uprising, is a firebrand tribal lady and a communist. Even after 50 years of the upsurge, she believes that the Naxalbari movement did not lie and has its reminiscences in modern India. Migration from one's homeland often isolates people from their traditions, but the immigrants always look for a new identity. Shanti Munda opted for a new life, which had risks. This Munda lady was a rebel communist and for the cause of her commitment to peasant liberty, she made a departure from the tribal tradition of community endogamy. She married a Bengali-speaking Naxalite leader, Keshab Sarkar, and started working for the movement at Naxalbari under the leadership of Charu Majumdar, Kanu Sanyal and Jangal Santal. The appearance of Shanti Munda into Naxalite political operations was instrumental in bringing thousands of tribal women from the tea gardens and villages into the orbit of the Naxalbari uprising.

Shanti Munda and Keshab Sarkar have three children, Mira, Jaya and Bablu. Of these, Jaya married Pradip Debnath, a Bengali, while Mira and Bablu are married to Mundas.

The Diverse Nagesias

The Nagesias are a Proto-Australoid tribe and, like the Oraon-Mundas, they, too, are an immigrant community in Bengal. They are often identified with the Kisans, a tribe of Chota Nagpur origin. The Nagesias consider themselves to be the descendants of the Nagbangsi-Khatriyas of Chota Nagpur. A section of the tribe migrated to the districts of Jalpaiguri and Darjeeling, in North Bengal, as tea garden labourers. Later, some of them settled in tiny groups in the rural villages of North Bengal. Though small in number, the Nagesias are also found in the forest-villages of the Duars. This tribe is socially divided into three sub-groups, the Telias, the Dhurias and the Sinduriyas.

These groups, however, are not the clans. The Nagesias worship the sun god and the tiger god while some of them worship the deity, Darha. Those residing in undivided Jalpaiguri and Darjeeling tea belts speak Sadri, like many other Adivasis

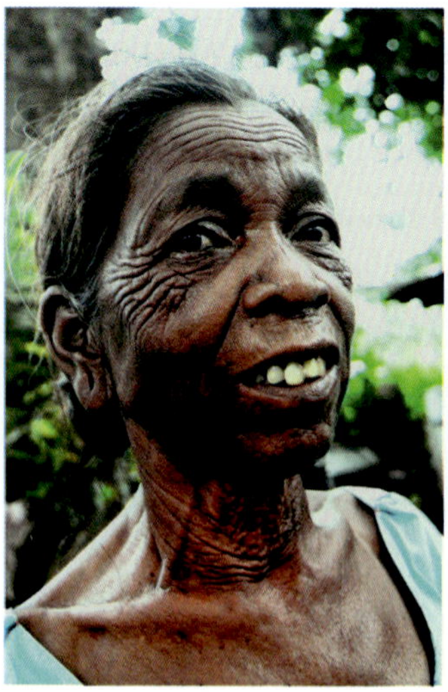

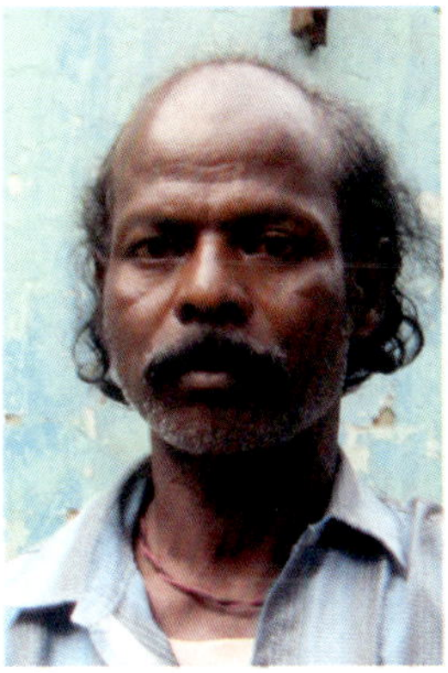
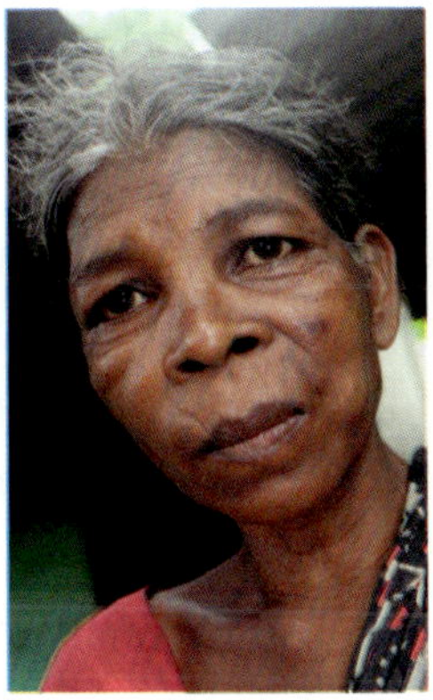
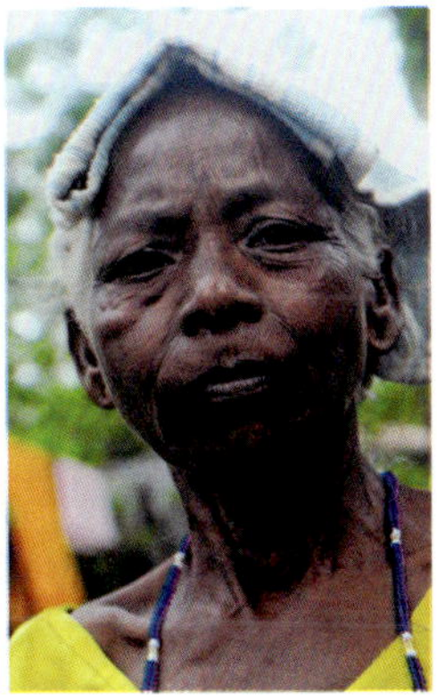
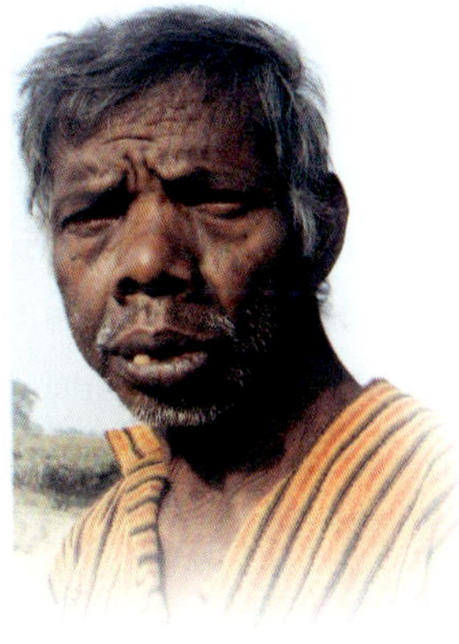

in North Bengal. Bengali and Hindi are also making inroads into the linguistic domain of the Nagesias. Among the Nagesias of the Terai and the Duars region, I found people who were earlier known as Kisans. As the term *kisan* is used to describe farmers, many of the Nagesias do not wish to identify with that; they would rather use their community name, Nagesia.

The census of 2011 recorded 16,378 Nagesias as the inhabitants of West Bengal. In North Bengal, Darjeeling and Jalpaiguri there are 48.33 per cent Nagesias with many inhabiting the district of Nadia; 29.15 per cent live in South Bengal.

The Clans and Totems of the Oraons

The Oraons are an important Dravidian-speaking tribe of India, which, according to researchers, is spread over a wide area of undivided Bihar and Madhya Pradesh, West Bengal and Tripura. They migrated to these states from the Deccan plateau and the western coast of India. During the Mohammedan invasion, they were forced to go down south from their earlier habitat and thus split into two groups —one went towards the Rajmahal hills, the other to the Chota Nagpur plateau. The large-scale Oraon immigration across different urban tracts, tea plantations and industrial zones of the various states, including West Bengal, is said to have originated from the Chota Nagpur plateau under economical hardship and other socio-political reasons. Most of the North Bengal Oraons were brought as labourers to the tea plantations a few generations ago; some of the tribe became railway labourers.

The Oraon community is the second largest (the Santals being the largest tribe of West Bengal with a population of 2,512,331 [47.42 per cent of the total tribal population of the state] in 2011) in West Bengal, with a population of 643,510 (12.14 per cent of the total tribal population). The majority are found in the Jalpaiguri district (368,413), according to the census of 2011.

The community is also known as Kurukh, though this name is used to identify the dialect of the Oraons. The word *oraon* is believed to have been derived from the Kurukh word *orgora*, meaning hawk, a totemistic object of the Oraons. The term *oraon* is also said to have originated from the Sanskrit word *uran*, denoting a spendthrift character. Some believe that the Oraons are the progeny of Ravana and the term *O-rawan* or *O-raon* has been derived from him. SC Roy, in his book, *The Oraons of Chota Nagpur* (1915), wrote about a significant story in the *Ramayana* that related to the origin of Sugriva, the leader of the *vanara*s (monkeys), suggesting that the Oraons formed part of the monkey-warriors of Lord Rama.

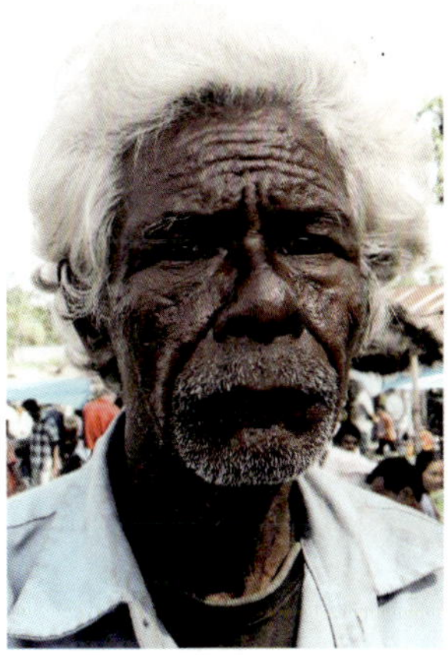

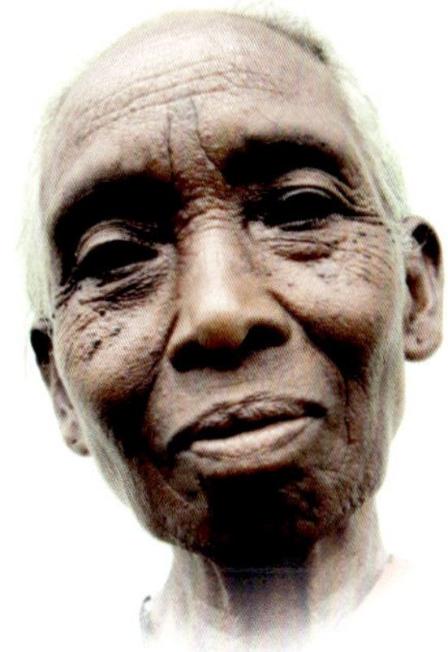

Though the Oraons have their own Dravidian dialect, Kurukh (a scriptless dialect like many other tribal speeches), a large number of them speak Sadri. Sadri is also a common language for most of the tribes that originated in Chota Nagpur, particularly in the tea gardens of North Bengal.

The religious beliefs and practices of the present day Oraons are found to be largely influenced by Hinduism. Some of them worship traditional deities such as Dharam Thakur or Dharmesh, the sun god. The other Oraon deities, Gaon-Deota, Bura-Buri and Sarna-Buri, are also worshipped but are losing their importance among the modern Oraon society. The Pahans and Bhagats among them are generally seen to perform religious ceremonies as priests. Bhelowaphari is regarded as the most important festival of the Oraons while Karam, Bandhna, Sarhul and Sohorai are celebrated in different seasons by the community. Bhelowaphari is observed not only as a celebration for the new crop but is also related to births, marriages, deaths and so on. The Karam festival, because of its wide range of acceptability, has already gained state recognition and, in North Bengal, there is a holiday on the eve of this festival in September. Many of the Oraons of North Bengal were found to have converted to Christianity.

The Oraon tribe is a patriarchal community and they have exogamous clans such as Kujur, Ekka, Lakra, Tirkey, Baxla, Panna, Kispotta, Toppo, Minj, Khalkha, Beck,

Khesh, Kerketta and Tigga. All these clans are related to some totemistic objects generally based on animals or plants. As a rule, an Oraon must abstain from eating, or otherwise using, domesticating, killing, destroying, maiming, hurting or injuring the animal or plant or any other object that forms his totem. Though the rituals continue till date, the taboos are not followed entirely. The clan names are generally used as surnames for all practical purposes.

The Oraons are held in great respect for their socio-religious movement, Tana Bhagat, which started in 1913–14 under the leadership of Jatra Oraon. A section of the community became Tana-Bhagats after the movement. The tribe has been incorporated in the list of Scheduled Tribes for West Bengal under the Constitution (ST) Order of 1950. They are also recognised as a Scheduled Tribe in Bihar, Madhya Pradesh, Maharashtra and Odisha.

Roy's book on the Oraons provides some serious insights into the people who I now frequently encounter in the Terai Duars. He saw this tribe in their Chota Nagpur-Ranchi homeland, while I see them uprooted in their new country of the Bengal Duars. It is interesting to observe that the Oraon people have adjusted so well in their new homeland, just as the uprooted Bengalis did in West Bengal and Assam after their forced migration from the then East Pakistan. Among the struggling Oraons in the tea gardens of the Terai and the Duars, I know very few who can remember their ancestor's village names.

Seth Ekka was among my Oraon friends during my boyhood. He was a peaceful and obedient boy studying in Kamakshyaguri Mission High School when I first met him. As far as I remember, Seth and I became friends when I was in Class VI. We were together till Class X, right up to the final (matriculation) examinations, which we both passed at the first attempt. Nuas Khesh, another Oraon boy, seemed to be Seth's closest friend. The boy was an introvert and did not know anyone else. Seth applied for a job with the Railways and never really discussed his tribal identity. He was conservative about conversing in his mother tongue in public. The Seths were Christian converts and had built a church close to their home. During Christmas, we were always Seth's family guests.

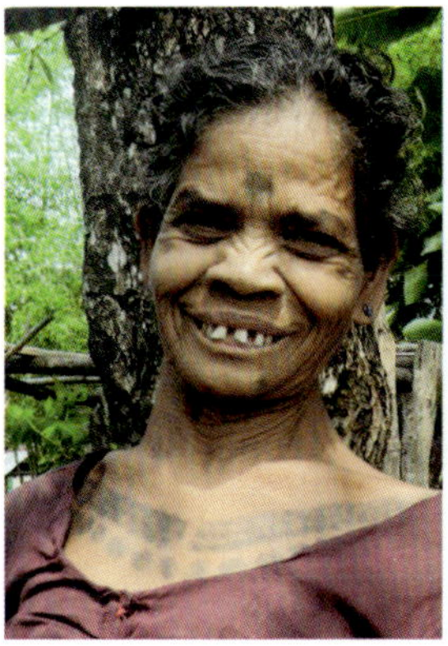

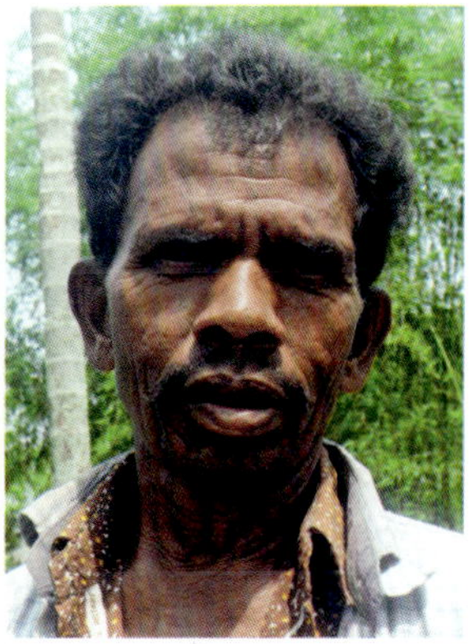

Another Oraon boy, Ganesh, was a dear friend of mine. We played football, watched movies, drank *tari* (date-juice) in the winter evenings and spent a lot of time together. Ganesh was older than me, but happened to be an academic junior in school. He was not as serious about his studies as Seth was. Instead, Ganesh was always engaged in dating girls, styling his hair and gossiping with friends in tea stalls. Unlike Seth, Ganesh ignited in me the desire to learn Kurukh. Kurukh is a difficult language for any Bengali-speaking person, as the dialect has a Dravidian linguistic origin. However, I managed to pick up the speech well. Ganesh was a hero in our school in his time because his fiancé, Gyanbati Narjeenary, was a real dream girl.

Sadly, his colourful and charismatic life did not last. His control over his family's wealth was questioned by other stakeholders and he virtually became a poor man in Telipara.

Roy observes, 'Towards Lohardagga many Oraons take the name of Bhagat, the corruption of Bhakt, and attach themselves to some Brahman or Gossain who gives them mantras. The Bhagats, without absolutely abandoning the religious observances of their ancestors, adopt the worship of Shiva or Mahadeo; have in

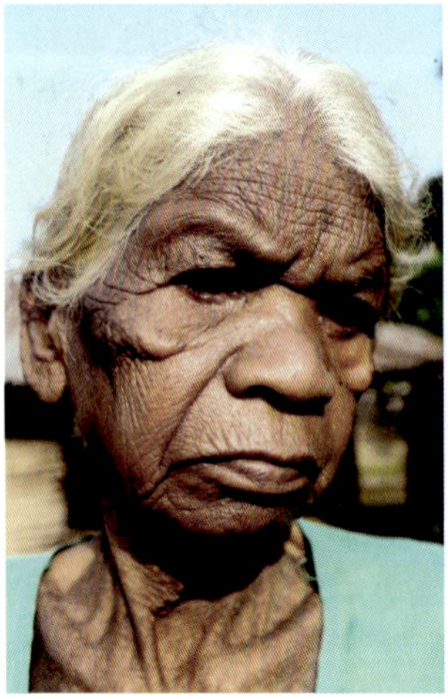

their houses, or on their premises, the usual monolithic emblem of that deity, and keep brazen images of Ganesh and other Hindu gods.... The Bhagats conform to Hindu notions regarding what should be considered clean and unclean for food, and they will not eat or drink with the people of their own tribe who are not Bhagats.... In some villages near Lohardagga, they annually make an image of a man in wood, put clothes and ornaments on it, and present it before the altar of Mahadeo.'

Another Oraon person who influenced my life immensely was my headmaster, Surendranath Bhagat. He founded my school's junior section and later Classes IX and X as well (today, the school has been elevated up to Class XII). The school was a Christian missionary enterprise, which later became secular. We had a big Mech (Boro) church nearby. Surendranath Bhagat was a Hindu Oraon and was very serious in maintaining discipline in the school. We were not allowed to organise Saraswati puja in the campus because all Hindu activities were banned. The headmaster, being a progressive man, did not contest this. Later, however, the restrictions were lifted. I was liked by my headmaster as he appreciated my love for English and, to this day, I hold him in great regard for his honesty and integrity. Our Sanskrit teacher, too, was an Oraon gentleman who was very interesting. He was a serious sort of man and we all had to be very particular during his classes. This gentleman, Marshall Lakra, later left our school and went on to join Indian Airlines as an officer. He was also from Telipara and made a great impact on me.

During my younger days I did not know that Dhangar is a synonym for the Oraons. Dalton mentions it while explaining the Oraons' ancient geography: 'The Khurnkh or Oraons of Chota Nagpur are the people best known in many parts of India as *dhangar*s, a word that from its apparent derivation (*dang* or *dhang*, a hill) may mean any hill men, but among several tribes of the southern tributary mahals, the term *dhangar* and *dhangarin* means the youth of the two sexes, both in highland and lowland villages, and it cannot be considered as the national designation of any particular tribe. The Oraons are found massed in the northern and western parts of Chota Nagpur proper, in the eastern part of Sirguja and Jashpur and scattered in Singbhum, Gangpur, Bonai and Hazaribagh, all in the Chota Nagpur province, and in Shambalpur of the Central Province; but all the scattered colonies are offshoots from the nucleus of the race in the districts first mentioned.'

In Oraon society, people are divided into a number of clans, which are exogamous. These clans are totemic and it is believed that the totems have emerged from the flora and fauna of the past. The totemic animals and plants are said to have protected or rendered some special service to their ancestors who, out of gratitude, took their clan names from these animals or plants. Roy has presented the origin of some of these clans in his book on the Oraons. The Kujur clan, for instance, got its name from the *kujur* plant. The story goes that once an Oraon had fallen asleep under a *kujur* plant when a flexible twig entwined round his body and protected him from molestation. Accordingly, the man took the *kujur* for his totem and his descendants now form the Kujur clan. In another story, an Oraon killed a pig and ate its flesh, but threw away its entrails. The life of the pig remained in the entrails, so that the slain pig was soon afterwards found moving in actual bodily form. From then onwards, pig's entrails became taboo to the slayer of the pig and his descendants who came to constitute the Kisputta (*kis* meaning pig and *putta* meaning entrails) clan.

An Oraon was fishing in a stream when a khalkho fish, which was caught in his net, managed to escape. Hence, the khalkho fish became taboo to the man and his descendants came to be called the Khalkho clan. The Ekka or Kachua clan began when an old Oraon was about to catch a tortoise and the latter exclaimed, 'I am your *jati* (caste).' The man desisted from catching the tortoise and his descendants came to form the Kachua (tortoise) or Ekka clan.

As for totemic taboos, Roy explains it in a scientific note: 'As a general rule, an Oraon must abstain from eating or otherwise using, domesticating, killing, destroying, maintaining, hurting or injuring the animal or plant or other objects that form his totem. Nor must he use anything made of it or obtained from it; and when practicable, he will prevent others from doing so in his presence. In the case of tree totems, the men of the clan will neither go under the shade of the tree, nor cut or burn its wood, nor use its produce in any shape.' In the book *The Oraons of Sunderban* (1963), Amal Kumar Das and Manis Kumar Raha state, 'If an Oraon finds the totemic object lying dead on the way, he covers it by some means so that it cannot be eaten up by some birds or beasts and goes away after saluting it.'

I have come across many more clans among the Oreans in the Terai and the Duars. These include the Bandos (wild cat), the Baras (ficus-indica), the Barwas (wild dog), the Baxlas (crocodile), the Becks (salt), the Binhas (fish), the Binkos (star), the Chermakos (tiger, rat), the Garis (common monkey), the Gidhs (vulture), the Godos (fish), the Hurhurias (snake), the Kerkettas (bird), the Khakhas/Xaxas (crow), the Khalkhos (fish), the Khanas (vulture), the Kheshs (paddy), the Khoas, Kindos (fish), the Kuhus (cuckoo), the Lakras (tiger), the Lendas (tortoise), the Lindas (flower), the Minzs (eel/snake-fish), the Nimas, the Pannas (iron), the Tiggas (monkey), the Tirkeys (mouse), the Toppos (bird), the Amris (bagh), the Baghs (tiger), the Bakulas (paddy bird), the Basas (tree), the Bhaklas, the Chigahs (jackal), the Chirras (squirrel), the Chouria Musa (field rat), the Dhans (rice), the Dhechuas (king crow), the Dirras (eel), the Doms, the Khakhas (raven, large crow), the Garwes (stork), the Gedes (duck), the Gislihis (bird), the Godos, (crocodile), the Golaias, the Gondraris (tree), the Induars (eel), the Kaiths (vegetable), the Kandas (sweet potato), the Kauas (crow), the Kendis (tree), the Kenus (fish), the Keonds (fruit), the Kheksas (vegetable), the Khettas (cobra), the Khoepas (wild dog), the Kindas (date palm), the Kosuars (fish), the Kundris (vegetable), the Kusuwas (fish), the Lakras (hyena), the Lilas (fish), the Lindas (eel), the Lohas (iron), the Mahatos (tittle), the Munjniars (wild creeper), the Murgas (cock), the Nagbans (cobra), the Orgonras (hawk), the Pusras (fruit), the Putris (tree), the Roris (fruit or tree), the Rundas (fox), the Sals (fish), the Sarnos, the Suars (hog), the Tig Hanumans (monkey), the Tirkuars (fruit), the Tirtias, Tirus (fish), the Topowars (long-tailed bird), the Bakhlas (grass), the Bandras (monkey), the Barlas (banyan tree), the Baros (wild cat), the Benjis (mangoose), the Dhanwars (paddy), the Indoors (rat), the Kinduars (fish), the Musas (mouse), the Nunuars, Saps (snake) and the Tetes.

Many more are mentioned by Dalton, Risley as well as Das and Raha, in their respective books. In his booklet, *Kurukh Benja Beeg,* Tej Kumar Toppo of Malbazar also provides a small list of Oraon clans. Tej Kumar has become a friend of mine and often I discuss my experiences with the tribal communities with him. Once he told me, 'It is only the Oraons who have totemic clans. No other tribal community of the Chota Nagpur plateau can claim such totemic genesis of their clans. Many of the communities took up our clans and renamed them. For example, the Mundas took our Toppo clan and renamed it Topno.' Tej Kumar was a government officer and after retirement from Kolkata, he has settled down in his original Malbazar home. Among his friends, there is Professor Virginious Xaxa. Whenever I find a new Oraon surname I try to locate its clannish version. In this way Tej Kumar is a bird while Xaxa happens to be a crow.

The stories of their clans and totems show how close the Oraon people are to nature. It is also amazing that a sizeable section is now actively involved in making a new and modern North Bengal. One cannot imagine that once these people were refugees from Lohardaga, Chota Nagpur and the Ranchi valley. Their identities as citizens of this land, in many cases, overruled their Oraon personality. As a result, their civilian roles influenced me much more than their tribal stereotypes. Thus, my Oraon story does not dwell upon the orbit of anthropology. It may, however, take frequent personal journeys.

For many reasons, the legendary Iswar Tirkey is central to my Oraon vision. Few people know that this Oraon man was a licensed pilot, the solitary tribal pilot of Bengal at that time. Being adventurous, Tirkey took on the training to become a pilot. He was a *zamindar* (landlord) of Naxalbari in the Indo-Nepal Bengal frontier and I never heard anyone discuss him as an Oraon. Tirkey, however, always remained a star in the political galaxy. He died a few years ago and has left a huge narrative of his illustrious activities between the 1960s and 1970s in West Bengal.

The story of Lalsukra Oraon also comes to mind when writing about the Oraons of North Bengal. Lalsukra was a legendary Oraon man in the Duars and the communist fraternity of Bengal would know him better than others. His fibreglass statue at Chalsa Tebhaga Park, near Malbazar, does not speak simply of his Oraon identity, but rather of his political personality. I was privileged to meet both, Lalsukra Oraon and Iswar Tirkey, just a few years before they died. Lalsukra was famous for his Tebhaga movement (a peasant upsurge during the 1940s in Bengal under the sponsorship of the undivided Communist Party of India) and as a composer and singer of revolutionary Sadri songs. In 2002, the West Bengal Government introduced an annual award in the name of Lalsukra Oraon for the conservation and promotion of tribal culture. Lalsukra's father, Balku Oraon, was a plantation labourer in Barodighi Tea Estate, near Chalsa in the Duars. For various reasons, Lalsukra did not manage to become famous among his own fraternity in the Duars.

Many people, over a period of time, contributed to the elevation of the Oraon gentry of North Bengal. Khudiram Pahan of Hamiltongunj (Duars) is one such gentleman. His Pahan surname resembled his forefathers' social ranking as priests. They were really the priests of Ranchi's Charima village and the Bhuihar Oraons who lived there. Bhuihar means those who settle a village themselves by clearing the jungles. I knew that Khudiram was from the Xaxa clan and that the crow was his totem. Though he was vastly knowledgeable about the tribal history of India and a very sensitive Oraon, it was his sacrifice of his empire in the Duars and his arbitrary exile that impressed me. I have known him since 1980.

I was surprised to learn that in his early life Khudiram was a timber merchant and a contractor. To me, he was more a public figure and less an Oraon in the true sense. Once, during a casual discussion at his Hamiltongunj house, he said, 'The Harappa civilisation was the civilisation of the Dravidians and Austrics, as the nomenclature "Harappa" itself resolves. In Mundari, *hor* means 'man' and in Kurukh, *erpa* means 'house'. So *hor* plus *erpa* is equal to Harerpa, which has been corrupted as Harappa.' Though he had several achievements to his credit across the tribal country of the Duars, Khudiram had seemingly a superiority complex as an educated and intellectual Adivasi. The status he achieved in the mainstream society of the Jalpaiguri Duars was not enough to make him happy. After some time at the Madhu Tea Garden near Hashimara, Khudiram settled at Satali-Nakadala tribal village and began a new life there. Later, he made Hamiltongunj his

home and everything seemed to be going well. We were, therefore, surprised to hear that he had left the Duars and settled back in Ranchi.

Khudiram Pahan became a tribal voice in North Bengal when he first organised the Adivasi-Gorkha League in order to bring the Adivasi and Nepali-speaking people together. Another of his achievements was struggling for the rights of the forest villagers. At that time forest villagers were as good as bonded labourers. This struggle was known as the Taungiya movement. What really made Khudiram famous was the demand to introduce the panchayat system in the tea gardens and the forest-villages of North Bengal.

The first lesson in creating modern Bengali poetry by an Oraon was given to me by my friend Sunil Lakra who also happens to be from Telipara, the village to which Ganesh and my headmaster belong. Sunil had a flair for writing poetry. Once he wrote in Bengali, '*Kanchan, ami tomay dekhechi; tokhon tumi suryasnane byasto chhile*.' (Kanchan [the peak of Kanchenjungha], I have seen you, when you were busy taking a sunbath.) Often we would sing the Bengali songs of Manna Dey or play football. Sunil later became the superintendent of a Divisional Railway Manager's office in Malda. His clan was Tiger and he, too, did not speak much about the Oraons.

There is an interesting story about John Arther Baxla of Kalchini in the Duars. He was an Oraon who became an MLA from Kumargram and belonged to the leftist Revolutionary Socialist Party (RSP). Once, in a fit of anger, he cut down the tea bushes of the Kalchini Tea Estate at night. He was protesting the suspension of a tribal worker. At that time he was a simple mechanic in the tea garden and his manner of resistance was noticed across the tea industry in the Duars. The RSP leader, Nani Bhattacharya, heard about this fiery young man and brought him into his revolutionary organisation. Later, he became John Arther.

Another Oraon personality whom I admired was Febianus Tirkey. Febianus fought for the restoration of tribal land from the clutches of brickfield grabbers in Ethelbari, at the Bhutan border of the Duars. He was an ordinary high school teacher in Dimdima and his cause could never draw the attention of the administrators of Jalpaiguri. However, it made him an Adivasi revolutionary in the Bengal Duars.

The Oraon fraternity had a kingpin in the Duars who once was a magician. His name was Besterwitch and people from the RSP caught him and made him a tribal leader of Madarihat. Later, Besterwitch's daughter, Kumari Kujur, also became a leader. All these people never really admitted to being Oraons. They played their role as citizens of the Bengal Duars.

In Alipurduar, there was Danish Lakra, an Oraon leader who was a minister during the Congress rule of 1972–77. Danish was a low-profile gentleman and, even after becoming a minister, he did not give up farming. I remember Salib Toppo, an Oraon leader from Kumargram who saw himself not as an Oraon but as a peoples' leader. We worked together at the Kumargram Block office during the 1980s. Salib gave me the name 'Mangra' when he came to know that I was born on a Tuesday.

The story of Manohar Tirkey is also an interesting one. He was a young goalkeeper at Saint Joseph High School, Damanpur. The RSP made him an MLA from Kalchini. He later became a Public Works Department (PWD) minister and a Member of Parliament (MP). He, too, did not publicise the fact that he was an Oraon.

The Oraon couple, Silvina and Sukra, of Rajabhatkhawa (the Duars), became famous for their love for wild leopards. They used to carry leopard cubs from the forest department's cave and affectionately bring them up at home, together with their own children. They named the cubs and, as soon as they were able to look after themselves, they would return them to the department. Durga Oraon, a mahout at Jaldapara's Hollong forest, was as friendly with the elephants as he was with human beings.

A village of the Duars, Laljhamela *busti* in Nagrakata, in the Jalpaiguri district at the Indo-Bhutan border, was named after two Oraons, Lal (red) Somra and Jhamela (trouble) Somra. Laljhamela's picturesque landscape attracts many picnickers during the winter months. Both these Oraons were firebrand leaders of the Communist Party of India, Marxist (CPIM) during the land reform movement of the 1960s in the Duars in North Bengal. Lal and Jhamela's struggle against the tea planters helped to recover the entire land of the village and a band of 400 tribal families settled here.

Today, the Oraon people of North Bengal seldom speak Kurukh, because in the tea gardens Sadri is doing well, while in the plain areas, Bengali and Hindi are being widely used. But, in some tea gardens, such as Panighata, Redbank and Gandrapara, Kurukh is the dominant language. In Ranchi, the Kurukh script, Tolong-Siki, is gathering momentum since 2000.

The Oraons had a culture of *dhumkuria* (bachelor's dormitory) in the past, which is not in existence any more. The *dhumkuria*s used to house unmarried young males and there were instances when girls used them as well. In 1872, Dalton wrote, 'I not long ago saw a *dhumkuria* in a Sirguja village in which the boys and girls all slept every night. They themselves admitted the fact, the elders of the village confirmed it, and appeared to think that there was no impropriety in the arrangement.' Recently I discovered an NGO named Dhumkuria in the Duars and found that it was an Oraon initiative.

The Forest-dwelling Parhaiyas

Originally from Bihar, the Parhaiyas migrated to Bengal in search of jobs in the tea plantations of North Bengal. They were actually the priests of the local chieftains of Palamou, former Bihar and were regarded as medicine people. The Adivasis of the then Bihar, Odisha and Madhya Pradesh came to North Bengal, settled here and ultimately made this country their second homeland. The entire tea country of North Bengal is this homeland of the Chota Nagpur-originating Adivasis.

In January 2017, I met Krishna Parhaiya at Salbari, near Siliguri. He had retired from a government job and now took care of his pet dog. While narrating his story, he said that his grandfather, Siucharan Parhaiya, had fled from Palamou to the Mohorgaon-Gulma Tea Estate, near Siliguri, in order to get rid of a British Police arrest warrant. Siucharan was then a boy of 18 years and was accused of having beaten up a British policeman in Bihar. Later, Siucharan married a Kharwar girl from Khaprail and this was the turning point of his life. They had a baby boy, Jamuna Parhaiya, who ultimately married an Oraon, Champa Minj, who gave birth to Krishna and Shankar. Krishna was educated in Siliguri; his brother, however, died in 2005. Krishna married a Nepali-speaking Chetri lady. This couple gave birth to a son, Paban, and two daughters, Mala and Shila. Both Mala and Shila are doing their Masters in Hindi.

The Parhaiyas are known to have had a few social divisions—the Pandavbanshis, the Narkatmas, the Pakfors, the Cherowans and so on. They are divided into *khut*s and these are further sub-divided into septs such as the Bags, the Gachats, the Gidhs, the Fanigas, the Kauas, the Maimas, the Ophiyas and the Tetengas. Apart from these, the Kashis and the Sinduriyas form other social divisions. Many of these are, perhaps, clans, as we understand in general, for a tribe or a community. But the young people, such as Mala or Shila, know very little of Parhaiya culture. They speak Hindi and are aware of how to get a job in a private English school. Their father told me that he had started writing on the Parhaiya culture for the future generations and had already taken notes from British authors. The most interesting thing about this Parhaiya family was their knowledge of at least five languages—Bengali, English, Sadri, Nepali and Hindi.

In a book brought out by the Anthropological Survey of India, *People of India*, it is said, 'The Parhaiyas believe that they are descendants from the Pandavas, heroes of the great Hindu epic, the *Mahabharata*, and hence they are known as the Pandavbanshi Parhaiyas. According to the dominant tribal population of the area, such as the Cheros and Kharwars, the Parhaiyas originated from one of the three *jhalaka*s (scarecrows) animated by Lord Shiva at the request of Goddess Parvati. As per the legend, they preferred to remain in the *pahari* (jungle) and since then they have been leading a forest-based life. According to Forbes, (1870) the Parhaiyas are the oldest residents of Palamou. They use Baiga as their title, which means priest.... They are a forest-dwelling community. The original habitat of Parhaiya was on the hilltop.' A question now comes to my mind: 'Who, then, are the Baigas?'

The ethnic Parhaiya population grew considerably during 2001 to 2011, from 688 to 921. But, if we look back a little, we find that their population has been falling significantly. According to the 1991 census, the Parhaiya population of West Bengal was 7,885. The district of Nadia showed 328 while Malda had 135 and Purulia, 106.

The Rich Cultural Heritage of the Raj Gonds

The Raj Gonds (Raj Gonr) are a section of the Gond tribe who once founded the kingdom of Gondowana. The prefix 'Raj' signifies their association with the Gond kingdom. Their early settlements were in Maharashtra, Andhra Pradesh, Madhya Pradesh and Bihar. They speak Gondi, which is a Dravidian language. The tribe has a rich cultural heritage of wood carving, body tattooing, wall painting, floor painting, basketry and pottery. In Odisha, Gond marriages with *mahul* trees were common practice. According to Gond legends, states Christoph von Fürer-Haimendorf (1979), they had divine ancestors who were nurtured by the Goddess Parvati, but Lord Mahadeo imprisoned them in a cave. These principal gods were ultimately liberated by the Gond cultural hero, Pahandi Kapan Lingal, with the assistance of Jangu Bai, a goddess well-disposed to the Gond and still worshipped regularly. When the primeval Gonds, referred to as the Parenda Khara Koya Wasi

Penk, literally meaning the 12 threshing floors of the Gond gods, emerged from the cave, they appeared in four batches; this division into four groups laid the foundation of the basic structure of Gond society.

This tribe has totemistic clans, which are exogamous. In the Motidhar Tea Estate of the Siliguri subdivision in Darjeeling, I came across the Karas (buffalo), the Dhamnas/Nags (snake), the Bags (tiger), the Kechuas (tortoise), the Sikras and the Lakras. The surnames they use include Pardhan, Majhi and Kalo. At the Gonr *busti*, near Typoo Tea Estate, they are found to belong to the Natia and Soratia clans who have migrated from the Siddhi district of undivided Madhya Pradesh. The people follow the traditional tribal religion and they subscribe to the Persa Pen cult or Baradeo, who is the supreme deity. They believe that they are the children of Baradeo. According to *People of India*, National Series, Volume III (1994), published by the Anthropological Survey of India and Oxford University Press, the Raj Gonds are a section of the great Gond tribe whose homeland extended from the Satpura range down to the Godavari, from Uttar Pradesh (Gonda district) and North Bihar to Andhra Pradesh, and from Maharashtra to Odisha. They have lent their name to Gondowana, a historical region that gained prominence during the medieval period. The Gonds established their political power, founded states and exercised

influence far and wide. There were as many as four separate Gond kingdoms in the Gondowana region, mentioned in the medieval accounts, which was bounded in the north by the Panna district, in the east by Ratanpur in the Bilaspur district and in the west by the Raisen district of Madhya Pradesh, while southwards it spread towards the Deccan in Maharashtra and Andhra Pradesh. These Gond kingdoms were located in the northern, central and southern parts. The southern and northern parts had independent kingdoms, with their capitals at Chandrapur and Mandla, while the two central kingdoms had their capitals at Deogarh (near Nagpur) and at Kherla (Betue).

The total Gond population of West Bengal was 13,535 in 2011, of which 5,065 of them were found in the district of North 24 Parganas. Next, in terms of Gond concentration, are undivided Jalpaiguri (2,157), Bardhaman (1,127) and Hugli (1,086).

The Origin of the Sabars

The term *sabar* is said to be a corrupt form of *sagaris*, which is the Scythian word for an axe. The letter 'g' has been interchanged with 'v' to form the term *savar*, which later became *sabar*. It has been argued that the tribe took their name from their habit of carrying axes such as the *khukri*, as in the case of the Nepali people. In Sanskrit, however, *sabar* or *savar* means hill people, barbarian, wild or uncivilised. Sabar is said to be a very old tribe that was found during 800 to 1200 BC, across Central and Southeast India. According to linguists, their dialect, Saora, belongs to the Austro-Asiatic language family.

In the Indian epics, the Sabars are the people who are mentioned, more than anyone else, as a tribe in Bengal. *Sabarir Pratikshya* is widely read and is a well-known part of the *Ramayana* where a Sabar woman was described as waiting to be blessed by Lord Rama. The Sabars are also said to be the descendants of the declassed sons of Viswamitra. According to the *Mahabharata*, the Sabars, the descendants of Kamdhenu of Basistha, were born to get rid of the angry Viswamitra. Some reckoned Jarasur as their ancestor. Jarasur once took the form of a deer and threw an arrow at Lord Krishna. Many people believe that members of the tribe emerged to carry the stones meant for the construction of Lord Jagannath's temple at Puri. They are the charioteers during the Rath Yatra festival and can still be seen drawing the chariot there.

According to a popular story, Lord Shiva wanted to train his people in agriculture. He created a plough and tied it to his ox, Nandi. The earth was full of jungles at that time so Shiva created a Sabar man and gave him an axe to clear the land. Shiva then went away for a while. The Sabar man got tired of clearing the jungles; he was hungry and thirsty and, unable to bear it any longer, he killed the ox and took its beef in a teak-leaf. The Sabars believe that grinded teak-leaves give out a red liquid in their tender age for this reason. However, Shiva was pleased to see the jungle clean and introduced the Sabar man to the plants, herbs and fruits of the forest. But Nandi lay dead nearby. The killer did not tell him the truth and as Shiva threw sacred water on Nandi, the ox came back to life and told Shiva what had happened. Shiva was angry and cursed the Sabar by saying that they will remain forest-dwellers forever. It is also believed that Shiva's curse made them poor.

According to the census of 2011, the total population of the Sabar tribe in West Bengal is 40,374. They are largely found in the districts of Paschim Medinipur (18,169), Purba Medinipur (3,666), Purulia (6,914), Bankura (2,500), Hugli (3,429), South 24 Parganas (1,156), Darjeeling (612) and Jalpaiguri (2,420). In the southern part, the tribe is basically an agriculturist community while in North Bengal they are tea garden workers. Their early homeland was at the bank of the river Mahanadi in Odisha. Many of the Sabars living in Bengal today are believed to have migrated here from the Ganjam, Ajaygarh and Pala areas of Odisha. It is said that once the Sabars had a kingdom there. Some say that the Kharias are their nearest kins and they also have a link with the Bhil tribe of Central India. The tribe was dependent upon the collection of forest products and hunting in the past but this has been virtually jeopardised with the promulgation of various forest laws.

The Sabars have a language of their own, which has been described as a dialect of the Mundari group of languages of the Austro-Asiatic linguistic family. Among their

musical instruments are the *tudung* (drum), *karing* (small leather instrument), *terete* (flute), *rogoigoi* (made from bamboo) and *neneng* (bell). They call their priest *kuran*. Like many other tribes, most of the Sabars in Bengal today are Hindus.

Various social festivals were once part of Sabar life and many of these are still celebrated. Gama Purnima in the Bengali month of Sravan is one such festival. The Sabars of South Bengal worship Bandurga, who is said to have been created by Lord Brahma. As Bandurga killed the powerful demon Gamasur and saved the Sabars from his attack, the Sabars became worshippers of this female deity. It is said that once they were known to be worshippers of Lord Jagannath, but after the idol was stolen, they stopped going to the temple. They do not go to Puri in Odisha for this reason.

Though they live amid many ethnically different communities in a pluri-cultural environment, the Sabars of the tea gardens of North Bengal follow interesting marriage rituals. A representative from the bridegroom's side, who is keen on negotiating the marriage, would initially go to the bride's house secretly with presents and hang them in front of the

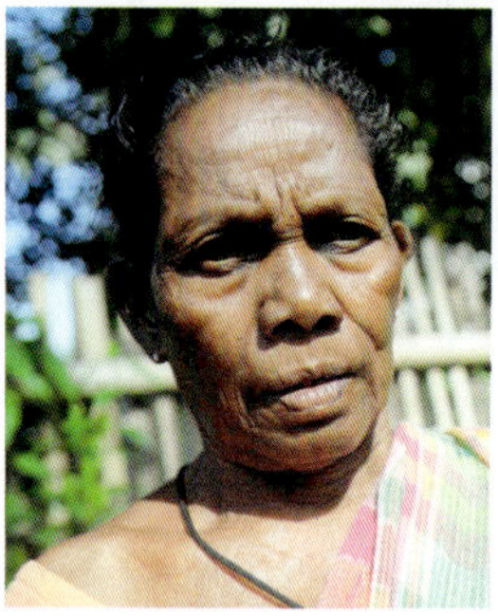

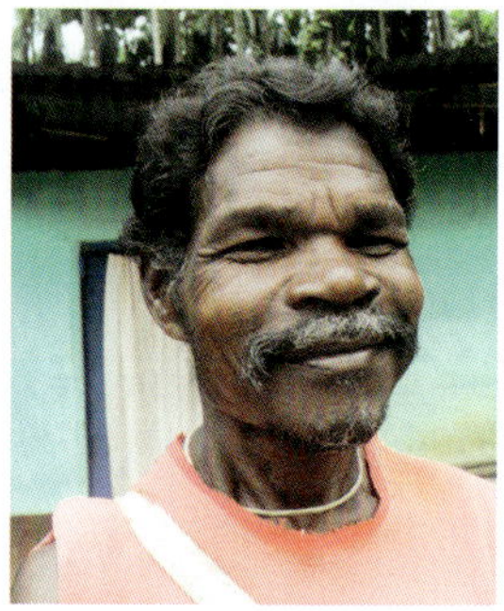

door. The gifts would usually include wine, bangles and an arrow. These, however, are not to be touched until the marriage is finalised. The bridegroom comes to the bride's house a couple of days before the wedding and the ceremony takes place before sunrise.

Twenty-five Sabar groups have been identified on the basis of occupation. Among these are the Jatis, the Arshis, the Jodus, the Kindals, the Kumbis, the Lanjias and the Sudhs. As for surnames, they use Gomana, Baya, Karji and so on. They have two major territorial groups, the hill Sabars and the Sabars who live in the plains. The Sabars of the Gungaram Tea Estate, in Siliguri-Terai, stated that they have clans such as the Roitos, Mannes or Monens, Jurais, Kinlongs or Kindals, Janglos, Kandodas and so on. I was told by Galanti Sabar of the Gungaram Tea Estate that she migrated here from Serong village of the Kumundia area of Odisha's Ganjam district. She also said that the Sabars are known as Saoras in Ganjam.

As far as the tribal literature of West Bengal is concerned, the Sabars of North Bengal have not yet been covered, perhaps because they are lesser known to the people involved in the tribal ethnography in this state. I have specific information about the Sabar concentration in the Terai Duars region of Bengal. According to a private survey in 2003, there were 141 Sabar families inhabiting the Darjeeling district while 667 families lived in the undivided Jalpaiguri district. The names of the tea gardens and villages where they were located were Pahargoomiah (6), Trihanna (80), Gungaram (32), New Champta (5), Durgapur (12), Fulbari Patan (2), Rohini (4) in the districts of Darjeeling and Jalpaiguri, Pathorjhora (15), Damdim (2), Rangamati (60), Songachi (150), Nakati (30), Nagrakata (14), Jiti (12), Kurti (35), Gathia (300), Haldibari (1), Redbank (15), Subhasini (7), Nepuchapur (5), Lataguri (3), Hatipota (5) and Turibari (3).

The Powerful Santals

The term *santal* is believed to be a corrupt form of the word *saontar*. It is said that, as Medinipur was known as Saont or Saonthbumi, the Santals were named after this region. Dr Suniti Kumar Chatterjee believes that the Santals derived their name from the Sanskrit word *samantapal*, which later became *samant-al*, *saontal* and finally *saotal*. The Santals, however, used to call themselves *hor* (meaning 'man').

This tribe, categorised as Proto-Australoid, is regarded as the third largest in India. For West Bengal, they are the largest tribe with a population of more than two-and-a-half million (2,512,331, according to the census of 2011). In this state, the Santal community constitutes 47.42 per cent of its total Scheduled Tribes population. Their concentration in West Bengal is ordinarily found in the

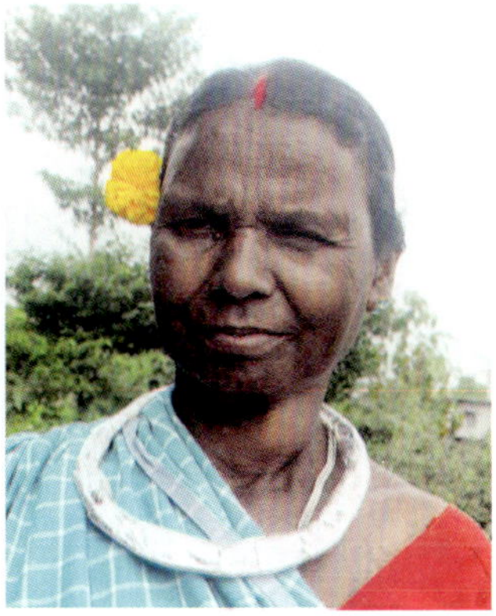
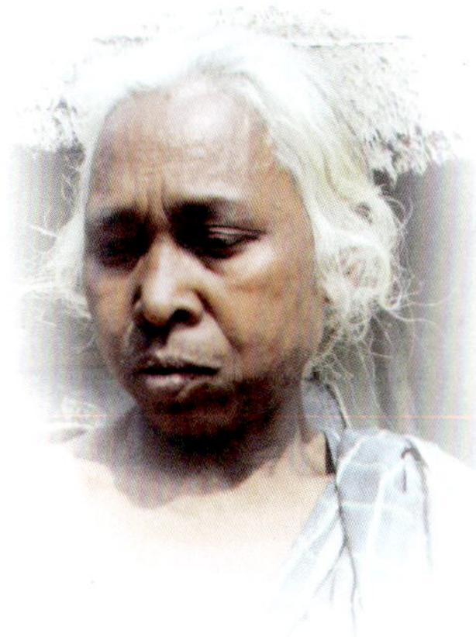

districts of Bankura, Birbhum, Purilia, Paschim Medinipur, Bardhaman, Malda, Uttar (North) and Dakshin (South) Dinajpur and undivided Jalpaiguri. The Santals are a dominating tribal group not only in West Bengal but across many regions in eastern India. It is said that they have contributed a lot to the development of settled agriculture in West Bengal, along with many other regions, by clearing the jungles over the last two centuries.

Though agriculture has become their primary source of livelihood, the Santals have been used to a nomadic life for centuries. Today, they can be found in the tea gardens of Darjeeling and a few villages in the plains of Jalpaiguri and Alipurduar. In the Bardhaman district, they are generally skilled coalmine workers and they can be seen as brick manufacturing labourers in several brickfields. Many have become government employees and teachers. In Uttar and Dakshin Dinajpur and in the Malda districts, the Santals are mostly farmers.

The Santali dialect is identified with the Austro-Asiatic Mundari language family. Apart from Santali, the West Bengal Santals are familiar with Bengali and Sadri while those of Bihar and Assam know Hindi and Assamese, respectively. The literature of the Santalis can also be seen in Roman, Bengali, Devnagri and the

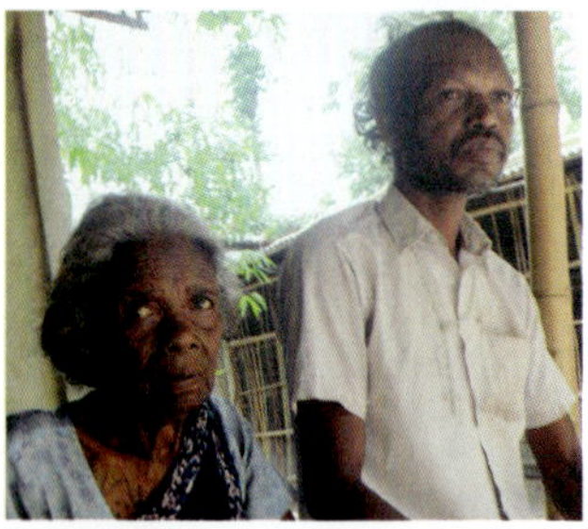

Ol Chiki script. The Santali language has very recently been recognised by the Government of India under the VIII Schedule of the Constitution. It has also been given official recognition by West Bengal.

The tribe is socially divided into 12 exogamous clans, though some of these no longer exist. Among the major Santal clans are the Kiskus, the Hembroms, the Sorens, the Mandis (Mardi or Marandi), the Murmus, the Baskeys, the Besras, the Hansdas, the Tudus, the Chonres and the Pauriyas. Except for the last two, these clans can be found in the Terai and the Duars of the Jalpaiguri district of West Bengal. Each of the clans has a series of sub-clans as they are believed to have emerged on the basis of totemistic objects. The Santals, like many other tribes, observe taboos of their own totems.

They have a very strong village organisation. *Majhi* is the traditional office of the village chief while the *paranik* is the assistant. The

village council appoints a *godet* (pronounced goret) for the purpose of discharging the job of a village messenger. Like many other tribal communities of India, the Santals have their own myths and folklores. According to some of these stories, their ancestors settled in the Dandakaranya area in Central India and later migrated to the eastern flank. At this stage, they were found to be scattered over a vast stretch of land around the Palamou, Chota Nagpur, Hazaribagh and Singhbhum belts. They later settled in the hill regions of Rajmahal. The Santal name for the Rajmahal hill was Damin-iko, the home of the tribe. Damin-iko was renamed Santal Parganas. The Santals organised the historic rebellion (*hul*) during 1855–57 against the British-sponsored native landlords and *diku*s (foreigners) at Bhagnadihi, of the Santal Parganas. During this battle many Santals died, including four great heroes, Sidhu, Kanhu, Chand and Bhairav (the Sidhu-Kanhu Dahar in Kolkata's Dharmatala area is named after the first two). This rebellion is regarded as the first organised indigenous people's upsurge against imperialism in British India.

The religion of the Santals is a form of tribal Hinduism. They worship supernatural powers or spirits during their festivals or at the time of any crisis. Their supreme deity is Thakur Jiu or Sin-Bonga or Dharam. Among the village spirits, the chief presiding deity is Marang-Buru, that is, the spirit of a mountain. Accordingly, Basuki or Basumata is the deity of agriculture while Burha and Burhi are considered to be the spirits of the ancestors. There are many more Bongas such as Gosea-Bonga, Jaher Era, Pargana-Bonga, Manjhi-Bonga and so on. Many Santals strongly believe in witchcraft and they have practiced the art for years. A sizeable portion of this tribe, like many others of eastern India, has been found to propagate their traditional way of magico-religious practices.

The Santals celebrate Saharai during the harvesting of crops and regard it as the largest, merriest and most important among their festivals; an occasion when the Santals show gratitude to their spirits. It is also known as Bandna Parab and is celebrated in the month of Pous (December-January) when they get winter paddy. Baha Parab is another important festival held in the month of Falgun (February-March) when the *sal* trees start blooming. The people observe Harior Sim for the plantation of paddy seedlings, Jom Sim to pay homage to the sun god or Sin-Bonga and so on. The Christians among the Santals observe festivals such as Christmas and Good Friday.

The Santals are a Scheduled Tribe in Bihar, West Bengal, Tripura and Odisha. A Santal Academy has been set up in West Bengal, under the aegis of the Government, which has its office in Salt Lake, Kolkata.

Mortgaging/leasing out their farm land to neighbours or money-lenders is a common practice in the Santal belts of North Bengal even today. A field survey

that I conducted during 1986-87 in the Duars revealed that 53.19 per cent of the Santal families had leased out their land for money that they needed for the renovation of houses, the purchase of livestock and agricultural implements, medical treatment, ritualistic expenses, children's education, among others. Mortgages were mostly reported from the Santal villages close to townships, which by then became multi-ethnic ones. In many cases, they had to lose land in the adjustment of outstanding loans and interests. The deals were found to take place mostly in unlawful private credit markets.

In February 1994, I was instrumental in organising a special land restoration court, which was held primarily for the toiling Santals at the Duars' Samuktala under the aegis of the district administration. The mission caused a huge sensation. The week-long camp was held at Baniagaon, which is still a Santal village. I later became the Area Inspector of the Integrated Tribal Development Project (ITDP) there. Fifty Santal land alienation cases were tried in that court under Chapter II of the West Bengal Land Reforms Act, 1955. The Sub Divisional Officer of Alipurduar, Vivek Bhardwaj and the District Magistrate of Jalpaiguri, Dilip Rath of the Indian Administrative Service, supported me and made some cases of land restoration possible. This, however, could not stop the mortgaging of land by the Santals in North Bengal.

The Passionate Sauria Paharias

The Sauria Paharias are also known as the Samariya Paharias, Males or Malers. Risley wrote that 'the Male of Rajmahal Hills have synonyms like Mal, Samariya Male, Paharia, Sauria, Samil Paharia, Asal Paharia and Sanghi. Their surnames are Singh, Malto, Pabaria and Sauriya Paharia. Their main concentration was found in the Sahebganj and Godda districts of Bihar.' In Godda, they are found in Sundarpahari, Boarijor and Pakur, particularly in the hill areas of Sahibganj. In the past, this tribe was largely found in the Rajmahal hills. The Sauria Paharias were once known to be close to the Oraons and were considered by some authors to be an isolated branch of the Sabar tribe. It has been said that they had identifying signs on their faces, which are, however, not seen today. They were among the earlier settlers of former Bihar's Santal Parganas and said to be one of the three sections of the Paharia tribe; the other two being the Malpaharias and the Kumharbhogs. This community is known to have been elevated as an advanced one during the time of Emperor Chandragupta Maurya of Magadha.

Chinese scholars such as Xuan Zhang and Fa-Hien wrote about this tribe in their travelogues on India. When going through a book, in Hindi, on the Jharkhand-

based Souria Paharias recently, I came across a field survey of eight Souria Paharia-dominated villages of the Godda district. The study reveals that the community has already become marginalised in Jharkhand, despite several development measures taken by the Government. Studies on this tribe are meagre in West Bengal, where they use 'Souria' as a surname. The Sauria Paharias are known to worship the earth and sun gods at the family level and the *sakua* tree at the village level. I have, however, found them assembling at a Lord Hanuman temple at Manjha Tea Estate's Karam line. In 2011, their population in West Bengal was 3,480; about 60 per cent (2,069) were found in the district of Malda. I also saw them in the Manjha, Simulbari and Mohorgaon Tea Estates in Siliguri, where they basically work as labourers.

Chandu Sauria is a tractor driver at the Manjha Tea Estate on the Nepal border of the Bengal Terai. Whenever I met him, he would say that he would help me to learn their mother tongue, Sauria, which has no script. It is a language that can only be learned through oral training. In Chandu's tea garden there live at least 30 Sauria Paharia families who speak their own language. It appeared to me that the dialect is bit like the Oraons' Kurukh. Chandu came to this tea garden from the Dabra village of Mohonpur area, in Jharkhand's Godda district, when he was just nine years old. His maternal uncle, Munshi Sauria, brought him here. Chandu went to a Naxalbari school at Chenga and went on to join the tea plantation as a labourer. He learned driving at Bagdogra. Later, he became a tractor driver. Chandu visits his motherland at Jharkhand occasionally and claims that the tribe has already become an endangered one as the Sauria population is on the decline. He gave me a book on his tribe, which he had brought from Jharkhand. Chandu's wife, Rahmi, is also from his tribe; their children are now going to school.

North Bengal's Ranghu Sauria has already become a star in the tribal galaxy of the Sub-Himalayan terrain for her bravery in tackling the cause of anti-trafficking

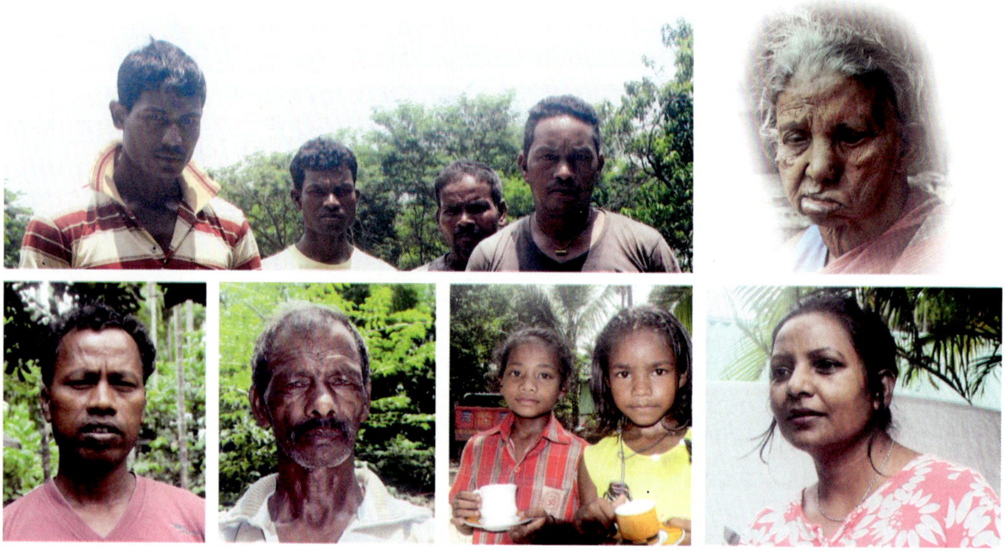

of women in North Bengal's tea gardens. She has been dedicated to this cause for the last 15 years. Her home is at Panighata Tea Estate (a closed tea garden now) near Dudhiya, which falls in the Mirik block of the Darjeeling district. She founded the Kanchenjungha Uddhar Kendra (KUK) in 2004 with its headquarters at Siliguri's Pradhannagar. Ranghu has a band of activists working with her and they already rescued 800 women from different parts of the country, even from the sex workers' dens of Dubai and Lebanon. KUK has also identified local and international trafficking gangs and handed them over to the police. According to Ranghu, five of the identified traffickers have been convicted under their initiative. This tribal lady has been threatened several times but that does not deter her from doing what she has taken up as her life's mission. After her graduation, she did not look for a job; instead, inspired by her mother, Etowasi Sauria, she decided to work for distressed women. Ranghu knows Bengali, Hindi, English, Nepali and Sadri well but cannot speak her own language, Souria-Paharia. Her dream is to build a home for the rescued women. She has received felicitations for her social work as well as an award from the President of India at Rashtrapati Bhawan, New Delhi.

Appendix One

State-level population of the different Scheduled Tribe communities of West Bengal and their concentration, according to the census report of 2011.

Name of the Community	Population	% to Total STP of the State	Concentration (districts where population found in larger numbers by 2011 census)
Asur	3,864	0.07	Jalpaiguri
Baiga	13,423	0.25	Paschim Medinipur
Bedia	88,772	1.67	Uttar Dinajpur, Dakshin Dinajpur, North 24 Parganas, South 24 Parganas
Bhumij	376,296	7.10	Bardhaman, Nadia, North 24 Parganas, Hugli, Bankura, Purulia, South 24 Parganas, Paschim Medinipur
Bhutia (including Sherpa, Toto, Dukpa, Kagatay, Tibetan, Yolmo)	66,627	1.25	Darjeeling, Jalpaiguri
Birhor	2,241	0.04	Jalpaiguri, Birbhum, Bardhaman, Hugli, Purulia
Birjia	1,123	0.02	Darjeeling, Jalpaiguri
Chakma	466	Ngl	Maldah, North 24 Parganas
Chero	5,477	0.10	Darjeeling, Jalpaiguri, Birbhum, North 24 Parganas, Paschim Medinipur
Chik Baraik	21,376	0.40	Darjeeling, Jalpaiguri, Uttar Dinajpur, Nadia, Purulia
Garo	2,039	0.03	Jalpaiguri, Cooch Behar
Gond	13,535	0.25	Darjeeling, Jalpaiguri, Bardhaman, North 24 Parganas, Hugli
Gorait	2,498	0.04	Purulia
Hajang	621	0.01	Jalpaiguri, Dakshin Dinajpur, Maldah
Ho	23,483	0.44	Darjeeling, Jalpaiguri, Dakshin Dinajpur, Maldah, Bardhaman, Paschim Medinipur, Purba Medinipur
Karmali	2,466	0.04	Maldah, Uttar Dinajpur, Dakshin Dinajpur, Bankura, Purulia, Paschim Medinipur
Kharwar	20,270	0.38	Maldah, Jalpaiguri, Nadia, Hugli, Paschim Medinipur
Khond	660	0.01	Darjeeling, Jalpaiguri, Nadia, South 24 Parganas
Kisan	98,434	1.85	Darjeeling, Jalpaiguri, Uttar Dinajpur, Maldah Murshidabad, Nadia, South 24 Parganas
Kora	159,404	3.00	Maldah, Birbhum, Bardhaman, Hugli, Bankura, Purulia, Paschim Medinipur
Korwa	2,912	0.05	Darjeeling, Jalpaiguri, North 24 Parganas, Paschim Medinipur
Lepcha	33,962	0.64	Darjeeling, Jalpaiguri
Limbu	46,847	0.88	Darjeeling, Jalpaiguri
Lodha, Kheria, Kharia	108,707	2.05	Jalpaiguri, Hugli, Purulia, Paschim Medinipur
Lohara, Lohra	24,783	0.46	Jalpaiguri, Dakshin Dinajpur, Nadia, North 24 Parganas, Purulia
Magh	8,032	0.15	Jalpaiguri, Bardhaman, North 24 Parganas
Mahali	81,594	1.54	Jalpaiguri, Bardhaman, North 24 Parganas, Purulia, Paschim Medinipur
Mahli	2,609	0.04	Jalpaiguri, Birbhum, Bardhaman
Malpaharia	44,538	0.84	Darjeeling, Jalpaiguri, Dakshin Dinajpur, Maldah, Murshidabad, Birbhum, Bardhaman, Nadia
Mech	41,242	0.77	Darjeeling, Jalpaiguri
Mru	197	Negligible	Jalpaiguri, Paschim Medinipur
Munda	366,386	6.91	Darjeeling, Jalpaiguri, Dakshin Dinajpur, Nadia, North 24 Parganas, South 24 Parganas, Paschim Medinipur
Nagesia	16,378	0.30	Darjeeling, Jalpaiguri, Nadia
Oraon	643,510	12.14	Darjeeling, Jalpaiguri, Dakshin Dinajpur, Nadia, North 24 Parganas
Parhaiya	921	0.01	Maldah, Birbhum, Nadia, Purulia
Rabha	27,820	0.52	Jalpaiguri, Cooch Behar, Uttar Dinajpur, Dakshin Dinajpur, Maldah
Santal	2,512,331	47.42	Jalpaiguri, Uttar Dinajpur, Dakshin Dinajpur, Maldah, Murshidabad, Birbhum, Bardhaman, Hugli, Bankura, Purulia, Paschim Medinipur
Sauria Paharia	3,480	0.06	Darjeeling, Dakshin Dinajpur, Maldah, Nadia, Purulia
Savar	40, 374	0.76	Darjeeling, Jalpaiguri, Hugli, Bankura, Purulia, South 24 Parganas, Paschim Medinipur, Purba Medinipur
Tamang	146, 203	2.76	Darjeeling, Jalpaiguri

Appendix Two

Scheduled Tribe Communities of West Bengal

(1) Asur (2) Baiga (3) Bedia (4) Bhumij (5) Bhutia (including Sherpa, Toto, Dukpa, Kagatay, Tibetan Yolmo) (6) Birhor (7) Birjia (8) Chakma (9) Chero (10) Chik-Baraik (11) Garo (12) Gond (13) Gorait (14) Hajang (15) Ho (16) Karmali (17) Kharwar (18) Khond (19) Kisan (20) Kora (21) Koewa (22) Lepcha (23) Lodha/Kheria/Kharia (24) Lahara (25) Magh (26) Mahali (27) Mahli (28) Malpaharia (29) Mech (30) Mru (31) Munda (32) Nagesia (33) Oraon (34) Arhaiya (35) Rabha (36) Santal (37) Sauria Paharia (38) Savar (39) Tamang (40) Limbu (Subba)

Primitive Tribe Groups of West Bengal (PTGs)

(1) Birhor (2) Lodha (3) Toto

Appendix Three

District/community-wise distribution of the Scheduled Tribe population of West Bengal, according to the census report of 2011.

Asur

District	Total Population of Asurs	Male	Female
Bankura	-	-	-
Barddhaman	2	1	1
Birbhum	3	1	2
Dakshin Dinajpur	1	1	0
Darjeeling	427	213	214
Haora	4	4	0
Hugli	14	9	5
Jalpaiguri	2,968	1,453	1,515
Cooch Behar	354	178	176
Kolkata	49	28	21
Maldah	1	0	1
Murshidabad	1	1	0
Nadia	15	8	7
North 24 Parganas	11	6	5
Paschim Medinipur	-	-	-
Purba Medinipur	-	-	-
Purulia	-	-	-
South 24 Parganas	12	4	8
Uttar Dinajpur	2	2	0
Total	**3,864**	**1,909**	**1,955**

Baiga

District	Total Population of Baigas	Male	Female
Bankura	-	-	-
Barddhaman	18	9	9
Birbhum	14	5	9
Dakshin Dinajpur	-	-	-
Darjeeling	65	34	31
Haora	19	9	10
Hugli	39	18	21
Jalpaiguri	42	20	22
Cooch Behar	-	-	-
Kolkata	85	42	43
Maldah	2	2	0
Murshidabad	4	3	1
Nadia	148	61	87
North 24 Parganas	80	42	38
Paschim Medinipur	12,845	6,490	6,355
Purba Medinipur	23	11	12
Purulia	-	-	-
South 24 Parganas	37	17	20
Uttar Dinajpur	2	2	0
Total	**13,423**	**6,765**	**6,658**

Bedia

District	Total Population of Bedias	Male	Female
Bankura	1,203	590	613
Barddhaman	3,244	1,605	1,639
Birbhum	3,021	1,514	1,507
Dakshin Dinajpur	16,153	8,302	7,851
Darjeeling	73	37	36
Haora	418	211	207
Hugli	1,105	568	537
Jalpaiguri	1,037	558	479
Cooch Behar	742	398	344
Kolkata	167	87	80
Maldah	2,237	1,101	1,136
Murshidabad	2,634	1,327	1,307
Nadia	3,485	1,811	1,674
North 24 Parganas	28,904	14,558	14,346
Paschim Medinipur	1,038	515	523
Purba Medinipur	213	110	103
Purulia	6,325	3,236	3,089
South 24 Parganas	8,519	4,250	4,269
Uttar Dinajpur	8,254	4,211	4,043
Total	**88,772**	**44,989**	**43,783**

Bhumij

District	Total Population of Bhumijs	Male	Female
Bankura	39,185	19,956	19,229
Barddhaman	12,553	6,300	6,253
Birbhum	55	30	25
Dakshin Dinajpur	19	10	9
Darjeeling	105	53	52
Haora	379	198	181
Hugli	21,303	10,493	10,810
Jalpaiguri	1,860	918	942
Cooch Behar	76	36	40
Kolkata	212	104	108
Maldah	153	81	72
Murshidabad	1,107	553	554
Nadia	31,577	16,056	15,521
North 24 Parganas	38,750	19,690	19,060
Paschim Medinipur	97,543	48,904	48,639
Purba Medinipur	3,997	2,007	1,990
Purulia	104,570	53,103	51,467
South 24 Parganas	22,178	11,248	10,930
Uttar Dinajpur	674	347	327
Total	**376,296**	**190,087**	**186,209**

Bhutia

(Bhutia includes Bhutia, Sherpa, Toto, Dukpa, Kagatay, Tibetan and Yolmo)

District	Total Population of Bhutias	Male	Female
Bankura	6	3	3
Barddhaman	91	44	47
Birbhum	26	14	12
Dakshin Dinajpur	19	10	9
Darjeeling	49,454	24,666	24,788
Haora	52	26	26
Hugli	66	32	34
Jalpaiguri	15,695	7,855	7,840
Cooch Behar	98	50	48
Kolkata	200	105	95
Maldah	38	19	19
Murshidabad	125	66	59
Nadia	41	21	20
North 24 Parganas	261	129	132
Paschim Medinipur	161	91	70
Purba Medinipur	95	48	47
Purulia	46	23	23
South 24 Parganas	79	42	37
Uttar Dinajpur	74	34	40
Total	**66,627**	**33,278**	**33,349**

Birhor

District	Total Population of Birhors	Male	Female
Bankura	97	52	45
Barddhaman	398	198	200
Birbhum	289	146	143
Dakshin Dinajpur	11	5	6
Darjeeling	55	31	24
Haora	42	23	19
Hugli	236	112	124
Jalpaiguri	272	137	135
Cooch Behar	45	12	33
Kolkata	86	85	1
Maldah	15	8	7
Murshidabad	40	20	20
Nadia	143	84	59
North 24 Parganas	61	37	24
Paschim Medinipur	72	40	32
Purba Medinipur	-	-	-
Purulia	288	145	143
South 24 Parganas	14	6	8
Uttar Dinajpur	77	35	42
Total	**2,241**	**1,176**	**1,065**

Birjia

District	Total Population of Birjias	Male	Female
Bankura	-	-	-
Barddhaman	37	13	24
Birbhum	43	21	22
Dakshin Dinajpur	28	28	0
Darjeeling	649	337	312
Haora	10	5	5
Hugli	11	6	5
Jalpaiguri	271	126	145
Cooch Behar	6	4	2
Kolkata	23	12	11
Maldah	-	-	-
Murshidabad	1	1	0
Nadia	13	5	8
North 24 Parganas	-	-	-
Paschim Medinipur	15	7	8
Purba Medinipur	7	4	3
Purulia	5	3	2
South 24 Parganas	4	1	3
Uttar Dinajpur	-	-	-
Total	**1,123**	**573**	**550**

Chero

District	Total Population of Cheros	Male	Female
Bankura	63	27	36
Barddhaman	159	82	77
Birbhum	353	173	180
Dakshin Dinajpur	13	6	7
Darjeeling	841	418	423
Haora	108	61	47
Hugli	79	40	39
Jalpaiguri	1,047	533	514
Cooch Behar	91	35	56
Kolkata	39	19	20
Maldah	59	34	25
Murshidabad	60	32	28
Nadia	28	13	15
North 24 Parganas	2,238	1,070	1,168
Paschim Medinipur	226	112	114
Purba Medinipur	-	-	-
Purulia	11	5	6
South 24 Parganas	6	2	4
Uttar Dinajpur	16	11	5
Total	**5,477**	**2,693**	**2,784**

Chik Baraik

District	Total Population of Chik Baraiks	Male	Female
Bankura	1	1	0
Barddhaman	59	34	25
Birbhum	1	1	0
Dakshin Dinajpur	45	23	22
Darjeeling	3,678	1,799	1,879
Haora	28	17	11
Hugli	147	74	73
Jalpaiguri	14,263	7,066	7,197
Cooch Behar	71	30	41
Kolkata	26	16	10
Maldah	51	29	22
Murshidabad	16	7	9
Nadia	1,292	641	651
North 24 Parganas	241	134	107
Paschim Medinipur	201	107	94
Purba Medinipur	14	6	8
Purulia	619	310	309
South 24 Parganas	98	51	47
Uttar Dinajpur	525	269	256
Total	**21,376**	**10,615**	**10,761**

Garo

District	Total Population of Garos	Male	Female
Bankura	-	-	-
Barddhaman	22	8	14
Birbhum	4	3	1
Dakshin Dinajpur	6	3	3
Darjeeling	41	19	22
Haora	13	7	6
Hugli	25	13	12
Jalpaiguri	1,117	549	568
Cooch Behar	553	268	285
Kolkata	31	15	16
Maldah	8	4	4
Murshidabad	3	1	2
Nadia	73	39	34
North 24 Parganas	19	9	10
Paschim Medinipur	57	28	29
Purba Medinipur	6	1	5
Purulia	-	-	-
South 24 Parganas	42	19	23
Uttar Dinajpur	19	11	8
Total	**2,039**	**997**	**1,042**

Gond

District	Total Population of Gonds	Male	Female
Bankura	2	2	0
Barddhaman	1,127	607	520
Birbhum	99	47	52
Dakshin Dinajpur	30	23	7
Darjeeling	929	469	460
Haora	421	242	179
Hugli	1,120	628	492
Jalpaiguri	1,971	1,043	928
Cooch Behar	388	192	196
Kolkata	636	360	276
Maldah	307	155	152
Murshidabad	59	36	23
Nadia	276	156	120
North 24 Parganas	5,065	2,591	2,474
Paschim Medinipur	495	242	253
Purba Medinipur	7	5	2
Purulia	29	16	13
South 24 Parganas	355	191	164
Uttar Dinajpur	33	20	13
Total	**13,535**	**7,122**	**6,413**

Gorait

District	Total Population of Goraits	Male	Female
Bankura	26	12	14
Barddhaman	90	43	47
Birbhum	-	-	-
Dakshin Dinajpur	15	8	7
Darjeeling	42	19	23
Haora	27	11	16
Hugli	27	17	10
Jalpaiguri	94	51	43
Cooch Behar	1	1	0
Kolkata	9	3	6
Maldah	2	2	0
Murshidabad	1	1	0
Nadia	62	31	31
North 24 Parganas	18	6	12
Paschim Medinipur	25	11	14
Purba Medinipur	-	-	-
Purulia	2,025	1,019	1,006
South 24 Parganas	14	12	2
Uttar Dinajpur	20	8	12
Total	**2,498**	**1,255**	**1,243**

Ho

District	Total Population of Hos	Male	Female
Bankura	10	3	7
Barddhaman	1,389	704	685
Birbhum	8	3	5
Dakshin Dinajpur	791	394	397
Darjeeling	855	442	413
Haora	81	40	41
Hugli	112	53	59
Jalpaiguri	2,905	1,414	1,491
Cooch Behar	10	6	4
Kolkata	68	39	29
Maldah	563	279	284
Murshidabad	73	40	33
Nadia	272	145	127
North 24 Parganas	121	67	54
Paschim Medinipur	14,656	7,360	7,296
Purba Medinipur	1,168	587	581
Purulia	267	139	128
South 24 Parganas	34	19	15
Uttar Dinajpur	100	52	48
Total	**23,483**	**11,786**	**11,697**

Karmali

District	Total Population of Karmalis	Male	Female
Bankura	404	200	204
Barddhaman	38	18	20
Birbhum	-	-	-
Dakshin Dinajpur	184	94	90
Darjeeling	103	49	54
Haora	7	4	3
Hugli	27	13	14
Jalpaiguri	70	42	28
Cooch Behar	6	3	3
Kolkata	29	17	12
Maldah	368	178	190
Murshidabad	23	9	14
Nadia	76	38	38
North 24 Parganas	49	24	25
Paschim Medinipur	229	117	112
Purba Medinipur	49	29	20
Purulia	576	292	284
South 24 Parganas	33	18	15
Uttar Dinajpur	195	104	91
Total	**2,466**	**1,249**	**1,217**

Kharwar

District	Total Population of Kharwars	Male	Female
Bankura	289	154	135
Barddhaman	630	314	316
Birbhum	25	17	8
Dakshin Dinajpur	11	8	3
Darjeeling	1,083	541	542
Haora	169	94	75
Hugli	1,113	561	552
Jalpaiguri	2,572	1,318	1,254
Cooch Behar	84	44	40
Kolkata	267	144	123
Maldah	10,438	5,403	5,035
Murshidabad	79	41	38
Nadia	1,440	721	719
North 24 Parganas	192	105	87
Paschim Medinipur	1,579	816	763
Purba Medinipur	23	8	15
Purulia	102	56	46
South 24 Parganas	65	33	32
Uttar Dinajpur	109	61	48
Total	**20,270**	**10,439**	**9,831**

Kisan

District	Total Population of Kisans	Male	Female
Bankura	4	2	2
Barddhaman	82	36	46
Birbhum	1	1	0
Dakshin Dinajpur	207	106	101
Darjeeling	2,106	1,043	1,063
Haora	67	34	33
Hugli	106	54	52
Jalpaiguri	532	268	264
Cooch Behar	16	9	7
Kolkata	146	86	60
Maldah	92,598	47,919	44,679
Murshidabad	462	251	211
Nadia	937	485	452
North 24 Parganas	61	35	26
Paschim Medinipur	101	46	55
Purba Medinipur	22	11	11
Purulia	12	5	7
South 24 Parganas	372	196	176
Uttar Dinajpur	602	310	292
Total	**98,434**	**50,897**	**47,537**

Kora

District	Total Population of Koras	Male	Female
Bankura	13,204	6,662	6,542
Barddhaman	37,315	18,624	18,691
Birbhum	14,980	7,513	7,467
Dakshin Dinajpur	1,959	969	990
Darjeeling	103	52	51
Haora	424	226	198
Hugli	12,345	6,177	6,168
Jalpaiguri	492	257	235
Cooch Behar	9	6	3
Kolkata	125	70	55
Maldah	7,105	3,506	3,599
Murshidabad	1,113	544	569
Nadia	185	100	85
North 24 Parganas	945	457	488
Paschim Medinipur	29,115	14,443	14,672
Purba Medinipur	148	75	73
Purulia	33,266	16,688	16,578
South 24 Parganas	1,701	890	811
Uttar Dinajpur	4,870	2,448	2,422
Total	**159,404**	**79,707**	**79,697**

Korwa

District	Total Population of Korwas	Male	Female
Bankura	3	2	1
Barddhaman	15	7	8
Birbhum	28	12	16
Dakshin Dinajpur	21	13	8
Darjeeling	659	326	333
Haora	13	5	8
Hugli	38	23	15
Jalpaiguri	959	469	490
Cooch Behar	38	17	21
Kolkata	12	6	6
Maldah	8	4	4
Murshidabad	11	5	6
Nadia	52	32	20
North 24 Parganas	469	243	226
Paschim Medinipur	419	199	220
Purba Medinipur	44	21	23
Purulia	11	3	8
South 24 Parganas	28	19	9
Uttar Dinajpur	84	41	43
Total	**2,912**	**1,447**	**1,465**

Lepcha

District	Total Population of Lepchas	Male	Female
Bankura	-	-	-
Barddhaman	25	12	12
Birbhum	25	12	13
Dakshin Dinajpur	8	5	3
Darjeeling	32,862	16,602	16,260
Haora	11	5	6
Hugli	10	5	5
Jalpaiguri	763	378	385
Cooch Behar	10	4	6
Kolkata	53	20	33
Maldah	12	7	5
Murshidabad	8	3	5
Nadia	27	15	12
North 24 Parganas	25	12	13
Paschim Medinipur	60	34	26
Purba Medinipur	8	5	3
Purulia	2	2	0
South 24 Parganas	19	9	10
Uttar Dinajpur	34	18	16
Total	**33,962**	**17,148**	**16,814**

Limbu

District	Total Population of Limbus	Male	Female
Bankura	1	1	0
Barddhaman	29	15	14
Birbhum	4	3	1
Dakshin Dinajpur	10	7	3
Darjeeling	41,284	20,527	20,757
Haora	4	3	1
Hugli	26	10	16
Jalpaiguri	4,812	2,358	2,454
Cooch Behar	2	0	2
Kolkata	33	18	15
Maldah	10	6	4
Murshidabad	12	8	4
Nadia	11	7	4
North 24 Parganas	7	4	3
Paschim Medinipur	230	124	106
Purba Medinipur	-	-	-
Purulia	11	6	5
South 24 Parganas	350	196	154
Uttar Dinajpur	11	6	5
Total	**46,847**	**23,299**	**23,548**

Lodha, Kharia and Kheria

District	Total Population of Lodhas, Kharias and Kherias	Male	Female
Bankura	2,096	1,040	1,056
Barddhaman	1,163	622	541
Birbhum	125	72	53
Dakshin Dinajpur	23	15	8
Darjeeling	2,516	1,219	1,297
Haora	172	77	95
Hugli	5,672	2,801	2,871
Jalpaiguri	34,481	17,312	17,169
Cooch Behar	346	169	177
Kolkata	82	49	33
Maldah	184	98	86
Murshidabad	26	7	19
Nadia	1,536	762	774
North 24 Parganas	1,229	600	629
Paschim Medinipur	51,772	26,267	25,505
Purba Medinipur	1,937	970	967
Purulia	4,940	2,405	2,535
South 24 Parganas	211	116	95
Uttar Dinajpur	196	91	105
Total	**108,707**	**54,692**	**54,015**

Lohara and Lohra

District	Total Population of Loharas and Lohras	Male	Female
Bankura	397	205	192
Barddhaman	167	88	79
Birbhum	196	100	96
Dakshin Dinajpur	2,136	1,051	1,085
Darjeeling	670	338	332
Haora	133	59	74
Hugli	110	57	53
Jalpaiguri	7,360	3,642	3,718
Cooch Behar	24	14	10
Kolkata	55	29	26
Maldah	133	66	67
Murshidabad	58	29	29
Nadia	3,097	1,548	1,549
North 24 Parganas	3,359	1,684	1,675
Paschim Medinipur	883	415	468
Purba Medinipur	24	12	12
Purulia	3,664	1,883	1,781
South 24 Parganas	1,211	628	583
Uttar Dinajpur	1,106	565	541
Total	**24,783**	**12,413**	**12,370**

Magh

District	Total Population of Maghs	Male	Female
Bankura	12	6	6
Barddhaman	1,017	528	489
Birbhum	150	77	73
Dakshin Dinajpur	1	1	0
Darjeeling	157	85	72
Haora	300	164	136
Hugli	883	431	452
Jalpaiguri	1,754	873	881
Cooch Behar	60	35	25
Kolkata	557	275	282
Maldah	60	32	28
Murshidabad	38	22	16
Nadia	172	90	82
North 24 Parganas	1,837	912	925
Paschim Medinipur	93	47	46
Purba Medinipur	23	12	11
Purulia	11	6	5
South 24 Parganas	897	436	461
Uttar Dinajpur	10	6	4
Total	**8,032**	**4,038**	**3,994**

Mahali

District	Total Population of Mahalis	Male	Female
Bankura	1,943	958	985
Barddhaman	5,939	2,998	2,941
Birbhum	2,483	1,247	1,236
Dakshin Dinajpur	2,749	1,394	1,355
Darjeeling	1,278	628	650
Haora	54	29	25
Hugli	2,118	1,064	1,054
Jalpaiguri	26,904	13,315	13,589
Cooch Behar	14	6	8
Kolkata	198	111	87
Maldah	2,317	1,132	1,185
Murshidabad	1,147	548	599
Nadia	3,313	1,670	1,643
North 24 Parganas	7,036	3,548	3,488
Paschim Medinipur	12,487	6,274	6,213
Purba Medinipur	155	88	67
Purulia	10,119	5,050	5,069
South 24 Parganas	940	486	454
Uttar Dinajpur	400	194	206
Total	**81,594**	**40,740**	**40,854**

Malpaharia

District	Total Population of Malpaharias	Male	Female
Bankura	155	64	91
Barddhaman	4,485	2,263	2,222
Birbhum	2,608	1,321	1,287
Dakshin Dinajpur	2,704	1,334	1,370
Darjeeling	2,550	1,269	1,281
Haora	16	9	7
Hugli	198	95	103
Jalpaiguri	2,680	1,334	1,346
Cooch Behar	38	21	17
Kolkata	8	4	4
Maldah	4,394	2,282	2,112
Murshidabad	14,064	7,045	7,019
Nadia	9,182	4,588	4,594
North 24 Parganas	237	123	114
Paschim Medinipur	52	24	28
Purba Medinipur	2	2	0
Purulia	255	127	128
South 24 Parganas	103	51	52
Uttar Dinajpur	807	408	399
Total	**44,538**	**22,364**	**22,174**

Mech

District	Total Population of Mechs	Male	Female
Bankura	1	0	1
Barddhaman	170	84	86
Birbhum	-	-	-
Dakshin Dinajpur	26	14	12
Darjeeling	2,508	1,266	1,242
Haora	7	4	3
Hugli	-	-	-
Jalpaiguri	37,726	19,077	18,649
Cooch Behar	287	134	153
Kolkata	64	33	31
Maldah	22	14	8
Murshidabad	10	6	4
Nadia	25	16	9
North 24 Parganas	64	34	30
Paschim Medinipur	190	90	100
Purba Medinipur	6	3	3
Purulia	2	1	1
South 24 Parganas	67	39	28
Uttar Dinajpur	67	36	31
Total	**41,242**	**20,851**	**20,391**

Munda

District	Total Population of Mundas	Male	Female
Bankura	1,714	858	856
Barddhaman	6,837	3,449	3,388
Birbhum	272	143	129
Dakshin Dinajpur	27,475	13,818	13,657
Darjeeling	18,307	9,070	9,237
Haora	1,625	820	805
Hugli	4,590	2,294	2,296
Jalpaiguri	86,223	43,086	43,137
Cooch Behar	1,439	754	685
Kolkata	1,136	561	575
Maldah	6,241	3,158	3,083
Murshidabad	3,428	1,747	1,681
Nadia	25,098	12,595	12,503
North 24 Parganas	61,215	30,888	30,327
Paschim Medinipur	67,069	33,734	33,335
Purba Medinipur	1,452	746	706
Purulia	10,221	5,177	5,044
South 24 Parganas	36,419	18,350	18,069
Uttar Dinajpur	5,625	2,850	2,775
Total	**366,386**	**184,098**	**182,288**

Nagesia

District	Total Population of Nagesias	Male	Female
Bankura	200	109	91
Barddhaman	22	16	6
Birbhum	-	-	-
Dakshin Dinajpur	196	88	108
Darjeeling	3,814	1,893	1,921
Haora	24	15	9
Hugli	740	375	365
Jalpaiguri	4,102	2,066	2,036
Cooch Behar	231	131	100
Kolkata	29	18	11
Maldah	405	206	199
Murshidabad	322	152	170
Nadia	4,775	2,397	2,378
North 24 Parganas	821	417	404
Paschim Medinipur	134	67	67
Purba Medinipur	68	32	36
Purulia	-	-	-
South 24 Parganas	388	207	181
Uttar Dinajpur	107	52	55
Total	**16,378**	**8,241**	**8,137**

Oraon

District	Total Population of Oraons	Male	Female
Bankura	311	159	152
Barddhaman	8,392	4,243	4,149
Birbhum	4,850	2,472	2,378
Dakshin Dinajpur	43,427	22,191	21,236
Darjeeling	72,487	35,543	36,944
Haora	2,505	1,265	1,240
Hugli	6,498	3,282	3,216
Jalpaiguri	368,413	183,985	184,428
Cooch Behar	6,722	3,506	3,216
Kolkata	1,001	500	501
Maldah	13,232	6,713	6,519
Murshidabad	9,277	4,694	4,583
Nadia	28,897	14,823	14,074
North 24 Parganas	41,679	21,362	20,317
Paschim Medinipur	2,670	1,302	1,368
Purba Medinipur	115	57	58
Purulia	8,481	4,377	4,104
South 24 Parganas	9,130	4,606	4,524
Uttar Dinajpur	15,423	7,853	7,570
Total	**643,510**	**322,933**	**320,577**

Parhaiya

District	Total Population of Parhaiyas	Male	Female
Bankura	-	-	-
Barddhaman	48	23	25
Birbhum	76	35	41
Dakshin Dinajpur	24	14	10
Darjeeling	14	7	7
Haora	9	4	5
Hugli	17	14	3
Jalpaiguri	61	25	36
Cooch Behar	-	-	-
Kolkata	-	-	-
Maldah	135	63	72
Murshidabad	6	4	2
Nadia	328	158	170
North 24 Parganas	62	26	36
Paschim Medinipur	-	-	-
Purba Medinipur	1	1	0
Purulia	106	59	47
South 24 Parganas	17	8	9
Uttar Dinajpur	17	10	7
Total	**921**	**451**	**470**

Rabha

District	Total Population of Rabhas	Male	Female
Bankura	18	10	8
Barddhaman	43	22	21
Birbhum	103	44	59
Dakshin Dinajpur	1,351	659	692
Darjeeling	44	29	15
Haora	18	7	11
Hugli	22	8	14
Jalpaiguri	14,487	7,410	7,077
Cooch Behar	3,801	1,936	1,865
Kolkata	27	16	11
Maldah	1,294	664	630
Murshidabad	625	329	296
Nadia	67	37	30
North 24 Parganas	433	219	214
Paschim Medinipur	248	124	124
Purba Medinipur	11	6	5
Purulia	2	2	0
South 24 Parganas	27	14	13
Uttar Dinajpur	5,199	2,719	2,480
Total	**27,820**	**14,255**	**13,565**

Santal

District	Total Population of Santals	Male	Female
Bankura	298,992	148,077	150,915
Barddhaman	375,263	186,137	189,126
Birbhum	206,329	101,581	104,748
Dakshin Dinajpur	163,696	81,424	82,272
Darjeeling	18,729	9,277	9,452
Haora	5,992	3,081	2,911
Hugli	153,809	75,652	78,157
Jalpaiguri	38,877	19,469	19,408
Cooch Behar	1,375	705	670
Kolkata	1,674	883	791
Maldah	161,991	79,473	82,518
Murshidabad	51,351	26,094	25,257
Nadia	20,765	10,300	10,465
North 24 Parganas	9,901	4,968	4,933
Paschim Medinipur	535,441	266,741	268,700
Purba Medinipur	13,726	7,024	6,702
Purulia	339,094	169,821	169,273
South 24 Parganas	4,376	2,205	2,171
Uttar Dinajpur	110,950	55,458	55,492
Total	**2,512,331**	**1,248,370**	**1,263,961**

Sauria Paharia

District	Total Population of Sauria Paharias	Male	Female
Bankura	35	15	20
Barddhaman	23	12	11
Birbhum	-	-	-
Dakshin Dinajpur	238	108	130
Darjeeling	546	273	273
Haora	4	3	1
Hugli	4	4	0
Jalpaiguri	13	7	6
Cooch Behar	-	-	-
Kolkata	12	6	6
Maldah	2,069	1,018	1,051
Murshidabad	49	16	33
Nadia	205	104	101
North 24 Parganas	43	25	18
Paschim Medinipur	7	5	2
Purba Medinipur	1	1	0
Purulia	128	67	61
South 24 Parganas	12	7	5
Uttar Dinajpur	91	44	47
Total	**3,480**	**1,715**	**1,765**

Savar

District	Total Population of Savars	Male	Female
Bankura	2,500	1,246	1,254
Barddhaman	293	152	141
Birbhum	240	117	123
Dakshin Dinajpur	3	1	2
Darjeeling	612	307	305
Haora	209	105	104
Hugli	3,429	1,676	1,753
Jalpaiguri	2,420	1,173	1,247
Cooch Behar	6	3	3
Kolkata	55	29	26
Maldah	13	9	4
Murshidabad	10	6	4
Nadia	169	92	77
North 24 Parganas	467	237	230
Paschim Medinipur	18,169	9,076	9,093
Purba Medinipur	3,666	1,810	1,856
Purulia	6,914	3,428	3,486
South 24 Parganas	1,156	574	582
Uttar Dinajpur	43	23	20
Total	**40,374**	**20,064**	**20,310**

Tamang

District	Total Population of Tamangs	Male	Female
Bankura	64	32	32
Barddhaman	175	97	78
Birbhum	15	6	9
Dakshin Dinajpur	38	23	15
Darjeeling	113,318	56,161	57,157
Haora	71	35	36
Hugli	101	52	49
Jalpaiguri	30,113	14,964	15,149
Cooch Behar	58	30	28
Kolkata	164	97	67
Maldah	31	22	9
Murshidabad	143	74	69
Nadia	50	29	21
North 24 Parganas	1,023	535	488
Paschim Medinipur	585	314	271
Purba Medinipur	51	31	20
Purulia	34	20	14
South 24 Parganas	102	46	56
Uttar Dinajpur	67	26	41
Total	**146,203**	**72,594**	**73,609**

Acknowledgements

So many people helped me with this book that it may just well be better to simply say, 'Thank you all, guys!' But there happen to be some people who are special and hence need a special mention! The first such name is my father, Krishnobijay Bhattacharya, who first awakened an interest in tribal people in me and made me aware of them. My father left us 37 years ago but his dedication to professionally introduce eri-culture for the sustainable development of the tribals of the locality, of the Mech (Boro) people in particular, gave me the vision to look at the tribals in a different way.

I am indebted to our dear departed writer-cum-activist, Mahasveta Devi, for always inspiring me to study the culture of the tribals. I miss her today not only because she was instrumental in helping me with my first book of this genre, *B for Bengal T for Tribes*, but because she also wrote a beautiful foreword and declared me as her friend in North Bengal. Professor Bengt G Karlsson of the Stockholm University, whose book, *Contested Belonging*, on the Rabhas of North Bengal, is a unique piece of research on Indian tribes, deserves a special mention because of his continuous follow-up on my work. I have been enriched by his advice in articulating my ideas for this work in many ways. Mr Nirmal Kanti Bhattacharjee of Niyogi Books is the man whom I would especially like to thank for his commitment towards bringing out this book. I am indebted to the great Bengali novelist, Sri Debesh Roy, for introducing me to him. My warm thanks to Mr Bikash and Mrs Tultul Niyogi of Niyogi Books for making this book possible. I am also grateful to Rajadipta Roy and Bijay De of Jalpaiguri, Tapash Chanda and Tapan Roy of Siliguri and Abhijit Roy of Alipurduar for supporting this study. I thank Sri Vivek Bharadwaj from the Union Home Ministry, New Delhi, for his valuable support. My gratitude to Write Media for editing and designing this book. Both Pritha, my daughter, and Jayashree, my wife, were very supportive while I was researching and writing. Another person who has always been very dear to me is my mother, Sujata, who passed away in February 2017.

During the last decade, many of my friends either accompanied me during my various field trips or gave me the necessary inputs for reaching the different communities. This book would not have been possible without their cooperation and generosity. They are Bijay Kujur of the Belgacchi Tea Estate; Sabita Kujur of the Ord-Terai Tea Estate; Belsing Karjee and Samarsing Thakur of Kamakshyaguri; Basanta Besra, Salomi Hembrom and Emanuel Mansing Hansda of Samuktala; Sanu Kharia of Dakshin Mendabari; Santosh Rajak of Bagdogra; Tileswar Rabha and Matol Rabha of Paro *busti*; Jogin Rabha of Uttar Mendabari forest *busti*; Rajesh Thapa of Champasari; Kundan Yolmo of Shivmandir; Ganga Beck of Malbazar; Sonam Tshering Lepcha, NT Lepcha and Dulal Chandra Roy of Kalimpong; Pradip Debnath and Bablu Saha of Hatighisha; Rabison Sangma of Kalkut forest *busti*; Bhakto Toto, Sanjib Toto, Bakul Toto, Dhaniram Toto, Bhabesh Toto and Asok Toto of Totopara; Dominique Dungdung of Birpara; Ratan Bomjan of Bagdogra; Garjan Mallik of Ketugabur (Naxalbari); SD Sherpa of Sonada; Sange Sherpa of Sreekhola (Darjeeling); Hemanta Narjinary and Mahadev Das of Siliguri. I am also indebted to Sushil Tirkey of Gayaganga (Siliguri-Terai) for his year-long support of this study.

Bibliography

Aajkaal, 15 January 1997, Kolkata and Tushar Pradhan's article in the Siliguri edition, 30 June 2017.

Bagchi Chandan, 17 and 18 October 2003, Siliguri, 'Nijeder Sanskriti, Lokachar...Sabar Janajati' (Bengali), *Uttar Banga Sambad*.

Baskey Dhirendranath, 1987, Kolkata, Paschimbanger Adibasi Samaj, Vol. I, (Bengali).

Basu Sunil Kumar and Others, 1980, 'Underdeveloped Tribes of West Bengal', Bulletin of Cultural Research Institute, Vol. XIV, Numbers 3 and 4, Government of West Bengal, Kolkata.

Beiteille Andre, 2000, 'What Should We Mean by Indigenous People?', seminar paper presented to Uppsala University, Sweden.

Bhattacharya Krishnabijay, 1964, 'Ericulture and the Tribals of Jalpaiguri', unpublished project paper, Kamakshyaguri, Duars.

Bhattacharya Krishnopriyo, 1984, 'Buxa Paharer Dukpa, Ekti Artho Samajik O Sanskritik Ruprekha', (Bengali), edited by Dibbyendu Sen, *Dabi*, special festival number, Alipurduar.

—, 1992, 'The Dukpas of Buxa Hills', Bulletin of Cultural Research Institute, Vol. XVIII, Numbers 1 and 2, Government of West Bengal, Kolkata.

—, 2004, *B for Bengal T for Tribes*: *Presentation of Tribal Communities of West Bengal through Texts and Photographs*, Papyrus, Kolkata.

—, 2007, *Silent Departure: A Study of Contemporary Tribal Predicaments in Bengal Duars,* Papyrus, Kolkata.

—, 2006, *Terai Duarser Lokayata Sabdokosh*, Papyrus, Kolkata.

Bhowmik Kanai and Others, 1989, *Paschimbanger Adibasi Chalchitra* (Bengali), Bengal Social Service League, Kolkata.

Bhowmik Suhrid Kumar, 1980, 'Ethno-Linguistic Study of the Kharias', Bulletin of Cultural Research Institute, Vols. I and II, Government of West Bengal, Kolkata.

—, 1990, *Arya Rahasya* (Bengali), Marang Buru Press, Medinipur.

—, 1994, *Jharkhande Mahaprabhu* (Bengali), Medinipur.

Bista Dor Bahadur, 1980, *People of Nepal*, Ratna Pustak Bhandar, Bhatahity, Kathmandu, Nepal (fourth edition).

Bose Nirmal Kumar, 1971, *Tribal Life in India*, National Book Trust, New Delhi (revised edition of 2002 by CB Tripathi).

Bright Eyes Global Action Project (BEGAP), 2013, CTEC, Totopara, project brochure.

Chakraborty B, 1979, *Cultural History of Bhutan*, Vol. I, Hilltop Publishers, Chittaranjan.

Chatterji Suniti Kumar, 1951, *Kirat-Jana-Krti*, The Asiatic Society of Bengal, Kolkata (1974 revised edition).

Chowdhury MK and Others, 1992, 'The Kharias in the Process of Development: A Study in Bankura District', Bulletin of Cultural Research Institute, Vol. XVIII, Numbers 1 and 2, Government of West Bengal, Kolkata.

—, 2003, 'Ethnographic Notes on the Scheduled Tribes of West Bengal', Cultural Research Institute, Government of West Bengal, Kolkata.

Dalton ET, 1973 (1872), *Descriptive Ethnology of Bengal; Indian Studies, Past and Present*, Kolkata (second reprint).

Das Amal Kumar, 1964, *The Koras and Some Little Known Communities of West Bengal*, Tribal Welfare Department, Government of West Bengal, Kolkata.

Das AK, 1969, *The Totos*, Cultural Research Institute, Government of West Bengal, Kolkata.

Das AK and MK Raha, 1967, *The Rabhas of West Bengal*, Cultural Research Institute, Government of West Bengal, Kolkata.

Das AK and Others, 1990, *Tribal Situation in West Bengal*, Firma KLM Pvt. Ltd., Kolkata.

Das Amal Kumar and Manish Kumar Raha, 1963, *The Oraons of Sunderban*, Cultural Research Institute, Government of West Bengal, Kolkata.

—, 1965, *West Bengal Tribes through Photographs*, Cultural Research Institute, Government of West Bengal, Kolkata (photographs by Dibyendu Chaki).

Das Amal Kumar and Others, 1966, *The Malpaharias of West Bengal*, Cultural Research Institute, Government of West Bengal, Kolkata.

Das Amal Kumar and Ramendra Nath Saha, 1989, *West Bengal Scheduled Castes and Scheduled Tribes, Facts and Information*, Cultural Research Institute, Government of West Bengal, Kolkata.

Das Amal Kumar and Sankarananda Mukhopadhyaya, 1976, *Paschimbanger Adibashi Loksahitya* (Bengali), Cultural Research Institute, Government of West Bengal, Kolkata.

—, 1977, *Paschimbanger Adibashi Nirdeshika* (Bengali), Cultural Research Institute, Government of West Bengal, Kolkata.

—, 1977, *Paschimbanger Adibasi Andolon* (Bengali), Cultural Research Institute, Government of West Bengal, Kolkata.

Das Amal Kumar, 1978, *The Lepchas of West Bengal*, Editions Indian, Kolkata.

Deb Arabinda, 1976, *India and Bhutan: A Study in Frontier Political Relations (1772–1865)*, Firma KLM Pvt. Ltd., Kolkata.

Debnath Asit Kumar, 1997, 'Social Life of Kharias', Bulletin of Cultural Research Institute, Vol. XIX, Number 2, Government of West Bengal, Kolkata.

Dhali Debendranath, 1987, 'Toto' (Bengali), Cultural Research Institute, Government of West Bengal, Kolkata.

Directorate of Census Operations, West Bengal, state level and district level census data and website.

Dutta Roy Sachchidananda, 2002, *Manab Unnayan* (Bengali), Seriban, Kolkata.

Goley Kajiman, 2001, 'Duarser Tamang Janajati O Tar Sanskriti', Paschimbanga, Special Jalpaiguri Number, Government of West Bengal, Kolkata.

Grierson G, 1903, *Linguistic Survey of India*, Vol. III, Part I (Tibeto-Burman family), Motilal Banarsidass, New Delhi (reprint).

Hodgson BH, 1849, 'On the Origin, Location, Numbers, Creed, Customs, Character and Conditions of the Koch, Bodo and Dhimal People, with a General Description of the Climate They Dwell In', Journal of Asiatic Society of Bengal, Vol. 18, Part 2, Kolkata.

Hoffmann John, 1930, *Encyclopaedia Mundarica, Ranchi* (1990 reprint by Gyan Publishing House, New Delhi).

Information and Public Relations Department, Government of West Bengal, 1970, *Paschimbanger Adibasi* (Bengali), Kolkata.

Karlsson BG, 1997, *Contested Belonging: An Indigenous People's Struggle for Forest and Identity in Sub-Himalayan Bengal*, Department of Sociology, Lund University.

Limbu (Subba) Vikash Samiti, 2010, souvenir in commemoration of the inaugural ceremony of 'Yuma Mangheem', Lookshan, Duars.

Majee Biplab, 2015, 'Umberto Eco, Boiyer Bhabishyat, Sahaj Path', Howrah.

Majumdar Bimalendu, 1998, *The Totos: Academic Enterprise*, Kolkata.

Miligan JA, 1919, 'Final Report on the Survey and Settlement Operation in Jalpaiguri District, 1906-1916', Bengal Secretariat Press, Kolkata.

Moitra Asish and Ranjan Sen (ed.), 2007, Jangal Saotal (Bengali), Radical Impression, Kolkata (second reprint, 2015).

Narjeenary Hiracharan, 1985, *In Search of Identity: The Meche*, BB Prakashan, Kolkata.

Norbu Thubten Jigmey and Colin Turubull, 1983, *Tibet: Its History, Religion and People*, Penguin.

Regmi Rishikeshab Raj, 1991, *The Dhimals, Miraculous Migrants of Himal: An Anthropological Study of a Nepalese Ethnic Group*, Nirala Publications, Jaipur.

Rennie David Field, 1866, *Bhotan and the Story of the Doar War*, John Murray, Albemarle Street, London (1970 reprint, *Bibliotheca Himalayica*, Series I, Vol. 5, Manjusri Publishing House, New Delhi).

Risley HH, 1891, *The Tribes and Castes of Bengal, Ethnographic Glossary* (reprint of Bengal Secretariat Press Edition, 1998), Firma KLM Pvt. Ltd. (distributor), Kolkata (Vols. I and II).

Roy Subhojyoti, 1997, *Jalpaiguri Under Colonial Rule 1765 to 1948*, School of Oriental and African Studies, University of London (thesis for Ph.D).

Roy SC, 1912, *Mundas and Their Country*, Kolkata (1995 Reprint by Catholic Press, Ranchi, Bihar with title, *The Mundas and Their Country*).

—, 1915, *The Oraons of Chota Nagpur*, Ranchi.

Roy Burman BK, 1961, 'Dynamics of Persistence and Change of a Small Community, the Totos', Ph.D thesis, Calcutta University.

Sanyal Charuchandra, 1973, *The Meches and the Totos, Two Sub-Himalayan Tribes of North Bengal*, North Bengal University in collaboration with Firma KLM Pvt. Ltd.

—, 1979, *The Limbu, the Kirata People of South-East Himalayas*, published by the author from Jalpaiguri.

Sengupta Promode, 1983, *Naxalbari and Indian Revolution*, Research India Publications, Kolkata.

Sharma B Deben, 2005, 'Lhops (Doya) of Bhutan', Akansha Publishing House, New Delhi.

Singh Bajrang and Dr Manohor Lal, 2016, *Souria Paharia*, BITM, Ranchi.

Singh KS (ed.), 1994, *People of India*, *The Scheduled Tribes*, National Series, Vol. III, OUP, New Delhi (on behalf of Anthropological Survey of India, Kolkata, 1997 paperback edition).

Singh KS, 2002, *Birsa Munda* (1872–1900), National Book Trust, New Delhi.

Singh KS (general editor), 2008, *People of India*, *Bihar Including Jharkhand*, Vol. XVI, Part I, edited by Surendra Gopal and Hetukar Jha, Seagull Books, Kolkata (on behalf of ASI, Government of India).

Srivastava ARN, 1986, *Tribal Freedom Fighters of India*, Publications Division, Government of India, New Delhi (1999 reprint).

Souvenir Sub Committee, Lalsukra Oraon Bust Unveiling Ceremony Organising Committee, Government of West Bengal, Chalsha (Duars), February 2009, Lalsukra.

Subba TB, 1999, *Politics of Culture: A Study of Three Kirata Communities in the Eastern Himalayas*, Orient Longman, Chennai.

Sunder DHE, 1895, Final Report of Survey and Settlement of Western Duars in the District of Jalpaiguri, 1889–95, Bengal Secretariat Press, Kolkata.

The Hindu (online edition), www.hindu.com, 29 January 2009.

The Telegraph, Siliguri edition, 21 November 2014, p. 9.

The Telegraph, Kolkata, 13 August 2016, p. 1.

Toppo Tezkumar, 2011, *Kurukh Beja Beg* (Hindi), published by author from Malbazar.

Toto Bhakto, 2011, 'Toto Upojatider Nana Ajana Tathya', *Lokoswar*, magazine in Bengali, Alipurduar.

Toto Dhaniram, 2011, 'Toto Janajatir Samagrik Parichay', *Lokoswar*, magazine in Bengali, Alipurduar.

Uttar Banga Sambad, 25 September 2016, 'Prayato Lalsomra'.

Verma RC, 1990, *Indian Tribes Through the Ages*, Publications Division, Government of India, New Delhi (second revised edition, 1995).

Index